*A New Paradigm for the Next Millennium*

# REVELATION
## for our time

# JOHN DAVIS

Jane —
You incarnated to
become the ultimate woman.
First: Defeat a man in
in many lives.
John

**Spiritual Unity of Nations Publishing**
Wyoming, Michigan

Spiritual Unity of Nations Publishing
1735 Pinnacle Dr., S.W.
Wyoming, Michigan 49509-4931

Publisher's Cataloging-in-Publication Data
Davis, John.
     Revelation for our time : a new paradigm for the next millennium /
     John Davis. – Wyoming, Mich. :
     Spiritual Unity of Nations Publishing
         p.  ill.  cm.
     Includes bibliographical references.
     ISBN 0-9664450-0-7
     1. Bible – Prophecies.  2. Eschatology.
     I. Title.

BS647.2 .D38    1998    98-90325
220.1'5         dc–21    CIP

02 01 00 99  ❀  5  4  3  2  1

Printed in the United States of America

*To the Spiritual Unity of Nations*

*We are presently living in a transitional period, a period that will see the disappearance of much that is old and the sudden emergence of much that is new. The seeds of the new era are already with us, and it is the task of those who know it is coming to convey the knowledge to humanity.*

Ryuho Okawa
*The Laws of the Sun**

# Contents

# ACKNOWLEDGMENTS

NO BOOK COMES into being without a great deal of collaboration and effort on the part of many people, and this book is no exception. It is the product of my own spiritual journey which has been in part shaped by my association with two men who have served as my mentors, Hamid Bey and Kurt Stanley. Both are great men I have been privileged to know and to whom I will be forever grateful.

I also wish to express my appreciation to my editor, Cynthia Weaver Dorman, for her professionalism and dedication to the task of writing this book. Many thanks, too, to Diane Hummel whose insightful and inspired artwork graces its cover and interior.

And, last but not least, my eternal gratitude to my wife, Nancy, whose unconditional support of my controversial work is appreciated more than she will ever know.

# INTRODUCTION

A TRIP TO Greece in September of 1993 changed my life dramatically, and was the final catalyst for initiating the process in which I conceived this book. As president of World Light Travels, I conduct tours to Earth's power places for the purpose of exploring the ancient spiritual traditions connected with them. We chose Greece as a destination because of its significant planetary history. Greece, the land of Pericles, Plato and Socrates, possesses a vibrant mix of color, texture and scenery: the brilliant blue-green of the Aegean, the verdant green of the countryside, and its magnificent bleached white monuments which stand as silent sentinels, bearing witness to the passing of the ages. To the ancient Greeks, as to ancient peoples everywhere, the Earth was a living entity, the source of life and rebirth. This belief was reflected in the art of their time, in the statues and adornments, as well as their myths, which revered the Great Goddess in all her many forms.

During our four-day Aegean Isles cruise I found myself transformed. As we traveled from island to island, we all were mesmerized by the beauty and history which we found at each port of call. One of our much-anticipated stopovers was the Island of Patmos, where John the Beloved was purported to have written the Book of Revelation during his exile. During a long and interesting tour of the island, we visited the place religious historians believe that John wrote his Revelation. However, to my surprise I felt no inner confirmation for this theory. Somewhat disappointed, I left Patmos wondering how I would proceed with the project of writing this book.

Later in our Aegean tour, I experienced a revelation of my own when we visited Santorini Island, part of a formerly existing landmass known by the ancient Greeks as Thira (Thera). A highly developed civilization known as Atlantis flourished on Thira until a series of volcanic eruptions shattered the island, creating the islands of Santorini, Aspronisi, Thirasia and Kaimeni.

The east coast of Santorini bears evidence of its volcanic origins in its black pebble beaches. At Akrotiri, the ruins of the Minoan city of the same name are found. The ruins of ancient Thira are home to classical monuments, temples and an Egyptian sanctuary, all bearing evidence of alternate occupation by Egypt, Rome, Byzantium, Venice and Turkey.

Interestingly, Santorini's official seal bears the image of two dolphins. This symbol can be said to represent the higher purpose of the island during the time of the Atlantean civilization. On a personal level the dolphins represent the merging of our masculine and feminine natures. On a planetary level, the dolphins symbolize cooperation and harmony between the function of political and governmental units, and the expression of the many and varied spiritual, religious and philosophical beliefs.

As our tour ship approached the island of Santorini, we were awed by its majesty. It was apparent that this island was the remains of a devastating earthquake, which carved its sides into great cliffs, requiring access by motorized cable car to reach the island's elevated interior.

During our tour of Santorini all participants of the tour reported experiencing great inner peace. There was something very special about the island's energy, even though what remained of the original landmass was but a small remnant of what must have been a land of great splendor. Whenever I visit a foreign land, as a matter of habit I investigate the vibration created by the name of the place as a first step in becoming familiar with it. My numerological analysis of "Santorini" revealed a striking and somewhat shocking result, the likes of which I had not experienced in all my twenty-five years of numerological practice, wherein I have analyzed literally thousands of subjects.

I found the term "the Devil" in two distinct places in Santorini. To be sure of my discovery, I deciphered the name Santorini several times, always yeilding the same result. This term, the Devil, has acquired such an intense negative interpretation, I felt compelled to investigate further. My investigation led me to a remarkable conclusion.

My conclusion was not arrived at without considerable research and consideration. It was clear to me that Santorini was the location of the governmental seat of Atlantis. Not only that, I concluded that the individual elected to the equivalent of President or Prime Minister was given the position of *Santorini* — an expression for both the title and physical location of the seat of power — which numerologically translates into "the Double Devil Seat" (the numerological energy of the word Devil appears twice in Santorini). It is important for me to stress at this point that "Devil" spelled backward is "Lived." This is an obvious anagram, or the rearrangement of the letters in a word to reveal another meaning. The Devil represents the past tense of the word "Live," or our past lives. This is the challenge to any present lifetime, to overcome the mistakes or failings of past lifetimes, in order to evolve to a higher spiritual level.

The dual authority of the Double Devil Seat existed in another form in ancient Egypt (originally a colony of post-cataclysm Atlantis), where the Pharaoh held rulership over upper and lower Egypt. Symbolically, this is portrayed as the figure of the Pharaoh holding in his left hand the flail, and in his right hand the Ankh, the Egyptian symbol of everlasting life. The left and right hand of Pharaonic authority in Egypt paralleled the governmental position of the Double Devil Seat in the earlier Atlantis civilization, the right hand symbolizing the authority of democratic government, the left hand symbolizing the position of spiritual leadership.

The misuse of power by the individual who held this position was the cause of the demise of Atlantis. When this ruler misused the power of the Double Devil Seat for his own purposes rather than for the benefit of the Atlantean people, Atlantis was destroyed, with the center of destruction located at this point of authority at Santorini. When we understand the source of the term Devil and its role in one of Earth's greatest cataclysms, there is little wonder such disdain for the name Devil has remained stored in humanity's collective subconscious throughout its long planetary history. While it remains real in symbolic terms, the Devil as an entity *does not exist* today.

Ultimately, this all led me to further investigate words which have acquired a negative interpretation to see if there may be similar misinterpretations, and finally to examine the Book of Revelation in light of this new information I had uncovered. The result of my work makes up the body of this book, and with it I hope to dispel the pervasive negativity that has been infused in our spiritual traditions.

# 1

# DECODING REVELATION

SYMBOLISM IS A universal language. It speaks to us in the mystic realms where archetypes don the costumes of our common human attributes, and myths are acted out on the stage of the collective unconscious. Symbols are present everywhere in our lives, indeed the letters which form our written language are themselves symbols. The ancients understood the power of symbols and that they were essentially representative of the higher spiritual principles which gave them form. To both preserve for posterity and conceal the sacred Mysteries from the uninitiated, the guardians of divine knowledge went to great lengths to symbolically encode higher truths in their writings and mythologies. While human cognitive powers are limited by perception, the unconscious mind has no limits to its comprehension, and it is to this mind that these symbologies speak.

The great sages of antiquity hid this divine knowledge in elaborate stone sculptures and artwork, the measurements of monumental buildings and mathematical formulae, and in their mythological stories and sacred texts. These truths were carefully preserved to ensure that humankind would not lose its access to the divine laws. Comprehension of these divine laws is essential to the reawakening of the slumbering spirit within the human form, a matter which was of supreme importance to the ancient mystics as it is to mystics of today.

The illumined Masters kept their secrets hidden and preserved through the establishment of the Mystery Schools. There existed many Mystery schools in ancient times, all of which required initiation and a devotion to secrecy. Their teachings have been preserved through the writings of such great thinkers as Pythagoras and Plato, both of whom were criticized for revealing the secret teachings to the uninitiated. While both philosophers studied at many centers of higher learning, they were greatly influenced by the teachings of Orpheus, who had been initiated into the Egyptian Mysteries. Pythagoras, himself an initiate in the Egyptian Mysteries and perhaps most well known for his work in mathematics, was also influenced by the Babylonian and Chaldean Mysteries. For our purposes we will focus on the Egyptian Mystery tradition, for it is from here that our Western traditions evolved.

The Egyptian Mysteries date back to 13000 BC and the tradition from which they sprang predates them by thousands of years. It has been said that the teachings originated with the Spiritual Hierarchy of our Solar System and were introduced to Earth during the time of the Lemurian civilization and later given to the Atlanteans. After the destruction of Atlantis, schools were established in Egypt by the survivors to carry on their sacred traditions. Inherited from the Atlantean Mystery Schools, Hebrew, a form of ancient Gaelic which carried mystery keys, was the sacred tongue of the Egyptian Mystery Schools. These keys are a system of numerical values assigned to the letters of the Hebrew language. This alphanumeric system was probably the model for Pythagoras' own system of Numerology. We will return to the subject of the Hebrew mystery keys when we discuss the Great Pyramid in detail in the next chapter.

Pythagoras wasn't the only Greek to influence higher learning in the ancient world. Hermes, believed to have been a man who was later deified, preceded Pythagoras by several thousand years. He was responsible for giving mankind the arts and sciences known as mathematics, chemistry, law, philosophy, geography, magic and astrology, among others. Hermes was known to the Egyptians as "Thoth", to the Jews as "Enoch" and to the Latins as "Mercury." *The Book of Thoth* was a volume of sacred teachings and its pages consisted of symbols and hieroglyphics which were purported to endow the initiated with great powers over the elements. A great deal of evidence exists that supports the claim of the ancient teachings that *The Book of Thoth* is the *Tarot*, the set of 78 cards of divination which has been preserved by the gypsies, who are believed to have descended from the blood line of the ancient Egyptian priests.[1]

The Mystery Schools of Egypt, where Pythagoras and many of his contemporaries, as well as other well-known initiates throughout our planet's history (Jesus was initiated in the Great Pyramid at Gizeh), chose to preserve their higher teachings through the use of coded language. Martin R. Anderson researched the subject of the use of hidden meanings in language for his *Tales of the Returning Messiah and the Universal Christ*, a self-published treatise on "The Roots of Christianity". He states:

> *The ancient Mystery School teachers ...chose to use language subtly as a screen or blind to hide the real meanings of their teachings behind. In a culture where most persons were not literate and unqualified to be temple initiates, guarded speech and secrecy were necessary to protect the purity of principles of the mysteries and prevent the misuse of the universal laws and powers that could be evoked by speech and sound....Unfortunately, the young Christian Church movement adopted the language and rhetoric of the mysteries, but not being qualified initiates, they did not have the keys for understanding the language and teachings of the Mystery Schools and so misapplied the teachings...*[2]

It is the probable misapplication of these teachings which is responsible for the misinterpretation of the Book of Revelation. Indeed, its very authorship has been in question for nearly 1,800 years. Manly P. Hall, in his *Secret Teachings of All Ages*, states that the authorship of the controversial Book of Revelation, regarded as an enigmatic example of Gnostic Christian writings, has been a matter of dispute since the second century A.D. That dispute raged on for centuries. In the third century, Dionysius of Alexandria and his contemporary, Eusebius, both argued its author was someone named Cerinthus who wrote under the name John the Divine. It has also been suggested that, owing to the contents of the Book of Revelation, it bears all the earmarks of pagan theology, which is additional evidence that its author was probably schooled in the Mystery tradition.[3]

The subject of biblical prophecy has been a difficult issue for theologians, biblical scholars and modern-day seers to resolve. This is as much due to the enigmatic nature of prophetic writings as to obvious differences in belief systems. Even those who prefer to interpret prophecy literally will concede that some symbolism is intermingled with what they believe is fact. The Book of Revelation is probably the most heavily debated book of the Bible. The identity of its author is a minor issue when we consider that the literal interpretation of the horrific scenes described in Revelation's twenty-two chapters has been such a great perpetrator of fear, our greatest enemy. It is precisely these fear-based interpretations which I intend to defuse, for we must conquer our fear if we are to realize our full potential as a people.

To fully understand the premise set forth in these pages an understanding is required of the manner in which the Bible has been altered over the past 2,000 years. Martin Anderson provides some insight into this subject:

> *After Moses received the Secret Doctrine, he promoted his secret order of Essenes among his elect of Israelites. The secret order of Essenes kept the wisdom pure throughout the Aryan Age until the time of the Messiah, Jesus Christ...*
>
> *The Essenes called all their literature the* Book of Enoch *[named after Enoch, an ancestor of Noah, and an Atlantean initiate]...The* Book of Enoch *predates Christianity by thousands of years...*[and] *parallels the* Book of Revelation *and* Genesis, *and there are indications that the* Book of Enoch *may have been the style manual for these first and last books of the Bible...*
>
> *It was at the end of the Fifth Century AD that the Church decided to replace the* Book of Enoch *with the* Book of Revelation, *because* [it was believed that] *John wrote the Revelation, and it fitted the mystical charismatic image the Church was creating for Jesus. The* Book of Enoch *did not fit into the political policies of the Church of that day...The reason apparent for withdrawing the* Book of Enoch *was that it pointed to pre-Christian beginnings of the doctrine upon which Christianity is based..."*
>
> [A version of the *Book of Enoch* was] *found in Quamran Cave Number Four* [Q-4] *in Palestine in the late 1950's by Dr. Josef Milik. Dr. Milik, a Jewish*

*archeologist, had searched for Dead Sea Scroll fragments for twenty years with good success as a team member with other archeologists...*

*After World War II, he developed the theory that the* Book of Enoch *may have originated in Palestine...He finally proved his theory to be correct after finding several scrolls and numerous fragments of the* Book of Enoch *in Quamran Cave Number Four. The Q-4 find of the* Book of Enoch *also satisfied his theory that the book had indeed originated with the Essenes.*[4]

Historically there is a great deal of evidence that the Bible as a whole was tampered with at different times to suit the purposes of the Church authorities. They were not initiated into the Mysteries, and therefore would not have understood the hidden meanings or higher purpose of the coded texts which served as a basis for Biblical scripture. Many are the critics who decry the rewriting of the Bible which has muddied the waters of knowledge concerning the true document. Turning again to Anderson we find more clues to the strategy behind this tampering:

*In the 325 AD Council of Nicea, it was determined that the Church should remove three Gnostic doctrines from its Canon beliefs and dogmas: 1. The Doctrine of Angels; 2. Psychic sciences and occult magic; and, 3. The Doctrine of Reincarnation. The belief in thousands of Enochian shining angels distracted from the monotheistic Son of God image of Jesus Christ. The gift of psychic seership and extrasensory perception, if taught to the people, would leave no church secrets the private property of the Church Fathers. If the Church believed in reincarnation and taught it, self-sacrifices in the name of Jesus Christ would have continued, and the slave and servant classes might not choose to serve their masters, even at the penalty of death, if they thought there was an alternative choice* [of freedom through death and reincarnation].[5]

The many revisions to the Bible brings into question the authenticity of the information contained therein and its doctrines. Anderson remarks that "many doctrines that are held as sacred, divine, 'original' scripture by today's Christian fundamentalists are actually doctrines established by the Roman Catholic Church Councils."[6] The Book of Revelation, as written, was likely a response to this unfortunate fact, and its author(s) undoubtedly drew upon the teachings of the Mystery Schools to encode a seemingly ominous scripture with sacred truth to preserve and further disseminate the true teachings under the noses of the unsuspecting Church authorities.

You may be wondering at this point how something that is composed of such terrifying images as the Book of Revelation could be anything *but* negative and fearful. The beauty of Numerology is its facility for revealing the true meaning of a word, no matter how negative or frightening the common or mundane definition may be.

This book will decode some of the more apparently negative passages of the enigmatic Book of Revelation with the help of Pythagoras. Pythagoras, through his system of Numerology, has provided us with a "code book" with which to translate the Revelation text.

Numerology is a system that was practiced in some form by initiates of the Mystery Schools and revealed to the world by Pythagoras. Pythagoras established his own school of higher learning where he taught that mathematics, music and astronomy were the foundation of all of the arts and sciences. He perfected the system of divining the sacred occult meanings of words by designating numerical equivalents to letters of the Greek alphabet, and rendering them with esoteric meanings much like the sacred Hebrew mystery keys, a system which assigned a number to each letter of the Hebrew alphabet. In simple terms, each letter is given a corresponding number and each number represents a principle or condition.

While the original system was based upon the Hebrew mystery keys, the system devised by Pythagoras used the Greek language, and an acceptable method for English has been adopted which has been proven to yield comparable results when compared with the Greek usage. This system has come to be known as the Pythagorean system of Numerology and the correspondences are as follows:

| **1** | **2** | **3** | **4** | **5** | **6** | **7** | **8** | **9** |
|---|---|---|---|---|---|---|---|---|
| A | B | C | D | E | F | G | H | I |
| J | K | L | M | N | O | P | Q | R |
| S | T | U | V | W | X | Y | Z | |

To find the subconscious or occult meaning of a word, the letters must be converted to numbers. The vowels, representing "Motivation," are added up separately from the consonants, representing "Personality," and then both are added together to find the natural "Expression" for that word. Thus the formula is:

**Motivation + Personality = Expression**

These terms are defined as follows:

## Motivation
The sum of the corresponding numbers of the vowels in a word. The drive or inspiration behind its outer actions.

## Personality
The sum of the corresponding numbers of the consonants in a word. The outer focal point through which the word expresses itself.

## Expression
The sum of the corresponding numbers of all the letters in a word. The manner in which the word most easily expresses itself—natural potential.

Once the numerical correspondences are understood, we can decode the esoteric meanings of words by adding the numerical values of each letter to reach a sum, in most cases reducing it to a single digit. Let's use the word "Revelation" as an example:

|  |  |  |  |  |  |  | | Personality |
|---|---|---|---|---|---|---|---|---|
| Consonants | 9 + | 4 + | 3 + | 2 | + | 5 | = | **23/5** *(2+3=5)* |
|  | **R** | **E V** | **E L** | **A** | **T** | **I O** | **N** | *Motivation* |
| Vowels |  | 5 + | 5 + | 1 | + | 9 + 6 | = | **+26/8** *(2+6=8)* |
|  |  |  |  |  |  |  |  | **49/4** |
|  |  |  |  |  |  |  |  | *Expression* |
|  |  |  |  |  |  |  |  | *(4+9=13; 1+3=4)* |

We can also assign the numerical position in the alphabet to any letter rather than its reduced Pythagorean number (which is actually the numerical position number reduced to a single digit). This gives us a more intricate interpretation and is useful in matters of complex esoteric principles. Then we translate that number into its esoteric meaning. An example of this is:

|  |  |  |  |  |  |  | | *(8+6=14; 1+4=5)* |
|---|---|---|---|---|---|---|---|---|
|  |  |  |  |  |  |  |  | **Personality** |
| *Consonants* | 18 + | 22 + | 12 + | 20 |  | + | 14 = | **86/5** |
|  | **R** | **E V** | **E L** | **A** | **T** | **I O** | **N** | *Motivation* |
| Vowels |  | 5 + | 5 + | 1 | + | 9 + 15 | = | **+35/8** *(3+5=8)* |
|  |  |  |  |  |  |  |  | **121/4** |
|  |  |  |  |  |  |  |  | *Expression* |
|  |  |  |  |  |  |  |  | *(1+2+1=4)* |

Notice that this method does not alter the inherent meaning of the numerological interpretation as the reduced values are unchanged.

We now need to look at the esoteric translation of the numbers as they are applied to our numerological analysis. These numerological meanings are as follows:

## Number              Esoteric Meaning

| 1 | Masculine, independent, new beginnings |
|---|---|
| 2 | Feminine, emotional, supportive |
| 3 | Communication—written and verbal |
| 4 | Practical, down-to-earth |
| 5 | Freedom, diversity, change |
| 6 | Duty, responsibility, service |
| 7 | Illumined intellect, mind, analytical process |
| 8 | Money, organization |
| 9 | Altruism, selflessness, compassion, philanthropy |

The word "Revelation" reveals a great deal when we analyze its meaning following the above guidelines. In it we find a blueprint for history leading up to the "Revelation," culminating in the birth of a new age. The word "Revelation" has elements of Buddha, the Great Pyramid, and King Arthur within its vibration. These apparently disparate subjects have a great deal in common when looked at through the lens of our deciphering tool, Numerology. Numerologically, Revelation expresses the energies of these names, indicating that they are all related in some way. The following analysis shows the relationship between Revelation and our three examples:

$$
\begin{array}{l}
2 \;+\; 4+4+8 \qquad = \; \mathbf{18} \\
\mathbf{B} \quad \mathbf{U} \quad \mathbf{D} \quad \mathbf{D} \quad \mathbf{H} \quad \mathbf{A} \\
21 \qquad + \qquad 1 \;=\; \underline{+22} \\
\qquad\qquad\qquad\qquad \mathbf{40}
\end{array}
\qquad
\begin{array}{l}
18 \;+\; 20+8 \;+\; 18 = 64 \\
\mathbf{A} \quad \mathbf{R} \quad \mathbf{T} \quad \mathbf{H} \quad \mathbf{U} \quad \mathbf{R} \\
1 \qquad + \qquad\qquad 21 \;=\underline{+22} \\
\qquad\qquad\qquad\qquad \mathbf{86}
\end{array}
$$

$$
\begin{array}{l}
\mathbf{18} \;+\; \mathbf{22} \;+\; \mathbf{12} \;+\; 20 \qquad +\; 14 \;=\; \mathbf{86} \\
\mathbf{R} \quad \mathbf{E} \quad \mathbf{V} \quad \mathbf{E} \quad \mathbf{L} \quad \mathbf{A} \quad \mathbf{T} \quad \mathbf{I} \quad \mathbf{O} \quad \mathbf{N} \\
5 \;+\; 5 \;+\; 1 \;+\; 9+15 \qquad =\; \underline{+35} \\
\qquad\qquad\qquad\qquad\qquad \mathit{121}
\end{array}
$$

$$
\begin{array}{l}
16+25+18 \;+\; 13 \;+\; 4 \;=\; 76 \\
\mathbf{P} \quad \mathbf{Y} \quad \mathbf{R} \quad \mathbf{A} \quad \mathbf{M} \quad \mathbf{I} \quad \mathbf{D} \\
1 \;+\; 9 \qquad =\; \underline{+10} \\
\qquad\qquad\qquad\qquad \mathbf{86}
\end{array}
$$

In numerological interpretation it isn't necessary for a word's elements (the Personality, Motivation and Expression) to be identical to those of another word. If any one of the elements are the same as any of the elements in another word, there is a significant relationship between the two words. If we think of the Personality as being the outer element, the Motivation as the inner element, and the Expression the manner in which the word naturally expresses itself as a result of these outer and inner elements, it is easier to understand how this can be so.

As an example, the fact that the Personality of Buddha is equivalent to the first letter of Revelation is important for the fact that the first letter of a word is many times more important than the remaining letters. This is because the first letter sets the tone for the energy of the word. In this example, the overall emphasis of the word Revelation is expressed by the Personality of Buddha, in other words, Revelation has the Personality of Buddha in its meaning.

If we examine the significance of the words Buddha, Arthur and Pyramid, we can gain greater insight into the meaning of Revelation, and greater comprehension of the historical events that have occurred as part of the process of the unfolding of the Revelation prophecy. Suspend the notion that Revelation is the prophecy of apocalyptic events, as fear-based interpretation is not part of this discussion.

Buddha was given the name Gautama at birth. According to the *Dictionary of All Scriptures and Myths* by G.A. Gaskell, Buddha experienced his initiation through "the six transcendent virtues" and reached a state of enlightenment under the Bodhi tree. Ascending from the plane of physical matter he became the Maitreya "whose very name implies love and tenderness toward mankind, and who was destined to become, like Gautama, a Savior of the world by teaching its inhabitants how to save themselves." Buddha represents the powers of the soul which are attained through personal effort. The Buddhic principle is "the source of all the higher emotions [relating to] Truth, Love and Wisdom."[7]

"The feminine Holy Spirit—Sophia [the goddess of Wisdom of the ancient Greeks]—and most of the great Goddesses of polytheism are symbols of [this principle]. She is the Divine Mother who gives birth to the Son of God on the buddhic plane, that Love and Truth may rule the soul in righteousness and peace when evolution is complete." The function of the Buddhic principle is the transmutation of "the lower emotions into higher emotions, so that the indwelling Self shall evolve itself and the lower nature of the Soul fall away."[8]

Thus the overriding energy of Revelation is that represented by the Buddha Personality; the transmutation of lower emotion to higher, to restore the feminine principle to its place of power, and the expression of Truth, Love and Wisdom. It is also significant that the number 22 is shared by Buddha (in its Motivation) and Revelation (as the letter "V"), as the number 22 is a Master Number representing the Master Builder—the principle of selfless service as part of the implementation of a great plan inspired by illumined vision.

"Arthur" also shares with Revelation the vibration of the number 22 in its Motivation. The legend of Camelot (Arthur's service to his people in compliance with Merlin's vision) and the quest for the Holy Grail (the knights' search for spiritual enlightenment) represent the transformative lessons of selfless service to humanity and the Great Quest—the individual's long search for his/her divine self. King Arthur lived around the beginning of the 6th century AD, during the turbulent time which was marked by the invasion of Britain by the Anglo Saxons. The Britons were a fragmented and disorganized people until Arthur arrived to unite them against their common enemy. He is said to have been brought to earth by the three queens known as Faith, Hope and Love, whose names evoke the exemplary traits of the universal teacher.

The Holy Grail, according to legend, was the cup used by Jesus and his disciples at the Last Supper when Jesus gave them his highest teachings. Legend also has it that Joseph of Arimathea, after the crucifixion, took the Grail cup to Britain and there placed it in a secret place which some have identified as the Chalice Well at Glastonbury. King Arthur's Knights of the Round Table left on their Quest for the Grail in search of spiritual fulfillment. The story of this Quest is about receiving membership into the mysteries of the Hierarchical teachings. This story reflects the teachings of the Mystery Schools, the unfolding of the long journey of the soul seeking its inner divinity through the struggles of earthly existence. An element of these teachings is the recognition of the power of the feminine. Symbolic of the devotion to the feminine or heart principle is Lancelot championing his lady, Guinevere.

Arthur created the round Table in order to ensure that no one in his assemblage of knights would be viewed as superior to the others, not even himself. This symbolized equality and unity among a diverse group established for the benefit of all. This principle is also, then, an inherent part of Revelation—the striving of humanity toward unity and bound by a common goal. And not only does "Arthur" relate to the vibration of the number 22, but the Expression of Arthur (86) is identical to the

Personality of Revelation, further emphasizing the principle represented by the relationship between these two words. Arthur was the great Peacemaker, who was delivered to earth by Faith, Hope and Love. Revelation, on a deep, symbolic level represents this same energy in its outer manifestation.

The word "Pyramid" represents the stages which humanity goes through to achieve oneness with the Godhead and it was upon the esoteric symbolism of the Pyramid which the Egyptian Mystery tradition was founded. This tradition was the foundation of the Christian teachings. Because the Great Pyramid is the centerpiece of the Mysteries it requires a deeper examination than we can give here and will therefore be discussed in greater detail in the next chapter. For our purposes here the importance of the principle symbolized by the Pyramid is clear when we see that its Expression is the same as that of Arthur and the Personality of Revelation.

Finally, the Expression of Revelation is 121. This number is very important as it tells us the overall meaning of Revelation, both the word and the Book itself. Another expression of this energy is found in the verse that holds the same numerical configuration: Rev. 12:1. This verse is the sum and substance of the entire Book of Revelation:

> *And there appeared a great woman in heaven;*
> *a woman clothed with the sun, and the moon*
> *under her feet, and upon her head a crown of*
> *twelve stars.*
>
> Rev. 12:1

To understand the meaning of Revelation we must decipher the symbolism of this passage. The "woman" represents the re-emergence of the feminine principle in human society. This full empowerment of the feminine will occur in the year 2000. The "sun" symbolizes the affirmation of life and the radiation of love to others. This principle is a requirement to the fulfillment of our spiritual destiny. "The moon under her feet" symbolizes mastery of the "moon," our subconscious mind. The subconscious is the source of habitual patterns which must be broken. The "crown of twelve stars" represents the 12-to-1 ratio so prevalent in our mythological archetypes: Jesus and his twelve disciples, Arthur and his twelve knights, Hercules and his twelve labors, and the twelve signs of the zodiac in the great circle of the heavens around the earth. All represent the twelve supporting energies present during the initiation of the individual pursuing spiritual evolution.A synthesis of the energies present in the word "Revelation" reveals a completely different meaning than has been attributed to it by literal translation. The book of Revelation is about the re-empowerment of the feminine leading to humanity's fulfillment of its spiritual destiny resulting in a new freedom for and unity among all people. This is the foundation of my premise and one which will be borne out upon examination of key Revelation passages which follow in subsequent chapters. As we shall see, in the esoteric tradition all things are related and this is especially true in the symbolism of language. It is here that we discover that a great plan is unfolding, heralding good news for humanity and the earth.

# 2

# THE GREAT PYRAMID OF GIZEH

As I STATED previously, the Great Pyramid is enormously important to any discussion of the Mystery School teachings, and therefore the Christian Mysteries, as it is the very symbol of the Egyptian Mysteries. This colossal limestone structure has endured the ravages of time for millennia, although its true age is a matter of dispute among researchers. In a remarkable feat of construction, someone of great intelligence and prophetic vision left us an enduring record of future world events, biblical history, and geophysical and astronomical knowledge.

The prophet Isaiah, while he wrote a millennium after the construction of the Pyramid, left us an important statement about the significance of the Pyramid in this scripture:

> *In that day there shall be an altar to the Lord in the midst of the Land of Egypt, and a monument at the border thereof to the Lord, and it shall be for a sign, and for a witness unto the Lord of Hosts in the Land of Egypt.*
>
> Isaiah 19:19-20

Isaiah wrote his scripture in the Hebrew language, each letter of which has a numerical value. The total sum of the numerical values of each word in these verses is 5,449. This is the precise height of the Great Pyramid when measured using the Sacred Jewish Inch. A coincidence? I think not. The Sacred Jewish Inch is equivalent to

1.00106 British inches, and its application to the Great Pyramid was discovered by Sir Isaac Newton.[1] This discovery enabled subsequent researchers to discover important Pyramidal measurements which revealed striking data.

Now, it is true that Isaiah wrote these verses well after the Pyramid was built, however, at the time of his writing, the base of the Pyramid was covered by sand and therefore not visible, which would have prevented him from measuring it or knowing exactly how deep the base lay. Another important point to recognize is that Isaiah wrote hundreds of years before Pythagorus gave geometry to the world and a calculation of the dimensions of the Pyramid would have required that knowledge.

While we're on the subject of the Pyramid's dimensions, let's examine the physical features of this great monument. We know already that the Pyramid is immense. Thanks to the work of researchers like physicist John Zajak, author of *The Delicate Balance*[2], we know some interesting facts about this wonder of the world. The following data and that on subsequent pages, unless otherwise noted, is from Zajak's work:

- The Pyramid's base has an area of 13.6 acres.
- The sides of the Pyramid each have an area of more than 5 acres.
- It rests upon a naturally existing solid granite base, and could not be supported by mere sand and earth, leaving us to conclude that its builders knew this precise location provided the support such a great structure required.
- The height of the Pyramid at its apex is 5,812.98 inches.
- The sides each measure 9,131 inches at the base.
- The sum of the length of the base's four sides equals 36,524 inches. If we move the decimal point over two places to the left, the result is 365.24, the exact length of the solar year.
- If an imaginary circle is circumscribed around the base, its circumference divided by twice the height of the Pyramid equals 3.14159, which any student of geometry will recognize as the value of *pi*.
- The exact height of the Pyramid, 5,449 inches, is equal to the average height of the earth's land masses located above sea level.

We have Sir Isaac Newton to thank for discovering the unit of measurement by which the Pyramid was constructed. His discovery was the result of his research into calculating the law of gravity, for which he needed to know the diameter of the earth. Knowledge of the Pyramid's keys to Earth's secrets and its history was well known even then by members of secret societies (to be discussed in Chapter 5) which were established to preserve the teachings of the Mystery Schools. Newton was most certainly a member of one of these secret groups, for he chose to seek the answer to the problem of the earth's diameter by investigating the Mysteries' vault of earth knowledge, the Great Pyramid. In verification of Newton's research, a remarkable discovery was made in the 1940's by a pilot who was shooting aerial photographs of the Pyramid. The pilot's photographs revealed that the four sides of the Pyramid have a concave surface. The degree of curvature of the surfaces is identical to that of the earth's curvature. Not only is it incredible that the architects of the Pyramid were capable of the precision this construction required, but they evidently knew vital geometric statistics regarding the earth when they built it.

Let's take a further look at Zajak's data on the Pyramid's features, as we have only begun to scratch the surface of this remarkable structure.

- The Pyramid faces true North.
- The Pyramid sits at the center of Earth's land mass; in other words, if you look at a globe, the Pyramid's East-West axis lines up with the earth's longest parallel, and the Pyramid''s North-South axis lines up with its longest meridian.
- The original surface of the Pyramid was constructed of 144,000 casing stones made of white limestone, an extremely hard substance, which were so highly polished that the reflection of the sun's light could be seen from as far away as Israel. (The significance of the number of stones will be discussed later.)
- The Pyramid is so huge that it can be seen from the moon (as reported by astronauts).
- The Pyramid's cornerstones are connected by a ball-and-socket joints, enabling the structure to adjust to the expansion and contraction associated with extremes of heat and cold, movement of the earth resulting from earthquakes, and normal settling.

- The precision with which the stones were cut resulted in a mere .01 inch of variance in nearly perfect right angles for each of the six sides of the stones. This precision in cutting 20-ton blocks of stone cannot be duplicated by today's technology.
- The Pyramid's stones were spaced .02 inch apart to allow them to be glued together. The glue used was a white cement that is still intact.

All this points to the fact that the technological know-how that was used to construct this great monument was advanced even by today's standards. Now that we have looked at the external features of the Pyramid, we turn to its interior to explore the secrets it holds.

The internal features include: two passageways, the Ascending and Descending Passages; a small room at the bottom of the Descending Passage called the Bottomless Pit; a larger open area at the end of the Ascending Passage called the Grand Gallery, which begins at the entrance to a smaller passage leading to the Queen's Chamber; the King's Chamber, which opens at the other end of the Grand Gallery; and the Construction Chamber, located directly above the King's Chamber. It should be noted that the Grand Gallery is a larger passageway that ascends from the Queen's Chamber level to the King's Chamber entrance. The construction of these internal structures is remarkable in itself:

- The Ascending and Descending Passages are both constructed at a 26.3 degree angle to the horizontal or ground level.
- The Queen's Chamber is finished in pristine limestone and has a gabled ceiling.
- The King's Chamber is finished in highly polished granite and has a flat ceiling.
- Above the King's Chamber, in the Construction Chamber, are five layers of single 70-ton stone "beams" that support the upper portion of the Pyramid.
- A massive plug was found wedged into the entrance from the Descending to the Ascending Passage that is composed of the same rare type of red granite as found on Mt. Horeb where Moses received the Ten Commandments.
- Air vents built into the main chambers help maintain a constant

internal temperature of 68 degrees Fahrenheit.

- A small, more crudely built passageway called the Well Shaft connects the lower end of the Grand Gallery with the lower end of the Descending Passage.

Again, the sheer dimensions of its construction evoke questions about the knowledge and technological capability that was required to build the Great Pyramid. The long-held answer that it was constructed by slaves using crude level-and-fulcrum technology doesn't hold up on close examination. But this isn't all. Let's take a look at some interesting related astronomical data:

- The Descending Passage, which extends to the exterior of the Pyramid, lines up with a Pole Star once every several thousand years. The last time this happened, it lined up with the star Alpha Draconis, the Dragon Star, in 2141 B.C. This date is actually inscribed, and is the only inscription that exists, in the Pyramid.
- At this time the new Pole Star, Polaris or the North Star, is the featured celestial player in the Pyramid's unfolding saga. In 1997 it illuminated the entrance to the Well Shaft, also called the Point of Last Escape.
- In 2004, the North Star will cast its light directly on the center of the floor of the Descending passage, the Bottomless Pit.

Additional astronomical information is discussed at length in the book *The Orion Mystery* by Robert Bauval and Adrian Gilbert. This book examines the relationship between the arrangement of the Gizeh complex structures and the constellation of Orion. Bauval and Gilbert establish, with aerial photographs and constellational maps, that the pyramids' arrangement exactly mirrors the stars which form the "belt" of Orion. In addition, the air shafts inside the Great Pyramid point directly toward this constellation. The authors also contend that the Pyramids were built much earlier than commonly believed. They date the Pyramids' construction at 10450 B.C., citing the fact that their positions reflect an exact alignment with the Orion constellation at that date. (Stars move very slowly over time so that presently this alignment is off somewhat.)[3] This date has been corroborated by the research of Robert Schoch which will be discussed in Chapter 4.

Another researcher, Alan F. Alford, has put forth yet another theory about the purpose of the Great Pyramid that supports the theory of extraterrestrial intervention on earth in ancient times. He agrees with Bauval on the date of construction, but goes on to say that the Great Pyramid likely served as a beacon to guide aircraft toward a huge stone platform at Baalbek in Lebanon, (discovered to have a geographical relationship by Zecharia Sitchin, author of *The Stairway to Heaven*), which was probably a landing site. The fact that this great structure can be seen from the moon supports this position. Alford's theory goes further, however, and presents a strictly functional interpretation of the features of the Great Pyramid. The function of the Great Pyramid according to Alford was that of a power generator which drew its power from water. He contends that the 15-foot-high Queen's Chamber Niche (a cavity in the Queen's Chamber wall) marks the position of a Water Fuel Cell which was removed at some long-ago date. The manner in which this powered the generator has to do with the separation of water into its elements, oxygen and hydrogen. Without going into the technical aspects of this device, suffice it to say that the gases were sent to the King's Chamber, probably via some kind of conduit, and burned to produce heat. The five granite beams located above the King's Chamber, in what is called the Construction Chamber, feature smooth bottoms and rough tops, a feature which has perplexed pyramid researchers. Alford states that this allowed the beams to give off more heat than they absorbed and concludes that the Construction Chamber was therefore a chimney. Alford also believes that the Grand Gallery, due to the nature of its construction, may have served as a radio-telescope. He cites the existence of 29 niches inside the Grand Gallery that are yet to be explained and suggests that they may have held crystals which would have served as important components of the communications function of a radio-telescope.[4]

I personally believe that the date of the construction of the Great Pyramid predates Bauval and Gilbert's theorized date by as many as 15,000 years. The foundation for this belief lies in the Astrological cycle known as the Precession of the Equinoxes in which the position of the vernal equinox makes a backward movement (at the rate of about $1°$ every 72 years) through the zodiac until it completes a full cycle. This cycle's duration—also known as a Great Age—is 26,000 years, a time period that was an intrinsic part of the Mystery School wisdom, as well as other ancient wisdom traditions including the classical Greek and Mesoamerican teachings. The significance of this 26,000-year cycle is represented in the very features of the Sphinx and its relationship to the Pyramid.

The Sphinx has the front paws of a lion, the back legs and tail of a bull, a human face, and, at the back of the head, the wings of an eagle. In ancient times fires were burned in firepits at night on the sides of the Sphinx, emphasizing and glorifying the wings. Metaphysician Joseph Robert Jochmans correlates the Lion, Bull, Human and Eagle of the Sphinx with the "four beings before the throne of the divine as described in the Books of Ezekiel and the Revelation [as well as] the four fixed signs of the zodiac—Leo, Taurus, Aquarius, and Scorpio."[5] A symbol of the achievement of God Consciousness, the Pyramid has a unique relationship to the Sphinx, a symbol of the human attributes which must be integrated and overcome. The Pyramid represents that which humanity will achieve when it has succeeded in integrating the symbolism of that figure which lies opposite to it, the Sphinx.

Interestingly, Jochmans also comments:

> *Most significantly, in the precession of the equinoxes, the distant Age of Leo...saw the burial of the Hall of Records beneath the Sphinx's front paws, as described in Egyptian, Hermetic, classical, Coptic and medieval Arabic chronicles...*
>
> *Today we have just entered the Age of Aquarius, and the face of the Sphinx symbolizes the face of global humanity joined in one mind and one heart, the goal of an evolving Aquarian civilization.*
>
> *Another 6,000 years into the future will complete the Sphinx's prophecy in the distant Age of Scorpio, when perhaps humanity's spiritual evolution will be complete. The flaming wings of the Sphinx may be more than just that of an eagle, they may signify the fire of the phoenix, the higher form of Scorpio that epitomizes its central themes of death and transfiguration.*[6]

Jochmans notes that Nostradamus predicted the end of his

prophecies for humanity and the end of the Pyramid's timeline both fall within the 83rd century—during the Age of Scorpio. This being the case, it stands to reason that if the structures in the Pyramid complex represent a complete cycle, and the archetype for that cycle is the precession (backward movement) of the equinoxes through the Ages, and if the end of the cycle is the Age of Scorpio, then the beginning of this cycle must be at the end of the Libran Age (one full turn backward through the zodiac).

Following the astrological model above leads to the suggestion that the first quarter of the cycle took Earth from the Libran Age to the Age of Leo, represented by the Lion's paws of the Sphinx; the second quarter brought us to the Age of Taurus, represented by the hind quarters of the Bull; the third quarter takes us to the Age of Aquarius, the Human face; and the fourth quarter—completing the cycle—will take us to the Eagle wings at the back of the head, the Age of Scorpio. This complete cycle, as mentioned above, takes nearly 26,000 years and the average length of time required to complete one astrological age is approximately 2,160 years. This being the case I believe that the Pyramid was built 19,440 years ago or roughly in 17400 B.C. As stated previously, the 26,000-year Great Age is an important feature in the time-keeping traditions in many cultures. The Mayans believe that at the end of a Great Age one world ends and another begins. This is in keeping with prophecies from around the world which speak of a succession of worlds through which humans must evolve.

Astrologically, Aquarius and Leo are opposite each other. The significance of this is that the key to successfully working with opposing energies, in this case Aquarius and Leo, is to consciously balance the tension that exists between them and integrate the qualities of the complementary elements in which each reside. In this case the elements are air and fire. Aquarius represents forward thinking and is the sign of universal consciousness and spiritual rebirth. The positive expression of this sign is humanitarianism on a grand scale. The negative is emotional detachment. Leo is the sign of self-consciousness and rules the heart. The positive expression of this sign is divine compassion and the negative is self-aggrandizement and arrogance.[7]

By integrating the positive expressions of each, the humanitarianism and spiritual renewal of Aquarius and the heart-centered compassion of Leo, humanity can overcome its tendencies toward destructive self-centeredness and arrogance. Then will humanity evolve to its next step—cosmic consciousness. Fire requires air to burn. As we cross the threshold of the Aquarian Age, we have the opportunity to ignite the fires of compassion for our fellow human beings with visionary humanitarian ideals and step into a future where all humanity is united "in one heart and one mind."

To understand how all of this relates to Revelation prophecy and our discussion of hidden symbolism, let's look a little deeper at some of the secrets that the Pyramid has yielded. Recall that Sir Isaac Newton discovered that the Pyramid's measurements were based upon the Sacred Jewish Inch. This unit of measurement has an esoteric meaning behind it, and if we substitute time for linear measurement—years for inches—(this is done in the Bible, Zajak points out) we can deduce that the Pyramid builders used the Sacred Jewish Inch to record time—an inch for a year.

The Pyramid's timeline yields some very interesting information. Again, let's look at John Zajak's data:

- The intersection of the Ascending and Descending Passages is the point that corresponds to the year 1453 B.C., the year of the Jewish Exodus from Egypt.
- The point where the Main Gallery begins corresponds to April 3, 33 A.D. (equating fractions of an inch to fractions of a year), the date of the crucifixion of Christ.
- The floor of the Queen's Chamber entry passage where it intersects the Ascending Passage corresponds to September 29, 2 BC, the birthdate of Christ. (The calculation of this date takes into account a two-year error in our calendar.)
- The horizontal length of the base of the Pyramid (one side) equals 30,043 inches, falling 3,469 inches short of the crucifixion date, or October 14, 29 A.D., the date Christ was baptised.
- The end of the Grand Gallery, where it meets the entrance passage to the King's Chamber, corresponds to the year 1914, the year in which World War I began.

Peter Lemesurier, as outlined in his book *The Great Pyramid Decoded*, interprets the timeline as extending until the 83rd century.

Note that this verifies Jochmans' end date of the Pyramid's timeline
and is the time of the end of Nostradamus' prophecies in the Age of
Scorpio. Lemesurier interprets the point where the limestone floor of
the Antechamber and the granite floor leading into the King's Chamber
meet as correlating to our present time. He suggests that this change of
material indicates a marked step upward in the spiritual evolution of
humanity, and places its beginning as February 21, 1999.[8] Other
researchers have provided additional chronographic information
relating to the Pyramid's internal structures, but a thorough discussion
goes beyond the scope of this book. It is significant to note that Edgar
Cayce verified the above dating system in one of his readings, saying
that the measurement/dating system represents the "periods through
which the world has passed and is passing, as related to the religious or
the spiritual experiences of man."[9]   The importance of the Sacred
Jewish Inch and its relationship to historical dates speaks for itself. A
thorough reading of the sources cited here will provide a more in-depth
understanding.

As in the fable of the twelve blind men each attempting to identify
an elephant by describing only one of its parts, the foregoing theories
each explain a small portion of the entire Pyramid story. It is likely that
all are merely pieces of the Great Puzzle. The Pyramid was certainly
built as a repository of knowledge, intended to preserve that
knowledge for posterity. Whoever built the Pyramid had a pretty
advanced knowledge of astronomy and vital statistics of the earth. And
it's a good bet that it served as some kind of beacon/generator device.
I will add with great confidence that the Pyramid symbolizes
humanity's need to overcome the past represented by the Leo
symbolism of the Sphinx, and embrace our future represented by the
Aquarian symbol, the Pyramid.

The previous examination of the Pyramid's features lead to the
conclusion that a tremendous amount of foresight, precision and
technological capability were possessed by the builders. If we look into
the symbolic significance of the Great Pyramid, we find it is a symbol
of man's aspiration toward divinity and his mystical union with
universal consciousness.

Breaking the Great Pyramid's outer features down to its individual
elements, we find more complex symbolism. The base of the Pyramid
represents a square with each side corresponding to the four cardinal

directions on the physical plane. On the spiritual plane, these four sides symbolize virtue, profundity, intelligence and truth. The four triangular faces consisting of a total of twelve linear sides symbolize the twelve signs of the zodiac.

We have already discussed the interior of the Pyramid and its physical features. The teachings of Coptic International, steeped in Egyptian tradition, reveal the symbolism of the materials used in its construction, and of the Chambers and Passages:

- Rock symbolizes the Living God.
- Limestone symbolizes the human.
- Granite symbolizes the Divine.
- Sandstone symbolizes things of an earthly nature.
- The Descending Passage and the Pit symbolize the descent of the soul into the material.
- The Ascending Passage symbolizes the upward climb of the soul.
- The Horizontal Passage leading to the Queen's Chamber symbolizes the lack of progressive spiritual growth and ascent at the time of the birth of Jesus.
- The Grand Gallery signifies the offering of high spiritual opportunity and resurrection. It is also symbolic of the soul's expansion into varied and greater planes of endeavor.
- The Great Step symbolizes a great step upward on the part of humanity in the middle of the past century.
- The illumination of the floor of the Pit by the Pole Star symbolizes man's illumination at his darkest hour.
- The Queen's Chamber symbolizes the birth of spirituality at the time of Christ—for woman represents Mother Nature—and the birth of a new era of feminine empowerment.
- The King's Chamber symbolizes divine protection.
- The Capstone is missing,symbolizing that humanity has for the most part rejected the teachings of Christ. But, the appearance of the New Messiah in the form of the Group Avatar will restore peace and harmony, and then the Capstone will be returned to its place atop the Pyramid.

Having examined the physical and symbolic aspects of the Great Pyramid, we turn to the practical application of the Mystery teachings, namely the initiation of a Master which was performed at the Gizeh complex. For this description we have Hamid Bey to thank, who was himself an initiate of the Egyptian Mysteries.[10]

The transition ceremony of the Masters that have been initiated into the Mystery tradition is a rite performed to usher the Master's soul from the physical body into the celestial realm of God Consciousness. The body was brought before the Sphinx for the ceremony, but it was understood that the soul had ceased to be earth-bound and was ready to seek communion with the Cosmic Spirit. The ritual of initiation began in front of the Sphinx and was completed inside the Great Pyramid.

It took three days and three nights for the astral body to take leave of the physical body, and that was the duration of the ceremony. The casket was prepared at the entrance of the Great Pyramid to receive the body of the great being. When the body had been placed within the casket it was then borne to the King's Chambe,if the Master was a man, or the Queen's Chamber, if the Master was a woman. Once the casket had been taken into the Grand Gallery seven Masters entered the Temple and the Master Mason sealed the passage. The Masters, or High Priests of the three natures of man bore the body into the King's or Queen's Chamber. The three priests then would retire to different chambers. The seven Masters required to perform this important ceremony were:

1.  The Master Mason—The Building Master
2.  The Astronomical Master—The Master Director of the Proceeding
3.  The Astrological Master—The Master who determines the position
4.  The Golden Master—The Master of Wisdom who went into the secret chamber, symbolizing spirituality, above the King's Chamber.
5.  The Sensation Master—The Master of Conscious Reasoning Power, who stayed with the body.
6.  The Silver Master—The Master of Memory or Records who went into a secret chamber that symbolized the subconscious part of man.
7.  The Christ Consciousness—This seventh Master is present in spirit. His was the body that lay in the casket.

When the Great Pyramid had been closed under the direction of the Master Mason and the body had been placed as indicated, the seven Masters took up their proper positions and remained for six days in meditation. The Golden Master, as stated, entered the special chamber which we know to be above the King's Chamber, although it has not yet been discovered.

In this particular chamber is kept the golden cap which, at the time of the ceremony was placed on top of the Pyramid, and I will add that this cap has remained hidden for a very long time. The cap symbolizes the superconsciousness or spirituality of man. While the Master of Sensations stayed with the body, the Silver Master entered into the Great Hall of Records which symbolized the subconscious mind of man. The Master Mason and the Astronomical and Astrological Masters prepared the way for the body to be taken into this great chamber. After six days of meditation, when the soul of the initiate had completely passed through the golden cap and became One with Universal Consciousness, the cap was removed and placed again in the superconscious chamber. Once completed, a silk covering that had been placed over the Pyramid for the ceremony was removed and the torches that had been burning were extinguished. All those that had been present for the ceremony returned to their homes.

At the completion of the initiation the six Masters descended with the body of the seventh into the great Archive Chamber to begin the preservation of the body. This procedure required three years to complete, and resulted in the petrifaction of the body. Food and water were supplied to them through a secret passage known only to the Master Mason. This ritual was only performed for those Masters who had attained Christ Consciousness. The last Master to have completed the great initiation at the Great Pyramid was Jesus the Christ.

This chapter has provided an overview of the traditions from which our present-day traditions began and an extensive discussion of the meaning of the Pyramid's secrets and how it applies to humanity's evolution on planet Earth. Now that we have an understanding of the connection between the Bible and the Great Pyramid as it relates to prophecy, we can now move on to the subject of the Book of Revelation, which, again, has its roots in the ancient Egyptian Mystery tradition. This tradition is rooted in the idea of the evolution of humanity. As humanity evolves, it gets closer to its destiny — the achievement of Christ Consciousness. The time is upon us for the return of the Christ Consciousness to Earth, but this time it will not be in the body of one individual. The return of Christ Consciousness will involve many, just as there were many Messiahs over the long course of human history before and after Jesus.

## 3

# REVELATION AND THE EGYPTIAN TAROT

THE EGYPTIAN TAROT was probably derived, as I indicated earlier, from *The Book of Thoth*, a sacred text that held within it the secrets of nature and life, and gave initiates in the Mystery Schools power over earthly phenomena. The symbols represented on the cards taken as a whole can be thought of as the blueprint of human consciousness which operate through the subjective state of the subconscious, much as the imagery in dreams. At the time that the Egyptian Mystery School was at the height of its glory, these symbolic representations were kept hidden from the masses to prevent the knowledge and power that went with it from falling into the hands of those who would abuse it. Eventually, however, the cards began to be circulated, perhaps to introduce their symbolism into the world so that the higher principles would begin to filter into the subconscious of humanity.

Tarot cards were probably introduced to Europe during the time of the Crusades by the Knights Templars on their return from the East. To conceal the mystical purpose of the cards it is likely that they were presented as playing cards, thereby ensuring both their secrecy and preservation, as the Church strictly forbade divination or pursuits in magic during that time. It is believed that all playing cards are derived from the Tarot.[1]

Numerology and the Tarot are both systems of divination employed by the Mystery Schools. Inasmuch as they both reflect a spiritual source for higher information and are basically part of the universal wisdom, it stands to reason that the two techniques would be practiced in tandem by the ancient Masters. This is in fact the case, as evidence shows that both systems, among others such as Astrology, formed the basis of the teachings of the sages of old.

The first twenty-two cards of the Tarot are called the Major Arcana, meaning "major teachings," and according to Angeles Arrien in *The Tarot Handbook*, they represent universal laws which each individual will experience during a lifetime in the form of events and circumstances. These laws are aspects of inner lessons which are universal in nature, referred to by Jung as *major archetypes* which are collectively experienced. In practical terms, the Major Arcana represent twenty-two aspects of our experiences which teach us and help us grow as human beings.[2]

The relationship between the Tarot and the Book of Revelation is fairly evident when we consider the common elements between the 22 Major Arcana and the 22 Chapters in Revelation. Manly P. Hall considers these commonalities when he states that in all likelihood the 22 cards of the Major Arcana of the Tarot each represent one of the 22 chapters of the Book of Revelation. He believes, however, that the order of the symbols on the cards are not in the same sequence as they were originally, having been deliberately altered with the likely intention of preserving their secret purpose.[3] I share this view and with the foregoing as a foundation, I will discuss the similar symbologies of the 22 Major Arcana of the Tarot and the corresponding chapters of the Book of Revelation. In subsequent chapters and in the Appendices key words and phrases will be decoded using the Pythagorean Numerology system.

To further illustrate the relationship between Numerology, the Tarot and the Book of Revelation,the chart at the end of this chapter gives the metaphysical correspondences between the 22 Chapters of the Book of Revelation, the 22 cards of the Major Arcana of the Egyptian Tarot, and their numerological values. I have rearranged the order of the cards to what I believe was their original sequence, exchanging the 5th and 6th cards for each other and placing the "0" card, the Fool, as the twenty-second card. This placement agrees with the *Sacred Tarot* of C.C. Zain, founder of the Church of Light, who, in 1919, modified the Egyptian Tarot of Paul Christian which was in common use at that time.[4]

The relationship between the 22 cards of the Major Arcana and the 22 Revelation chapters can be more easily seen when we compare the higher meanings of their respective symboligies. The following meanings given for the Major Arcana of the Tarot were inspired by Angeles Arrien's *The Tarot Handbook.*

| *Major Arcana Card* | *Revelation Chapter* |
|---|---|
| **1  The Magician**<br>The Magician represents the positive energy of the Male principle. The principle of inspired communication. Original and creative. Our link with Universal Wisdom. | **Chapter 1**<br>Jesus Christ—undisputably a great Magician—is the first person named in Revelation; represents an ideal for which to strive. Activation of the 7chakras. (See Appendix I) |
| **2  The High Priestess**<br>Represents the Feminine Principle. Receptive energy, intuition and gestation. Creative self-sufficiency. Balance and objective judgment. | **Chapter 2**<br>Overcoming our reluctance to express our feminine nature, represents the future of feminine leadership. The feminine will find balance in forgiveness of the masculine side. (See Appendix II) |
| **3  The Empress**<br>Represents love combined with wisdom. Emotional discernment. Nurturance and healing of self and others. | **Chapter 3**<br>Feminine communication from heart, mind in the context of global leadership. Altruistic nurturing of others to empower them. (See Appendix III) |
| **4  The Emperor**<br>Represents, personal power and enlightened leadership. The patriarch. Start of a new venture. Resolution of conflict. Responsibility for personal well-being | **Chapter 4**<br>The right use of masculine power in leadership. Practical approach toward achieving earthly success. Attending to the details in management of personal affairs. (See Appendix IV) |

| *Major Arcana Card* | *Revelation Chapter* |
|---|---|
| **5 The Lovers**<br>Represents the principle of family and social responsibility, love, passion and compassion, healing | **Chapter 5**<br>Empowering others by fostering freedom. Freedom through diversity. The beginning of the opening of the "seven seals." (See Appendix V) |
| **6 The Hierophant**<br>Represents learning, the initiator; the four gifts of practicality, creativity, originality, and passion. | **Chapter 6**<br>Importance of responsibility and service. Mastery of the "4 Horses": Spiritual, Emotional, Mental, Physical. (See Appendix VI) |
| **7 The Chariot**<br>Represents change and variety, contemplation. Balance between quietude and activity. | **Chapter 7**<br>Disciplines of meditation and contemplation. Acceleration of mental processes to achieve greater awareness. (See Appendix VII) |
| **8 Strength**<br>Represents personal gifts and talents with which we can conquer our inner beasts. Creative power. Passion, lust, charisma. | **Chapter 8**<br>Focus on practical matters. Acceptance of worldly responsibility leading to material reward and inspired creativity. (See Appendix VIII) |
| **9 The Hermit**<br>Represents contemplation, introspection. Completion of unfinished business from the past. | **Chapter 9**<br>Altruism, dedicatoin to higher service. Power is acquired and karma repaid through service to empower others. (See Appencix IX) |

| *Major Arcana Card* | *Revelation Chapter* |
|---|---|

**10 Wheel of Fortune**
Represents opportunity, abundance, prosperity. The beginning of a new cycle at a higher level. Awakening to possibility.

**Chapter 10**
The quest for perfection. Potential of inner angelic force. Vocal expression of the seven thunders to awaken others. (See Appendix X)

**11 Justice**
Represents completion of a venture that has been begun. Balance in all things, integrity, the truth of the individual's identity.

**Chapter 11**
The two pillars symbolizing past and present are represented by **1 1**. The left = past lifetimes; the right = the present. (See Appendix XI)

**12 The Hanged Man**
Represents sacrifice, independence achieved when the self surrenders to a higher power. Breaking of old patterns, adopting a new perspective. Sacrifice of the ego.

**Chapter 12**
The feminine principle attaining the true Christ/ Buddha essence. A new freedom for all resulting from liberation of the feminine. (See Appendix XII)

**13 Death**
Represents an ending, rebirth and renewal, transformation. Detachment and release. Letting go and moving forward.

**Chapter 13**
The death of old ideas and emotions; the birth of new ones. Shamanic death— release of old, outworn patterns. (See Appendix XIII)

**14 Temperance**
Represents balance between polarities. Integration. The union of opposites resulting in a higher expression of their energies. Creative visualization.

**Chapter 14**
The personal energy of the symbolism of 144,000. The right use of higher freedom and wisdom to awaken others to their potential. (See Appendix XIV)

*Major Arcana Card*                    *Revelation Chapter*

**15  The Devil**

Represents stability. The evocation of creative power through the law of attraction. Centered approach to problem solving.

**Chapter 15**

Confronting our "Devil"— past-life karma. A Capricornian/responsibility issue. Individual freedom leading to higher service. (See Appendix XV)

**16  The Tower**

Represents healing and restoration. Awakening to false beliefs, and the destruction of old ways to make room for renewal.

**Chapter 16**

The concept of Armageddon. Connfronting the tests of money, sex and power. Facing and conquering past-life issues. (See Appendix XVI)

**17  The Star**

Represents self-esteem and confidence which is recognized by others. Trusting in inner guidance to actualize balance and clarity.

**Chapter 17**

Liberation from addiction and self-deprecating behavior. In-tegration of the $1^{st}$ and $7^{th}$ chakras activating the feminine. (See Appendix XVII)

**18  The Moon**

Represents intuition, choice-making and expression of the authentic self. Feminine power.

**Chapter 18**

Expressing altruism and philanthropy. Assisting the birth of Baby Christs through nurturance (the feminine). (See Appendix XVIII)

**19  The Sun**

Represents teamwork and partnership. The life force and creativity directed toward a shared vision between inner masculine and inner feminine nature.

**Chapter 19**

Expression of the life-giving power of the inner sun to empower others and negate karma. (See Appendix XIX)

| *Major Arcana Card* | *Revelation Chapter* |
|---|---|
| **20 Judgment** | **Chapter 20** |
| Represents discernment, end of suffering, revival, objectivity, resolution. Realization changing personal consciousness. | Resolution of differences betwen inner masculine and inner feminine natures. Achievement of equality among a diverse population. (See Appendix XX) |
| **21 The World** | **Chapter 21** |
| Represents totality, individuation, and union of polarities resulting in achievement of life purpose, wholeness. | Activation of superconscious. Multi-dimensional inner worlds supported by Prayer. The feminine as world teacher. (See Appendix XXI) |
| **22 The Fool** | **Chapter 22** |
| Represents youth, mysticism, innovation, courage, absence of fear. Spontaneity, unlimited possibilities. Spiritually enlightened consciousness. | The birth of the inner child. Freedom to explore new levels of existence; faith while stepping into the unknown; world service. (See Appendix XXII) |

These descriptions are by design brief and sketchy, offered only to illustrate the general symbolism shared by the Tarot and the Chapters of Revelation. Subsequent chapters and the Appendices will explore in greater detail the meanings of specific Revelation verses. We turn now to explore the symbolism of the Sphinx and the "Tests of the Nile" to offer more insight into the symbolism associated with the Eqyptian tradition and its influence on biblical interpretation.

| Letter | Numerical Equivalent | Revelation Chapter | Tarot Major Arcana Card | Astrological Association | Elemental Relationship | Mental Function | Quality or Principle |
|--------|---------------------|--------------------|--------------------------|-------------------------|------------------------|-----------------|----------------------|
| A | 1 | 1 | Magician | Mercury | Mercury | Creativity, Initiation | Wisdom |
| B | 2 | 2 | High Priestess | Moon | Silver | Receptive energy, Gestation | Intuition |
| C | 3 | 3 | Empress | Venus | Copper | Growth, Sociability | Productivity |
| D | 4 | 4 | Emperor | Aries | Fire | Discipline, Practicality | Authority |
| E | 5 | 5 | Lovers | Gemini | Air | Freedom, Change | Union |
| F | 6 | 6 | Hierophant | Taurus | Earth | Service, Love, Healing | Organization |
| G | 7 | 7 | Chariot | Cancer | Water | Introspective, Philosophical | Triumph |
| H | 8 | 8 | Strength | Leo | Fire | Power, Responsibility | Success |
| I | 9 | 9 | Hermit | Virgo | Earth | Compassion, Selflessness | Self-reliance |
| J | 10 | 10 | Wheel of Fortune | Jupiter | Tin | Change, Transformation | Destiny |
| K | 11 | 11 | Justice | Libra | Air | Idealism, Illumination | Guidance |

| Letter | Numerical Equivalent | Revelation Chapter | Tarot Major Arcana Card | Astrological Association | Elemental Relationship | Mental Function | Quality or Principle |
|---|---|---|---|---|---|---|---|
| L | 12 | 12 | Hanged Man | Neptune | Water | Reversal, Surrender to Spirit | Inner Peace |
| M | 13 | 13 | Death | Scorpio | Water | Death of old, Evolution | Rebirth |
| N | 14 | 14 | Temperance | Sagittarius | Fire | Balance, Harmony | Resolution |
| O | 15 | 15 | Devil | Capricorn | Earth | Overcoming bondage | Anger |
| P | 16 | 16 | Tower | Mars | Iron | Awakening, Grace | Dominion |
| Q | 17 | 17 | Star | Aquarius | Air | Revelation, Meditation | Inspiration |
| R | 18 | 18 | Moon | Pisces | Water | Intuition, Altruism | Serenity |
| S | 19 | 19 | Sun | Sun | Gold | Regeneration, Wholeness | Emergence |
| T | 20 | 20 | Judgment | Pluto | Fire | Realization, Judgment | Renewal |
| U | 21 | 21 | World | Saturn | Lead | Liberation, At-one-ment | Completion |
| V | 22 | 22 | The Fool | Uranus | Air | Conception, New Experience | Spontaneity |

# 4

# Decoding the Secrets of the Sphinx
## and
## the Tests of the Nile

AN IMPOSING TWO hundred feet long and seventy feet high, the
mysterious Sphinx has intrigued mankind for thousands of years. The
central portion of its body is carved of one massive stone, while the
front paws were constructed of smaller pieces of rock. It originally was
painted red, evidenced by the bits of red remaining in places. The nose
was broken by a Mohammedan zealot to discourage idolatry, but its
enigmatic presence remains regardless of the ravages of man and time.[1]
Many researchers and laypersons hold the view that it is the original
entrance to the Great Pyramid, a belief that is supported by the writings
of Iamblichus, a Greek chronicler of the 4th century A.D. Iamblichus
wrote that the Sphinx was the portal through which the initiates of the
Mysteries passed to reach the hidden vaults within the Pyramid where
initiation took place. Galleries leading to the underground chambers of
the Pyramid were constructed like a maze, which could not be
successfully traversed without a guide.[2]

In 1991, Dr. Robert Schoch, a geologist at Boston University,
conducted some exciting studies concerning the Sphinx and the Great
Pyramid at Gizeh. His findings show a direct correspondence between
the age of these structures and the time-line given in *The Book of
Knowledge: The Keys of Enoch*. Dr. Schoch estimates that the Great
Sphinx is at least 8,000 years old, which is considerably older than the
traditionally accepted age of 4,500 years. It is his belief that the Sphinx
was at times allowed to be swallowed up by drifting sand, only to be
later re-excavated and subsequently repaired. Schoch gives as
evidence of the ability of such an ancient civilization to construct a

monument of the complexity of the Sphinx the existence of the ancient cities of Jericho and Catal Huyuk, dating from at least the ninth and seventh millennia BC, respectively. Both were sophisticated societies demonstrating a high level of civilization.[3]

Manly P. Hall writes that the Sphinx is a typical Egyptian construction. The face was carved in the likeness of the reigning Pharaoh, but was said to represent the Sun God, Harmackis, who appeared to Thutmosis IV in a vision and told the Pharaoh he was distressed by the weight of the sand around his body. Thutmosis IV responded to his vision by having the Sphinx re-excavated and restored. During re-excavation, the Sphinx's broken beard was found between its paws. The steps, temple and altar between the paws are probably Roman additions, for it is known that the Romans were responsible for the reconstruction of many Egyptian monuments. An indentation at the crown of the head originally held a headdress. The Sphinx represented strength and intelligence to the Egyptians and possesses androgynous features to represent both outwardly directed (male) and receptive (female) creative energies.[4]

The Sphinx represents the material plane while the Pyramid represents the spiritual plane. The connection between the material and spiritual plane is represented by the undiscovered sealed passageway between the Sphinx and the Pyramid. This seal cannot be broken until man has overcome the material side of his nature thus leading to unity with God.

The Sphinx is a symbol of man's evolutionary progress. As previously stated, the Sphinx's lower body is that of a lion, the upper body is that of a human being, and it bears the face of a man and the head of a woman. In back of the head are two wings. These features represent man's progression from animal to human over the ages.

The process of evolution is motivated by suffering and the subsequent awakening of a desire for knowledge. As this process progresses we gradually acquire a more perfect body. Hence the upper body of the Sphinx is that of a human being. Since the soul may incarnate either as a man or a woman, male and female characteristics are shown in the face and head. Indeed, each soul must exist both as man and woman in order to achieve full development, for we must all acquire the dual qualities of reason and spiritual power.

The law of Duality (Nature and God) is symbolized in the Sphinx by the male face and female head. When a human being has attracted to himself a member of the opposite sex and assimilated theknowledge from that polarity, he is liberated from primal desire and enjoys a new sense of freedom. In the Sphinx this sense of emancipation is illustrated by the presence of the eagle wings at the back of the head.

The wings also indicate that the sixth sense has been awakened and that man has entered into the spiritual realm. The seat of the sixth sense is the Pineal Gland situated in the back part of the head, represented by the King's Chamber of the Great Pyramid.

The ancient Egyptian texts state that if a person breaks the code of the Sphinx that he/she will understand the meaning of life. The following discussion is based upon my own interpretation derived from the numerological decoding of the word "Sphinx."

An analysis of "Sphinx" reveals the principle of six tests that exist on the Earth plane which the initiate must face and eventually pass before graduating from third-dimensional reality. The letters in the complete birth name of an individual reflect in symbolic terms the past-life experience accumulated by the individual. The letters S-P-H-I-N-X, when occurring in the birth name, indicate the tests the individual has already gone through, and on a subconscious level, they reveal the influence the letters have on the present life. These tests and influences are as follows:

### S—(Power Test)

The letter "S" represents the misuse of male power in another life-time. If the letter "S" is found in the present name, the individual must face this male power test again in this life, either directly or vicariously. This test usually comes through males the individual knows. The way men treat him/her in the present life is the same way that individual (as a male) treated others in other lives. As long as that male is present in the current life, this test is being mirrored back to the individual. If that powerful male leaves any time during the present life, the test represented by that individual is over. The way to pass this test is to become a symbolic Sun. A Sun disc once existed above the head of the Sphinx symbolizing the overcoming of the beastial desires of the Sphinx and the exemplification of Sun principles—unconditional love, non-judgment and selfless giving. The individual expressing the Sun shines on everything and everyone he/she meets. The expressed Sun energy is the inner attitude as well as the outward action.

## P—(Sex Test)

The letter "P" represents the misuse of sex in another life. If the letter "P" is found in the present name, the individual must face, directly or by indirect observation, the issue of sexual misconduct in this life. The test usually comes through family contacts or by being put into the position of having to deal appropriately with sexual advances. Depending on the circumstances, the appropriate response is to resist the temptation of sexual misconduct. This test could even mean obstinacy relating to or suppressing sexual desires in a past life. If the "P" is found in the last name (the spiritual lineage name) the individual behaved much like the priest in the monastery where all the nuns wore smiles on their faces.

## H—(Money Test)

The letter "H" is the blessing or responsibility of possessing large amounts of wealth in another life. It could be called the CEO Syndrome since having great wealth brings its own unique set of challenges and temptations only understood by the person of great wealth. The money test this life may come in the form of struggling through life with limited funds. When the letter "H" occurs in the name, the wealthy person in a past life had difficulty understanding how the lower and middle classes dealt with everyday matters. This lifetime the individual finds him/herself in situations where lack of abundance affects personal values. Generosity in the form of giving to charities such as organizations benefitting the homeless, hungry and disenfranchised are examples of the successful passing of this test.

## I—(Ego Test)

The letter "I" is the only vowel in the name "Sphinx." Two facets of "I" exist in the human condition. The first aspect is the "me" syndrome, ie."What's in it for me?"arising in relationships with family, business as well as all other worldly interactions. The other side of "I" is altruism and generosity, the number 9 (the numerological value of "I") represents the 1990's. The laws of the 1990's follow the overtone of philanthropy and selfless giving. The successful 1990's businesses who are tithing generously to charities of their choice are usually successful themselves because they are following the laws of the letter "I" on a conscious level. The letter "I" test is passed when the individual consciously realizes that the great joy of life is giving.

### N—(Freedom Test )

The letter "N" in the name represents the misuse of freedom in another lifetime. The individual played to the extreme in recent lifetimes, experiencing too much freedom with not enough time devoted to responsibility, job, family, or personal attention to the physical/mental/emotional laws of balanced living. This individual usually bears tremendous responsibility on all levels with a pre-occupation toward performing a job well. The individual with the letter "N" in his/her name secretly desires freedom from these weighty responsibilities; however, the surpassing of the test of the "N" is to discover the balance between the responsibility of freedom and the freedom of responsibility.

### X—(Service Test)

The test of the letter "X" is confronted after the tests of power, sex, money and freedom of responsibility are passed. This test represents the expression of the practicality of the feminine nature leading to a new type of responsibility. This responsibility is the "X" factor and usually manifests in the form of transcendence. The individual follows the laws of successful living and finds that leadership and care of others is their predominant pre-occupation. He/she focuses on service to others and uses every opportunity to lessen the burden of others on a regular basis. The expression of the "X" factor principle is the rewarding of others with praise and this is the overriding goal. Life is good and they want to share it with others as much as possible. The "X" factor represents unlimited power if it is shared with others.

The tests of the Sphinx are but one small part of the esoteric teachings of the Mystery Schools. The entire geographic area surrounding the Gizeh plateau and the relationships between the colossal monuments built millennia ago bear significant symbolic lessons for the initiate. The Nile River is itself a physical representation of the personal spiritual tests that must be undertaken by the initiate if he is to transcend the physical plane. The physical body of the Nile possesses places of power that correspond to the chakras in the human body and each corresponds to an archetype or initiatory energy:

| SYMBOLIC INITIATOR | VERTICAL CHAKRAS | LOCATION IN EGYPT |
|---|---|---|
| Buddha/Jesus/ Mary Kwan-Yin | Crown | Alexandria |
| Thoth/Hermes (feminine counterpart) | Pineal | King's Chamber, Great Pyramid |
| Serapis Bey (feminine counterpart) | Pituitary | Queen's Chamber, Great Pyramid |
| King Zoser (feminine aspect) | Throat | Sakkara |
| Ahknaton/Nefertiti | Heart | Tel-Amarna |
| Moses/Elijah (feminine aspect) | Solar Plexus | Karnak |
| John the Baptist (feminine aspect) | Navel | Komombo |
| Mary/Joseph Osiris/Isis | Base (Root) | Aswan |
| Ramses/Nefertari | Knee | Abu-Simbel |
| Present mother & father | Feet | Headwaters of the Nile |

The personal spiritual tests of the Nile relate to parts of the human body. Each of these parts represent higher plane principles and energies as follows:

FEET—
### Symbolic Initiator:  present father and mother

On the inner planes before physical birth, we choose our earth plane parents by locating our children from a previous lifetime on earth who can best teach us the lessons we have chosen for the upcoming lifetime. These children (previously our parents) in turn will help us learn our karmic lessons by serving as the mirror of ourselves in the parent role. At the time of our conception, we overlight our mother for nine months using her brain to create our fetus and familiarizing ourselves during that nine months with the eventual family environment into which we will be born. At our physical birth and during our childhood, we experience through our parents' example, the manner in which we demonstrated parenting behavior in a previous lifetime.

**Test: Personal Karma** (resulting from the parental experience in past lifetimes). We incarnate as our parents' children. However, as our parents age the roles are reversed and we play the role of our parents' parents as they prepare for their eventual transition.

KNEE—
### Symbolic Initiator:  Ramses and Nefertari, represented by Abu-Simbel, Egypt

At Abu-Simbel, Egypt, two beautiful temples exist which represent Ramses/Pharaoh (the masculine principle) and Nefertari/Queen (the feminine principle). Ramses, the most famous Pharaoh in ancient Egypt is commemorated with his Queen Nefertari to represent the collective past lifetimes in which humanity struggled to ascend to higher consciousness. On a personal level, individual past lifetimes are revealed to the initiate for spiritual testing purposes. Many times, what the initiate does with knowledge and wisdom revealed to them is more important than the actual knowledge and wisdom itself. These past lifetimes are usually lifetimes spent as famous or powerful persons or royalty and can tempt the initiate's ego, presenting interesting options for use of this information, which has been revealed to stimulate soul growth.

### Test:  Resolution of Karma

The way to successfully pass this test is to not reveal personal past lifetime information to others. The possession of this knowledge should not be used to psychologically elevate the self above others, as the overall purpose of this lifetime is to empower others.

## BASE (Root)—
**Symbolic Initiator:  Isis, represented by the Isis Temple, Aswan**
At the Base chakra center in Egypt is the Isis Temple, the Egyptian birthplace of the principle of immaculate conception. The Christian story of Jesus' birth is legendary, and the spiritual virgin birth within each individual is the second coming of Christ (Buddha). The light body is activated at this spiritual birthing in a similar manner to the birthing of the physical body on the physical level. Present at this light body birth are the archetypal Mary and Joseph, or Isis and Osiris, and their baby Christ/Buddha is an inner birth. The Three Kings are also archetypally present at this birth representing a new beginning on the mental, emotional and spiritual planes, resulting in the birth of a new King on each level.
**Test: Ego**
The trap here is that the new adult spiritual body believes it is the only Christ. Each of us is a potential avatar, and when the new avatar in male or female form is reborn, he/she recognizes the divine potential in everyone else, dedicating him/herself to assisting others in the light body birthing process.

## NAVEL—
**Symbolic Initiator:  John the Baptist, represented by Komombo, Egypt**
The navel chakra represents the emotional nature and is symbolized by the water sign Pisces. John the Baptist used baptism by water during the advent of the Piscean age. Jesus activated his emotional nature when he was baptized at the River Jordan. It took 29 years (at his Saturn return) for his consciousness to rise from his Root chakra (Bethlehem) to his accelerated emotional center (Jordan).
**Test: True outward expression of emotional nature**
We often stuff our emotional issues and allow our intellect to dominate our soft emotions to protect our vulnerable feeling nature. The challenge is to risk exposing our feminine self by freely expressing our emotional feelings and assist the nurturing of others in the pro-

cessing of their own emotional issues.

## SOLAR PLEXUS—
**Symbolic Initiator:  Moses/Elijah, represented by Karnak, Egypt**

Our power center is located in the solar plexus. This test requires a reexamination of true power and how this concept relates to us in our daily life. Moses and Elijah appeared to Jesus at the time of his transfiguration. An individual symbolically representing Moses/Elijah appears to us at the time of our own transfiguration—a dramatic change to a more positive lifestyle: regular exercise, balanced diet, dedication of service to others.

**Test:  Motivation**

The solar plexus is the Sun center and this test requires the use of our power center for the benefit of others. Its keynote polarity is: Am I here for others' growth and development or am I here for my own personal self-aggrandizement?  As an example, Alexander the Great failed the Power Test. He conquered the outer world, but without the commitment to serve.

## HEART—
**Symbolic Initiator:  Ahknaton and Nefertiti, represented by Tel-Amarna, Egypt**

Here the Gnostic Christian crucifixion is symbolized in its entirety. Each initiate must experience mental and/or emotional crucifixion on a personal level. The personal crucifixion usually is processed on the initiate's nearest and dearest center of interest:  business, family (wife or child) or personal avocation. Another individual/organization, real or imagined, threatens the very foundation of the individual's existence. The heart, the center of the personal cross which we carry with us throughout our earth life, is challenged to achieve a purification of motive.

**Test:  Forgiveness**

Jesus serves as the ultimate example of the power of this test. When he made the plea, "Forgive them, father, for they know not what they do," he passed this critical spiritual test. It is the supreme act of forgiveness to forgive one who crucifies us, threatening the very core of our being. Our heart is in the key position at the center of the four directions, centered in the vertical plane of the seven chakras (Heart) and horizontal plane of the Father/Sun axis (Holy Spirit). Forgiveness of our crucifier (our symbolic Judas) is the key to passing the Heart Test. The heart is the opening of the inner pyramid and allows the initiate to ascend the Grand Gallery of his inner Great Pyramid.

## THROAT—

**Symbolic Initiator:  King Zoser, represented by Sakkara, Egypt**

Hamid Bey wrote that in ancient days the Pyramid of Sakkara, 18 miles south of the Pyramid of Gizeh, was a center of great religious pilgrimage. This pyramid was the first Egyptian pyramid built and it was here that the first philosophy of spiritual guidance was practiced. Here were set forth principles of human behavior and disciplinary measures for non-compliance of those principles. The throat is the portal through which the power of the word is expressed. The power of the word is manifested through the intellect and the activity of speech. What we think and feel returns directly to us from the mirror of the I Am/First Cause plane. We create our personal karmic destiny with our thoughts and words. We achieve our spiritual destiny when we have learned to use the power of the word to benefit others by prayer, action and word.

**Test:  Silence**

On a personal level, this symbolizes keeping our communication with others on a totally positive plane. The expression "accentuate the positive, eliminate the negative" can be applied in our communication with others and is mandatory for the passing of this test. On the planetary level, revelations of supreme importance are given only to the initiated, requiring the test of silence. If the initiate reveals the divine wisdom the test is failed. This test requires judgment to communicate only what is appropriate and no more.

## PITUITARY—

**Symbolic Initiator:  Serapis Bey, represented by the Queen's Chamber of the Great Pyramid**

This test represents the opening of the subconscious mind. Revelation 12:1 is, again, the essence of this principle.

> *And there appeared a great wonder in heaven; a*
> *woman clothed with the sun and the moon under her*
> *feet, and upon her head a crown of twelve stars.*
>
> Rev. 12:1

The pituitary gland is symbolized by the phrase "and the moon under her feet." The moon (subconscious mind) is in her control because it is beneath her feet. The opening of the subconscious mind affirmation. This phrase also symbolizes the planet Venus, which, at certain times of the year, appears in the pre-dawn or evening sky above the moon.

**Test: Emotional Support**

The pituitary gland represents our feminine side, representing unconditional love and the support of others emotionally. This test requires that we love others as we love our own flesh and blood. The goal is to open the subconscious mind and perfect the intuition, in order to nurture others. It requires seeing beyond personal family boundaries, perceiving others as part of one's family, and giving to others unconditionally.

## PINEAL GLAND—

**Symbolic Initiator:  Thoth/Hermes, represented by the King's Chamber of the Great Pyramid**

The sixth chakra represents the responsibility of the mind. The ancient Egyptians thought so much of the symbol of the sixth chakra that they built the Sphinx and Pyramid in dedication to this ancient principle. Responsibility is a primary lesson for each person on Earth. "The responsibility of freedom" and "the freedom of responsibility" are two phrases which express an apparently contradictory relationship between the two principles of responsibility and freedom. The key to succeeding in this test is to balance these two principles.

**Test:  Responsibility**

We are responsible for all we are given at birth and earn during the course of our lifetime. Whether it is only a dollar in our pocket or the coat on our back, it is our privilege to use (for we are ultimately borrowing) these earth objects during our lifetime. How responsibly we handle these earth possessions during the course of our life is the criteria we use when, at death, we evaluate our lifetime.

## CROWN—

**Symbolic Initiator: Buddha/Jesus/Mary Kwan-Yin, represented by Alexandria, Egypt**

It is here that the initiate receives the crown of enlightenment and wisdom. How long did Buddha meditate under the Bodhi tree before he achieved illumination? Meditation is the key to the opening of the crown chakra and without a dedicated daily commitment to this inner plane activity, rarely is the seventh chakra opened. The lotus flower of the seventh level gradually unfolds through the daily discipline of meditation.

**Test: Presenting the "crown" to others—an act of empowerment**

As soon as the initiate receives the crown, he gives it away. "As I am lifted up, I lift all men and women unto me" is a famous biblical quote. It is an exquisitely appropriate passage for expressing the seventh level of crown attainment as it requires the ultimate in philanthropy and altruism.

The attainment of global peace, unity, sharing, prosperity and healing are achieved when the crown chakra and the feet chakra are merged. Illumination is the reward, providing that the initiate shares the precious gift of knowledge and emulates the Master prototype. This is the ultimate goal of the Tests of the Nile. Understood in conjunction with the Secrets of the Sphinx we have a basic formula for the initiation of the spirit to a higher evolutionary level. A key principle embodied within these tests is the power of the feminine, for too long suppressed in a patriarchal society. Thus, in order for humanity to successfully achieve these desired goals, we must return the feminine to her rightful place alongside the masculine in a co-creative and co-ruling capacity. It is this re-empowerment of the feminine which we will address in the next chapter.

# 5

# THE RETURN OF THE FEMININE
## AND
# THE SECRET DESTINY OF AMERICA

FOR THE PAST 5,000 years civilization has been dominated by the masculine, both secularly and spiritually. This male dominance has resulted from the conqueror mentality that has predominated this period. But in the recesses of humanity's collective unconscious there lives a memory of a more gentle and peaceful time when men and woman lived in partnership with each other. Archaeological discoveries are revealing that there existed thousands of years of peaceful prosperity where civilization was not dominated by the male. These discoveries are supported by the images and writings that have survived from the earliest period of recorded history. The ancient Greeks (i.e. Plato, who wrote of the civilization of Atlantis) told of such societies in their prose and poetry, and evidence is mounting that these stories are not merely fictional accounts as has long been believed.[1] An example of such stories that were originally thought to be pure myth is the story of Troy. Not until an archaeologist by the name of Heinrich Schliemann discovered the city of Troy under centuries of earth was it accepted that the ancient Greek tale of this great city was a true accounting of an historic place.

But it is not only in the field of science that we can find verification for the existence of a prehistoric partnership society. We can even find evidence in the religious traditions of today. Riane Eisler, in her groundbreaking *The Chalice and the Blade*, states that both the Bible and the Tao Te Ching make references to a time when man and woman coexisted in a harmonious partnership, where the feminine was revered.[2] This observation leads her to her "Cultural Transformation Theory" in which Eisler theorizes that humanity originally was partnership oriented and peaceful in its social organization, and that after a chaotic period that was initiated by the invasion by a warrior people, the dominator society was imposed on them and has continued to serve as the model for nations to the present.[3]

Two thousand years ago the incarnation of a spiritual Master initiated an effort to return humanity to the partnership ideal and restore peace on earth. Jesus' mission was to bring the vibration of love and compassion to a humanity who had for too long lived with fear and oppression. Love and compassion are considered "feminine" emotions; indeed, emotions in general are considered by many to be the realm of the feminine. The spiritual Hierarchy saw the need for these principles to be reindoctrinated into the consciousness of the human species and sent Jesus as an emissary to teach them. In the *Occult Christ*, Ted Andrews writes:

> *Part of the function of the true Christian Mysteries was to restore the Divine Feminine. Every mystery school taught the balance of the male and female within the individual. Only by accomplishing this could the divine child be born within. Unfortunately, the scriptures, as we have seen them, are relatively thin in regard to the function of the feminine energy in general, but also of the female initiates in particular...*
>
> *Students of the more traditional mystery systems rendered homage and reverence to the feminine aspects of life as equally as the masculine. Within the Mystery Schools were many myths of the Divine World Mothers: Isis of Egypt, Tiamat of Babylonia; Gaia of Greece, the Navajo Changing Woman, Mu Kwa of China, and many others... The early Christian Initiates knew that living the Christian Mysteries would awaken the Feminine once more in the ages to come, opening increasing numbers to higher vision and illumination.*[4]

The purpose of Christ's teachings was to restore balance between the feminine and masculine. Jesus focused on the Feminine Mysteries which reveal the subconscious and subjective aspects of life. These teachings are revealed in the use of images and language which are symbolically feminine (i.e. the moon, caves, rivers, female animals such as mares and sows, and various birds) and emphasizing such feminine attributes as compassion and the practice of service. All this points to the feminine as a "profoundly significant" force in the universe that needs to be restored to its rightful place alongside, and in equal partnership with, the masculine.[5]

Andrews states that "the scriptures are an allegory for the redemption of the Divine Feminine"[6] and their purpose was to lay the foundation to accomplish this task. It is now up to us to take the necessary steps to accomplish it. It may not come without a struggle, but we are equipped with the tools to succeed, as we, in fact, have begun to demonstrate.

Riane Eisler contends that for there to ever be a real peace on earth, we must evolve to a partnership model of society where both sexes are truly equal, and points to various other sources which share her view. The futurists Robert Jungle, David Loye, and John Platt as well as the Baha'i Universal House of Justice all see the connection between true equality for men and women and world peace.[7]

Going a step further, Eisler states that although it may seem a daunting task, all great causes had their modest beginnings in the mind(s) of only a few but a relentless pursuit for social justice eventually brought them into fruition. She cites as examples the abolition of slavery, the movement from monarchial governments toward democracies, as well as many other social reforms gained over the past several hundred years.[8] Additionally, it seems that the ultimate symbol of the feminine, Earth, is rising in rebellion as well. The years of unchecked degradation of the planet is resulting in serious consequences which have become more widely recognized as people are literally finding evidence of them in their own backyards. Ecological imbalance is the cause for the dramatic change in our weather patterns and climate, not to mention the quality of our water and land resources. Moreover, our problems are drastically worsened by a population that is growing beyond the planet's ability to sustain it.

This can all be attributed to a lack of respect for the feminine. The unenlightened attitudes of governments which enact laws that deny women access to family planning education and encourage procreation are a major contributing factor in overpopulation. Even if family planning were more universally accessible, Eisler reports, population experts are warning that for a curbing of population growth to succeed, roles for women beside that of housekeeping and parenting must be honored by the society in which they live and must be available and promoted alongside birth control education and guarantees of reproductive freedom.[9]

There is hope. Humanity is evolving—in positive ways—in spite of attempts by some to maintain the status quo. Science is revealing that evolution is in large part self-directed. Theorists like Erwin Laszlo contend that we humans have a choice about the direction that our evolution takes.[10] *We can choose our next step.* Add to that the fact that our social consciousness is becoming more partnership oriented, and that science is "focusing more on relationships than on hierarchies,"[11] and we have the recipe for a new model of male-female relationships. Humanity is beginning to comprehend the need for balance between the feminine and the masculine, and is choosing in ever-increasing numbers partnership in relationships, both individual and global.

Eisler indicates that there is a growing awareness of the ideal of partnership and that science is discovering the possibilities for the expansion of consciousness of our species and the subsequent evolution of society.[12] Scholars and theorists are predicting a rebalancing of the roles of men and women where there is equal sharing of the responsibilities of child-rearing as well as career opportunities. This will result in a healthier society and economy and humanity will begin to realize its full potential.[13] This in turn will lead to the end of the threat of war and the degradation of the planet, not to mention the more personal social problems we are faced with today.[14]

Eisler projects even farther out from this vision and sees the dissolution of the idea of nation-states and an increased spirit of cooperation worldwide relating to food production, space exploration (which we are already seeing in the US-Russian partnership in the Mir project), scientific discoveries and artistic endeavors.[15] The future world will be one where fear will no longer be a tool for manipulation and control, rather children will grow up in a world with an understanding of the inherent goodness in a peace-loving people and where creativity is nurtured and love is the guiding principle.[16] Over the past couple of centuries or so a trend has emerged toward a partnership model and away from the dominator model. This trend is evidenced in the various movements for social justice and equality, which can be viewed as steps in humanity's evolutionary quest for survival.[17] Among these movements is the founding of a nation on the edge of a pristine wilderness where people would experience true religious and civil freedom, a nation which was forged by men who held a higher ideal than the pursuit of dominance and power. The societal model for the future exists in the democratic ideal established during the latter part of the 18th century in the western hemisphere on the North American continent, an ideal which has its roots in the sacred traditions of our ancient forbears.

Down through the ages, the esoteric traditions of the Mystery Schools have been kept alive by individuals directed toward the evolution of mankind to achieving a higher spiritual ideal. These traditions were adopted by secret societies, whose membership boasted many high-ranking and learned members of the cultures of their time. Manly P. Hall has concluded after studying ancient records of various cultures that there has existed over millennia a group of enlightened souls which works toward the goal of world democracy. It is fair to say that these individuals often operate within the traditions of secret orders. Hall believes that a decision was made by these illumined minds, sometime "prior to the time of Plato," to create a "philosophic empire," based upon the democratic ideal, in the Western hemisphere, citing references to such a plan in Plato's writings on Atlantis.[18]

Organizations such as the Freemasons and Rosicrucians are prominent examples of secret societies established for the promotion of democratic principles and equality for all humanity, and both have had such astute persons as George Washington, Benjamin Franklin, Sir Francis Bacon and probably Thomas Jefferson in their ranks. A thorough examination of the esoteric influences acting at the time of the founding of the American colonies and the subsequent birth of the United States reveals the exquisite design underlying the development of the American nation.

Sir Francis Bacon was the architect of the English colonization of

America and undoubtedly saw it as the perfect environment in which to incubate the seeds of democracy. Bacon was a primary proponent of colonization of the New World and exerted a great deal of influence on Queen Elizabeth I to do so, his prime motivation being to prevent Spain and the Catholic League from dominating the Western hemisphere. He established Freemasonry and Rosicrucianism in the colonies before the middle of the 17th century and took great pains to indoctrinate the colonists with the ideals of religious tolerance, democratic government and social equality. [19]

In 1627, Bacon wrote the *New Atlantis*, a novel which was never published in total, but according to Hall, a second unpublished part exists and is well-known among the secret societies of Europe. The book gives a blueprint for world democracy where each nation is equally represented and all share in new discoveries in the arts and sciences and great libraries hold all the world's knowledge. Interestingly, an illustration on the title page represents a great creature symbolizing Time leading a female figure out of a dark cave.[20] Isn't that a fitting symbol for the emergence and empowerment of the feminine principle in the consciousness of our planet?

When the Founding Fathers convened to sculpt the foundation for the new nation, it was not without a great deal of consideration and deliberation. At least nine of the signers of the Declaration of Independence were Freemasons. Some historians claim as many as 50 of the Founding Fathers were Freemasons. While missing records make verification of this claim difficult if not impossible, records do exist that show unquestionably that George Washington, Benjamin Franklin and probably Thomas Jefferson were Freemasons, and that Jefferson was most certainly a Rosicrucian, as evidenced by the discovery of a very old Rosicrucian code in his personal papers.

Freemasonry was in widespread practice in the 18th century, in both the New World and in Europe. Lafayette and Voltaire, both close associates of the Founders, were prominent Freemasons as were twelve of Washington's generals, who held membership in what were called "military lodges." All of this points to a grand esoteric design operating at the birth of the new republic, a design that had as its core the ideals of freedom of information and the elimination of political and religious tyranny.[21]

The occult was an important element in the lives of the three aforementioned Founders. Benjamin Franklin was well-known to have been proficient in astrology and alchemy, and his *Poor Richard's Almanac* was a popular publication that featured astrological information which was of great interest to the colonists. Franklin also subscribed to the principle of reincarnation, the evidence for which is contained in his epitaph, which he wrote after a close brush with death due to an acute illness:

> *The Body of B. Franklin Printer (like the cover of*
> *an old book, its contents torn out and stript of its*
> *lettering and gilding) lies here, food for worms, but*
> *the work shall not be lost; for it will appear once*
> *more, in a new and more elegant Edition Revised and*
> *corrected by the author.*[22]

George Washington was no stranger to the occult either and, in fact, was the subject of two prophecies. One was a vision he had while stationed with his troops at Valley Forge in which an angel appeared to him and revealed America's future. The second was an Indian prophecy which foretold that Washington would be the founder and "chief" of a great nation of a diverse people. [23]  And Thomas Jefferson, who was well-versed in a variety of subjects, designed the University of Virginia, the structure of which, according to one researcher, contains the teachings of the Mystery Schools, leading one to conclude that he, too, had more than a passing interest in occult philosophy.[24]

Further evidence for the hidden spiritual agenda operating at the time of the nation's founding were the many intriguing events documented at the time of the founding of the United States. One concerns a mysterious gentleman who participated in the design of the flag. He was a boarder at the home of a friend of the committee members assigned the task of designing the flag. This friend's home was chosen as the meeting place for the flag committee, a circumstance curious in itself. During the meeting, it was decided that the 6 men present did not constitute "an auspicious number" and so the hostess was included in the meeting to raise their number to 7. (The number 7, numerologically, represents wisdom, in particular spiritual wisdom, and faith in a higher plan.)  The stranger, known only as the "Professor," made suggestions as to the flag's design, discussing at length the significance of each element, which was unanimously adopted by the committee. The Professor was not seen again after this meeting even though he had had such an important role in designing the new nation's symbol.[25]

An even more mysterious event occurred at the time of the signing of the Declaration of Independence. A strange man, unknown to all others present, somehow entered unobserved the old State House in Philadelphia where the signers were gathered. This was a time of great trepidation for those present, as they knew the penalty that would be imposed by the Crown, if they were caught, was sure to be swift and merciless. The debate became heated as members argued the pros and cons of the instrument that would sever their ties to England. Suddenly, the stranger, as if possessed by some great power, bellowed out with a voice that resonated through the hall. He spoke eloquently and with great conviction, saying, in part:

> *Sign that parchment! Sign, if the next moment the gibbit's rope is about your neck! Sign, if the next minute this hall rings with the clash of falling axes! Sign, by all your hopes in life or death, as men, as husbands, as fathers, brothers, sign your names to the parchment, or be accursed forever! Sign, and not only for yourselves, but for all ages, for that parchment will be the textbook of freedom, the bible of the rights of man forever...God has given America to be free![26]*

He collapsed into a chair as the glamour left him and the mood in the room changed from discord to harmonious enthusiasm for the task the Founders had come to perform. As the signers crowded around the document that would declare their freedom from tyrannical rule, the mysterious stranger departed unseen, even though the doors were locked and guarded.[27]

The Great Seal of the United States is another example of the secret societies' influence on the symbolism that was chosen to represent the essence of the new nation. After two committees tried and failed to approve the design of the United States' Great Seal, a third committee approved the emblems designed by Charles Thomson and William Barton on June 20, 1782. The front of the seal is an eagle (or phoenix) and a shield, the reverse is a pyramid without a capstone over which the all-seeing eye is placed.

The reverse side of the shield went unrecut, even though the front side was recut several times, until Henry A. Wallace, the former Vice-President and Secretary of Agriculture, submitted a proposal to then-President Franklin D. Roosevelt to have the entire front and reverse sides recut in 1934. Wallace enticed the President by interpreting the seal's motto *Novus Ordo Seclorum* (New Order of the Ages) to mean "The New Deal of the Ages." In any event, the fact that both men were Masons most certainly played a part in their interest in having the seal recut. They would have recognized the Masonic symbolism in the pyramid/all-seeing eye image on the reverse, which would explain why Roosevelt decided, in 1935, to have it placed on the one dollar bill.[28]

It is clear from the symbolism in our national icons, including those depicted on our one dollar bill, that the United States of America was founded on spiritual principles. The stated purpose was to create "a government of the people, by the people and for the people." On a deeper level, there existed a planetary vision for democracy, the pursuit of which has not been without its dark moments — we can cite the horrendous crimes committed against the native people who originally inhabited the North American continent as an example — but which has survived in the hearts of those who hold its ideals dear.

The date that was chosen for the birthdate of this nation was arrived at only through careful consideration. When we decode the July 4, 1776 date numerologically we arrive at a striking result:

**J U L Y   4 — the 7th month + the 4th day, or 7·4**

This **7·4** is an expression of the Messiah vibration:

$$
\begin{array}{ccccccc}
13 & + & 19+19 & + & 8 & = & 59 \\
\mathbf{M} & \mathbf{E} & \mathbf{S\ S} & \mathbf{I} & \mathbf{A} & \mathbf{H} & \\
5 & + & 9 & + & 1 & = & +15 \\
& & & & & & \mathbf{7\cdot4}
\end{array}
$$

The Founding Fathers selected the only day of the year that could bring Messianic proportions to the new nation's birthdate. They knew the time had come for the energy of the Messiah to be introduced into governmental structure. As long as the independence and freedom of the individual was of paramount importance in the language of the Declaration of Independence, this Messianic purpose would be transferred to the governance of the people on a symbolic and subconscious level. Even though this energy was introduced on a symbolic level, its power was firmly grounded in the July 4, 1776, birthdate, ensuring the fulfilment of the higher purpose. This birthdate was the first time in history that the Messianic power of altruism, to be manifested in the form of the Group Avatar, was grounded at the governmental level. The Founders' vision was extraordinary for their time in history. They knew the Messianic energy would mature to become a group initiation for not only the citizens of the United States, but for the Earth as a whole. We are now at the threshold of this maturation process. Our planet is on the cusp of the completion of three major cycles which are maturing at the same time, a phenomenon that has only happened once before in the last 8,000 years. These cycles are the end of a century (and millennium); the end of a great Age, the Piscean, roughly a 2,160-year cycle; and the completion of a great age, or a 26,000 year cycle marking the precession of the equinoxes.

The 7·4 principle continues to manifest with the revelation of the overlighting seed of God-consciousness to inspire the United States to manifest its highest ideals.

The sum of the consonants in a word represent the outer personality of that word. In the case of the word "God" the letters G and D (7 and 4) are equivalent to the birthdate of July 4th (7 +4) as well as the essence of the word "Messiah" (7 · 4). In other words, the letters G and D are the outer expression of the Messianic purpose on earth through the destiny of a nation, in this case the United States, whose birthdate was intentionally chosen to activate the personality of God on the earth plane. July 4 is the only date of the year which possesses the correct energy, that of the 7 · 4 expression. Inherent in the establishment and implementation of the US democratic governmental structure is the compelling desire to reflect God in its foundation and all facets of its existence.

Another important dimension of the July 4, 1776, birthdate is the symbolic significance of the statement "I Am That I Am," an ancient vibrational energy introduced to Moses on Mt. Sinai.

$$
\begin{array}{ccccccccc}
& 13 & + & 20+8 & + & 20 & + & & 13 & = 7 \cdot 4/11 \\
\mathbf{I} & \mathbf{A} \quad \mathbf{M} & & \mathbf{T} \quad \mathbf{H} \quad \mathbf{A} & \mathbf{T} & & \mathbf{I} & & \mathbf{A} \quad \mathbf{M} & \\
9 & + \quad 1 & + & & 1 & + & 9 & + & 1 & = \quad +\underline{21} \\
& & & & & & & & & 32
\end{array}
$$

If we add the double digits of this mystical Hebrew energy, we find the result exactly reflects the vibration of the July 4, 1776 birthdate, when added in traditional numerological fashion.

### JULY 4, 1776

**(Month) (Day)        (Year)**
$$7 + 4 + 1 + 7 + 7 + 6 = 32$$
**(Destiny #)**

Numerologically, the number 32 represents the communication of the feminine leading to a new freedom.

It is no coincidence that the US Founders selected this date. If they had waited one more day to sign the Declaration of Independence, birthing the new democratic government, the United States would have been the first country on earth to have as its birthdate the highest level of Masonic initiation, the number 33. Based on the esoteric interpretation of the mystical number 33, the United States would have instantly achieved ultimate world-dominating power. To put it simply, they faced, on a governmental level, the power test. If the Founding Fathers had selected July 5th as the birthdate of the new nation, the US would have become the dominating world power on the same level as England, certainly a tempting proposition since it would have given the new state a power equal to that by which the colonists had been oppressed. As Masons, the Founding Fathers would have found this to be the ultimate test (the World Power Test), the achievement of the coveted 33rd degree of the Masonic order.

It goes without saying that the men who fashioned this new government were great thinkers and visionaries, seeking only the best for their citizenry and new republic. The choice they made speaks highly of their integrity considering the tremendous potential for power that was available to them at that moment. The July 4th birthdate was chosen for its potential to liberate the feminine, over the promise of male world domination offered by the July 5th date. Their choice was made with the long view toward the realization of true freedom as they were acutely aware of the fact there remained only 224 years until the year 2000—the birth of a New Age, the time of the re-emergence of feminine power and the principle of compassion.

As the young country grew and began to achieve status as a world power, it became necessary for intervention from the higher planes to keep the nation directed on the chosen path. When circumstances occur that necessitate such an intervention, occasionally an exchange of souls for a physical body occurs or the individual has some other peak experience. Such was the case of Abraham Lincoln, who, at the age of 22, either became a walk-in or experienced what is known as a "Sinai experience."

An exchange of souls early in Abraham Lincoln's life may have been a karmic necessity stemming from the time of the dawn of the new republic. At that time, even though the Founders believed in the equality of all men and women, it was commonplace for landowners to own slaves. The economy depended greatly upon the institution of slavery to maintain the supply of goods sufficient to meet demand at a low cost. These landowners, including the Founding Fathers, had grown accustomed to a certain standard of living which using slave labor afforded them. Their great Declaration that "all men are created equal" created a dilemma for them, testing their conviction and forcing them to evaluate their belief in the equality of all. If the model of equality was to work, it had to be demonstrated by their own example. Some of the Founders did free their slaves, others rationalized keeping them for humanitarian reasons, that their slaves would not be able to care for themselves or support themselves if they released them. Thomas Jefferson was one of those that held this view. The failure to free slaves created a karmic debt for the Founders (including Jefferson) who did not do so. This karmic debt resulted in a confrontation between ideals and economics, one that exists to this day.

Numerologically, the end of an important cycle occurs after every 81-year period. The important cycles for the United States occur every 81 years subsequent to July 4, 1776. At these points, any karmic debts that are owed become due and payment is exacted in the form of significant events.

|            |                                                  |
|------------|--------------------------------------------------|
|            | **1776 — Birth of the United States**            |
|            | **+ 81 — Cycle-ending period**                   |
|            | **1857 — End of cycle**                          |
| **(event)**| **1860 — Civil War begins — karmic payment**     |
|            |                                                  |
|            | **1857**                                         |
|            | **+ 81**                                         |
|            | **1938**                                         |
| **(event)**| **1939 — World War II begins — karmic payment**  |
|            |                                                  |
|            | **1938**                                         |
|            | **+ 81**                                         |
| **(event)**| **2019 — The prophecy of world peace and unity** |
|            | **and world healing attained**                   |

It is clear from examining both the historical and esoteric evidence that America was chosen to serve as the incubator in which the seeds of freedom, equality and religious tolerance would be planted and allowed to grow, at first serving as an example to the world and then, as it flourished, to become the standard by which the greatness of men and nations would be determined. It is no accident that the democratic ideal came to the New World at a time when there were such tyrannical forces at work within both governments and the Church. The spiritual hierarchy of the planet has pressed forward with its plan for a universal democracy century after century with its sights set on the approaching millennium, when a new era of peace and unity among peoples begins. It is time now to banish the tool of oppression —fear—and what better place to start than with the ultimate representative of fear, also known as Satan, the AntiChrist, or the Devil.

# 6

## THE S.A.D.* SYNDROME
### (*Satan, Anti-Christ, Devil)

*To become, one must overcome.*

THE CONCEPT OF a supernatural evil being has been part of
humanity's consciousness since earliest times. Paul Carus wrote in *The
History of the Devil and the Idea of Evil* that religion arises as a
response to the fear of evil, and it was humanity's fear that gave rise to
the creation of an anthropomorphic representative to embody the evil
it so feared. And, Carus contends, this figure that plagued pagan
peoples was the seed for the prototype of the Devil.[1]

All cultures have had their demonic representatives: to the
American Indians encountered by Captain John Smith it was *Okee*, to
the early Haitians it was *Jocanna*, to the Aztecs it was *Huitzilopochtli*,
to the ancient Egyptians, *Set*. The transformation of Egypt's Set into
Satan occurred at the time Osiris began to be worshiped as a god,
evidence of the pronounced influence exerted by the Egyptian tradition
on Christianity.[2]

The beginning of the Christian era was marked by the development
of religious beliefs which presented the ideas of sin atonement and soul
redemption, but the ideas of "evil, sin, hell, salvation, and immortal life
were familiar to the Greek mind even before the days of Plato,
[although they] were still mixed up with the traditional mythology."[3]
This fact is merely an example of the manner in which ancient myths
were adapted and transformed into Christian tenets. In some cases
entire mythological stories were borrowed from pagan traditions and,
with a little reworking of the characters, adopted by the early Christian

writers. For example, Hesiod's tale of the battle between Zeus and the monster Typhon, or Typhoeus, is strikingly similar to Revelation 7:7-9. Compare this passage from Hesiod's *Theogony,* written centuries before the birth of Christ, with the aforementioned Revelation verses:

> *...huge Earth bare her youngest born son Typhoeus...whose hands, indeed, are fit for deeds on account of their strength...On his shoulders there were one hundred heads of a serpent, of a fierce dragon...The huge monster would have reigned over mortals unless the sire of gods and men quickly observed him...Jove smote Typhoeus and scorched all the wondrous heads of the terrible monster. When at last the monster was quelled, smitten with blows, it fell down lame, and Zeus hurled him into wide Tartarus.*

The resemblance of this passage to the Revelation passage that follows leaves little doubt that the former served as the inspiration for the latter.

> *And there was a war in heaven. Michael and his angels fought against the dragon; and the dragon fought and his angels; and prevailed not; neither was their place found any more in heaven. And the great dragon was cast out, that old serpent called the Devil and Satan, which deceiveth the whole world; he was cast out into the earth, and his angels were cast out with him.*[4]

The old Greek demons were transformed by the early Christian writers into the fearsome Devil or Satan and were inducted into the New Testament canons, becoming fundamental to the Christian religion that was beginning to dominate the world.[5] It is important to understand that the early Christians were the most common members of society, not the nobility or ruling classes. It was in the lower stratum of society that Christianity first took root and the earliest Church leaders were neither cultured nor well educated. While some Christian writers were comparatively sophisticated, few members of the Church hierarchy could make the same claim.[6]   These writers drew upon the familiar pagan traditions from which they arose and modified them to harmonize with the teachings of Christ, creating the canonical literature that composes the Old Testament.

The period during which the New Testament emerged was marked by increased cultural exchange between the civilizations of the Middle East and Western Asia. This cultural exchange had a pronounced, if subtle, influence on the respective religious views of the contributing societies, having a marked impact on the writings of the day. These writings were no longer accepted as canonical Old Testament literature and were thus relegated to the New Testament apocrypha.

Carus wrote: "It is noteworthy that Satan, in the canonical books of the Old Testament, is an adversary of man, but not of God, he is a subject of God and God's faithful servant [whose office it is to accuse and mete out punishment]."[7]   However, as time passed and new books were added to Bible, "the conception of Satan grew more mythological and at the same time more dualistic. He developed into an independent demon of evil, and...became the adversary of God himself."[8]

As the Christian tradition developed, magic in the form of miracles became central to its doctrine, owing to the miracles performed by Jesus during his ministry. However, the Church held that the performance of miracles was within the jurisdiction of the son of God and of God himself, and not of the faithful. This attitude gave rise to the suppression of magic and witchcraft, which were believed to be the work of the Devil unless specifically sanctioned by the Church. The papacy was central to the enforcement of its laws against magic, and proscribed severe punishment for the breaking of those laws.[9]

The superstitious people of the thirteenth century saw the Devil in nearly every extraordinary occurrence in their lives. As a response to this, people began to practice magic rituals of their own design to ward off evil. The practice of pagan rituals and natural healing methods by the common people had also continued even though the Church had extended its influence by this time to nearly all of the Western world. The Church saw these practices as a threat to the foundation of its power, and resulted in a comprehensive campaign to root out and destroy the guilty infidels, a campaign that became known as the Inquisition. As we well know, the Inquisition is one of the darkest periods in history, and one which contributed to an obsessive fear of the

Devil by Church followers.[10]

During the Reformation, in addition to the split in the institution of Christianity, a gradual change occurred in the view of the Devil whereby he became to be interpreted in more psychological terms rather than physical. This change continued to escalate during the rise of science in the eighteenth century. As Carus wrote, "The free-thought movement of the eighteenth century and a better scientific conception of nature relieved [humanity] of the unnecessary fear of the Devil and the nineteenth century could begin to study the question impartially in its historical and philosophical foundations...[and] theologians began to give a rational explanation of the Devil" owing his existence as real only if it is believed he exists.[11]  Perhaps a bit caustically, Carus states that today the idea of the Devil as a real force is only alive "among the uneducated."[12]

Humanity's obsession with the idea of a demonic figure who is responsible for all the evil in the world has been a long-standing one. Naming this figure and giving it a personality makes it all the more real. It can be said that personifying the Devil has provided humanity with a mirror for itself. Mirroring has been an inherent human behavior from the moment spirit took human form. Each individual attracts to him/herself through the law of attraction a mirror to gauge his/her personal evolution at any point of time. Beginning in infancy with mother and father, we attract their protective maternal and paternal energies to assist our growth into adulthood. Mom and Dad are the first influences to be placed in our consciousness at birth. We appear to have no choice in this matter, but the truth is that we chose our parents and thus selected the adult models that would shape our early life experiences before we took embodiment, much as they chose each of us in previous lifetimes to serve as their parental models. As we grow into maturity, these models serve as the blueprint for our development and are integrated into our personal tree of life. The end result is that we emulate the traits of our parents.

When we delve into our childhood, we blame Mom and Dad for our challenges as adults. Psychologists spend extensive time exploring the childhoods of their patients to discover dominant attitudes that have created adult problems. Mom and Dad are too often the scapegoats for our difficulties. Blaming someone else for our mistakes or self-destructive behavior has been an easy way of putting off the resolution of our personal issues. The many collective issues on this planet that await resolution are directly related to the personal issues that have gone unresolved by individual people, for global problems are the extrapolation of personal problems. The time has come for us to take responsibility for their resolution so we may make the next step in our evolution. We can begin by ridding ourselves of the fear of this ultimately nonexistent evil being, called by many names but most commonly known as the Devil, the AntiChrist or Satan.

## SATAN

The word Satan was created originally as an instrument of wisdom and selflessness and the Eygptian Tarot initially reflected this symbolic meaning. Through centuries of misuse and abuse, the term "Satan" has become so imbued with the idea of evil that it has evolved to symbolize the ultimate fear for humanity to overcome. In the ancient Egyptian Mystery Schools, where the Tarot originated, this term had another meaning. Breaking it down esoterically according to Tarot symbology we arrive at the following interpretation:

| Letter | Number | Tarot Card | Light Side | Shadow Side |
|--------|--------|------------|------------|-------------|
| S | 19 | The Sun | Shines down on all; gives selflessly | Past-life misuse of male power |
| A | 1 | The Magician (left hand) | Ultimate creator of reality (Heart) | Self-serving creation based on emotion |
| T | 20 | Judgment | Wisdom governs judgment | Unwise, unfair judgment |
| A | 1 | The Magician (right hand) | Ultimate creator of reality (Mind) | Self-serving creation based upon intellect |
| N | 14 | Temperance | Excellent Management | Over-emphasis on freedom |

How can a word such as "Satan" take on and perpetuate negativity? We humans have a habit of creating a scapegoat, someone or something which we can blame for the world's ills. It is easier to point outside oneself and say, "They did it. They are responsible," than it is to accept personal responsibility and take action to correct the problem. Satan is a convenient catch-all for all the negativity expressed on Earth and has been capitalized upon by power mongers of all kinds. It is also an effective control device. "If you don't subscribe to our doctrine, this evil force will devour you." This is power that even Satanic cults have tapped into. They use fear to control their members and commit unspeakable acts to instill fear in those who oppose them. Neale Donald Walsch, in his *Conversations with God, Book One*, points out that the seductive bait these power mongers hold out is approval:

> *...All you have to do to get instant approval is to agree. Agree and you have instant approval. Some will even sing and shout and dance and wave their arms in hallelujah!*
> *That's hard to resist. Such approval, such rejoicing that you have seen the light; that you've been saved!*[13]

Walsch's book is a series of conversations with God in which God expounds on all manner of subjects, not the least of which is the subject of Satan and fear. The following passage from God relates to our discussion of fear:

> *And so you must reduce yourself to a spirituality which teaches fear and dependence and intolerance, rather than love and power and acceptance.*
> *You are filled with fear—and your biggest fear is that My biggest promise might be life's biggest lie. And so you create the biggest fantasy you can to defend yourself against this: You claim that any promise which gives you the power, and guarantees you the love, of God must be the false promise of the devil. God would never make such a promise, you tell yourself, only the devil would—to tempt you into denying God's true identity as the fearsome, judgmental, jealous, vengeful, and punishing entity of entities.*[14]

And then God goes on to say that the mythologies that were created by early man to explain the cosmic nature of creation and existence were told in the only language that humanity could understand at that time: the ideas of good and evil, light and dark, and terrible battles between angelic and devilish forces. It is about time we abandoned these archaic and naive mythologies and adopt a new set of beliefs that are fitting for our level of sophistication and intelligence. We no longer wear animal skins and sit huddled around campfires at night for warmth.

Ideas and beliefs are the power behind all reality. If we are to move into a golden era of peace and prosperity we must dissipate the negative energy that has been attributed to the idea of Satan and the only way to do that is to stop believing in it. This will, in effect, "bind Satan for a thousand years," as is stated in Revelation 20:1-3:

> *And I saw an angel come down from heaven, having the key of the bottomless pit and a great chain in his hand.*
>
> *And he laid hold on the dragon, that old serpent, which is the Devil, and Satan, and bound him a thousand years.*
>
> *And cast him into the bottomless pit, and shut him up, and set a seal upon him, that he should deceive the nations no more, till the thousand years should be fulfilled: and after that he must be loosed a little season.*

This "thousand years" is not a description of a period of time, but is an expression of the 1000th power of the concept of a New Beginning. These verses relate to the "T" in Satan, corresponding to the Judgment card of the Tarot. These passages represent that the idea of Satan has outlived its purpose and has only been kept alive by continued misinterpretation. Let us as a society not only put the outmoded thoughtform of Satan to rest, let us end all belief in negativity, so that we may experience our birthright, true freedom.

Satan (fear) is first mentioned in the Book of Revelation in Chapter 2. The number 2 represents our feminine nature and our reluctance to express the Love aspect of that nature. If we personalize the Book of Revelation as the description, written in a secret code, of a symbolic, subconscious journey that the individual undertakes, it can be understood to  describe the attainment of higher consciousness during a lifetime. It describes the challenge, or test, of the empowerment of the feminine aspect, which is sensitive, loving and vulnerable.

On the mundane level, this Satan test may present itself in the form of an unappreciative spouse or boss at work, who disregards our hard work and dedication to our home or job. We pass our Satan test by providing emotional support to our spouse even though it is not reciprocated, and dedicate ourselves to excellence on the job regardless of the lack of recognition for our hard work. These are the kinds of challenges we face on a daily basis which test our vulnerable feminine nature.

In Revelation Chapter 3, the Satan test appears in verse 9.

> *Behold, I will make them of the synagogue of Satan, which say they are Jews, and are not, but do lie; behold, I will make them to come and worship before thy feet, and to know that I have loved thee.*
>
> Rev. 3:9

The number 3 symbolizes communication, and here the test deals with our use of words. This is the opportunity to rise above the tendency to criticize others in our lives, accepting them as they are and using our words to inspire and uplift them. A few kind words spoken can work miracles. Each person we meet provides us with the opportunity to act as an empowering agent, requiring from us only a few kind words of encouragement.

In Chapter 1, I stated that Revelation 12:1 expresses the essence of the entire Book of Revelation. A more detailed discussion of the meaning of its symbolism will reveal just how this is so.

> *And there appeared a great wonder in heaven; a woman clothed with the sun, and the moon under her feet, and upon her head a crown of twelve stars.*
>
> Rev. 12:1

As previously stated, the ratio 12:1 is a mystical number whose meaning is represented by Jesus and his twelve disciples; Hercules and the twelve labors; Arthur and his twelve knights of the Round Table; the astrological relationship between the twelve planets and the individual; and the twelve months composing one year. Each of these relationships relate to the twelve powers of mind the individual can potentially activate through altruistic service, selflessness and compassion.

The crown of twelve stars in the aforementioned passage represents these 12 powers of mind and the significance of their activation. In astrological terms, each individual has a symbolic male and female lifetime occupying the position of one of the twelve powers of mind represented by the twelve signs of the zodiac. For example, when an individual has an important decision to make a male and/or female representative of the zodiacal sign symbolizing a previous lifetime will come forth to offer the available options. The decisions we make this lifetime are continuously influenced by our experiences from past lifetimes.

The passage, "a great wonder in heaven; a woman clothed with the sun," refers to a major step in soul development where we balance our male and female polarities. Risking our feminine nature and demonstrating our nurturing, motherly love is the major key in attaining Christ Consciousness. The feminine polarity is clothed with the sun of higher consciousness and serves as the expression of the Sun on earth. In other words, to achieve Christ Consciousness, a person must reach a highly developed feminine consciousness performing the inspirational role of the Sun in thought and deed. Because the word "Revelation" also vibrates to the frequency of 12:1, the essence of the entire book is captured by Verse 12:1. Each of us can become the woman clothed with the sun, by activating our twelve powers of mind and subordinating the subconscious mind (mastering our moon) for the benefit and service of others.

Another important passage which at first glance appears to possess a negative meaning is Verse 12:9. This is another form of the Satan test. Twelve is the number of the master communicator, the ability to reach the subconscious mind:

> *And the great dragon was cast out, that old serpent called the Devil, and Satan which deceiveth the whole world; he was cast out into the earth, and his angels were cast out with him.*

When we take a closer look beneath the facade of mundane language and examine this verse in the light of the occult system in which it was written, we find some interesting correlations:

```
          45              +              43              =   88
    7 + 18     +    20        4 + 18  +   7   +   14
    G  R  E  A  T             D   R   A   G   O   N
       5 + 1     +               1    +  15
         6        +              16                      =   +22
         |                        |                         110
         |                        |                      (The Christ)
        51                       59
    (Michael)          (personality of "Messiah")

         13   +   19 + 19    +     8   =   59
         M    E    S    S    I    A   H
```

And again, we can see the underlying positive message in the phrase "That old serpent" when we compare its vibration with that of "Holy Spirit":

```
                                                              [Personality]
        48        +        16       +              87       =   151
    20 + 8   +   20      12  +   4      19   +  18 + 16  +  14 + 20
    T   H   A   T        O   L   D      S    E   R   P   E   N   T
        1     +   15          +          5   +       5       =   +26
                                  (Christ  Consciousness)       177
                                                              [Expression]


                                                              [Personality]
           45          +              73                  =    118
       8  +  12 + 25      19 + 16  +   18   +   20
       H   O   L   Y      S    P    I    R    I    T
       15          +                  9   +   9           =    +33
                                                               151
                                                              [Expression]
```

The Personality of the phrase "That old serpent" is the same as that of the Expression of the term "Holy Spirit." In a literal interpretation the phrase "that old serpent" would be considered negative and the name "Holy Spirit" highly revered. In the esoteric language of numbers, both are in truth positive.

It bears repeating, the origin of Satan is fear; it is not a physical manifestation. Satan in its form as fear does not exist unless we give it energy. Fear is non-productive, it depletes productive energy on the physical, mental and emotional planes, individually and collectively. We can put our energy to better use by focusing on positive solutions to our global problems, and at the same time cease the counterproductive activity of giving energy to negative thoughtforms.

In the bible, Satan appears as a symbol of fear to the biblical characters it confronts. In 1st Corinthians, Satan appears to David as a symbol which has meaning to him and to Israel, and David's challenge is to overcome both his own and Israel's fear. When he faced his challenge of fear and overcame it, Satan ceased to exist in David's life. David did the thing he feared to do and dealt a death blow to fear itself.

Each of us are David facing our personal Goliath, our Achilles heel from past lifetimes. Whatever tripped us up in past lifetimes will appear again this life in one or more forms representing the following earthly issues: money, sex or power. In the biblical book of Job, Job was tested on the physical plane when his livelihood was challenged by natural catastrophes. Satan appeared to him in a form that would best test him. Job did not blame God for these unfortunate circumstances. He faced the earth fears and overcame his adversities.

In Matthew, Chapter 4, Jesus was tempted by Satan in the form of earth power, one of the many tests Jesus had to face before attaining messiahship.

> *Then was Jesus led up of the spirit into the wilderness to be tempted of the devil.*
>
> Mark 4:1

After having been weakened by a 40-day fast, the Devil came to him and attempted to get him to perform miracles and worship himself, and at each turn Jesus refused.

> *Then saith Jesus unto him, Get thee hence, Satan: for it is written, Thou shalt worship the Lord thy God, and him only shalt thou serve.*
> *Then the devil leaveth him, and, behold, angels came and ministered unto him.*
>
> Mark 4:10-11

Jesus faced his fears (Satan), overcame his Devil ( past lifetimes) and reached full Christhood.

## *Examples of Devil/past life, Satan/fear experiences:*

| *Individual Tested* | *Satan(fear)* | *Result of Experience* |
| --- | --- | --- |
| Jesus | the Cross | Power Test won |
| John the Baptist | Salome | Sex Test failed |
| David | Bathsheba | Sex Test failed |
| Samson | Delilah | Sex Test failed |
| David | Goliath | Power Test won |
| Julius Caesar | Cleopatra | Sex/Power Tests failed |
| Moses | Ramses II | Power Test won *(Declined Pharaohship)* |
| Buddha | Unknown | Power Test won *(Declined title of Prince)* |
| Humanity | Devil *(past lifetimes)* | To be completed |

Just as in David's slaying of Goliath, the illusion of fear can be banished by doing that thing you fear to do. The karma accrued from past lifetimes can be repaid in this lifetime, and once a karmic balance is achieved between the past and present lifetimes, the law of Dharma (or spiritual life purpose) takes effect. Dharma has already been realized by many. Accepting your dharma and giving in service to others and the performance of all philanthropic endeavors in general are the keys to the path to fulfillment, and the gifts of happiness, joy and abundance will be yours.

The word Satan does not appear again in the Book of Revelation after Verse 12:9, signifying the fact that with the new-found ability to communicate and act in an altruistic way and eliminating the illusion of fear, Satan no longer exists. Once we have cast fear out of our lives, we feel compelled to help others eradicate fear from their own.

## ANTICHRIST

Many people, mostly those of the collective Christian world, are looking for an *Anti*Christ figure to appear before the return of the Christ. According to their perspective, the AntiChrist is to return and will represent in individualized form the qualities and characteristics diametrically opposed to the Christ.

I do not agree with this conception. The word AntiChrist was a mistranslation from the original Aramaic word which means *Ante*Christ. Webster's Dictionary defines *ante* as "before, in front of, prior, earlier than." In other words, the AnteChrist appeared before the coming of Christ. Examples of this principle would be Moses coming before Joshua, and John the Baptist coming before Jesus.

However, I believe that "Christ" is a consciousness to be attained rather than the name of an individual, and therefore the AnteChrist is a circumstance or condition or group of people which precedes the birthing of Christ Consciousness within the individual. The AnteChrist may take the form of an initiation at a conference, the interpretation of an astrology chart, or a dream in which a baby is born to the individual. The form the AnteChrist takes is chosen by our individual souls which best will serve the purpose of preparing the way for the birth of the Christ Consciousness within each of us.

If we take the AnteChrist symbology to a planetary level, the AnteChrist is a planetary thoughtform similar to the story of David's confrontation with Goliath. To diffuse this and all negative planetary thoughtforms (such as the AntiChrist prophecy) we can project light, love, and positivity on a daily basis to the Earth's Akashic plane, the mass consciousness of the planet. By changing our focus from negative to positive we can, much as David did, ensure the preservation of our planet. World peace can prevail as we replace misguided ideas such as the existence of an AntiChrist with the positive vibrations of thoughts of world peace, world sharing and world unity.

Verse 13:18 has been mistakenly interpreted as providing the identity of the AntiChrist. If we examine the verse in light of the science of numbers we find a very different identity hidden within it, one that is contrary to common biblical interpretaion.

> *Here is wisdom. Let him that hath understanding count the number of the beast; for it is the number of a man, and his number is six hundred three score and six.*

The number 666 has been termed the number of the Beast, or the AntiChrist. As all the terms in Revelation, when interpreted correctly, are positive, so too is this number 666. It is significant that it is composed of 3 identical numbers. What is its significance? We know that a birthdate consists of 3 numbers also: the month, day and year. A person's full name traditionally consists of three parts: the first, middle and last names. Therefore, we can conclude that these three numbers do in fact represent an individual symbolically, and is further verified by the phrase "it is the number of a man." It is the number of every man and woman who take responsibility for their lives.

In the language of numerology the first name represents the physical nature. The second name represents the mental and emotional natures, and the last symbolizes the spiritual nature. Similarly, the date of birth represents the means by which the characteristics of the individual will manifest on the earth plane. In the case of the biblical 666 symbolism, the physical, mental/emotional, and spiritual natures of the individual symbolized in Revelation all vibrate to the energy of the number 6.

In Numerological analysis a number can be analyzed on several levels. This analysis reveals the higher meaning behind the number's basic interpretation. By adding the various components of a multi-digit number in different combinations, a refined interpretation can be made.

The following complex analysis of the number 666 reveals the many levels of meaning contained in what at first glance appears to be merely a three-digit number representing a finite value:

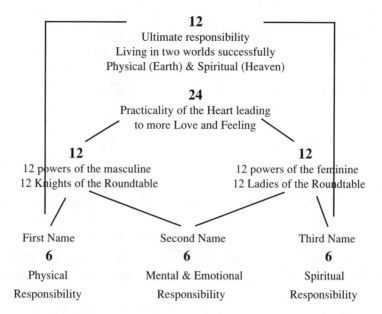

**12**
Ultimate responsibility
Living in two worlds successfully
Physical (Earth) & Spiritual (Heaven)

**24**
Practicality of the Heart leading
to more Love and Feeling

**12**
12 powers of the masculine
12 Knights of the Roundtable

**12**
12 powers of the feminine
12 Ladies of the Roundtable

First Name
**6**
Physical
Responsibility

Second Name
**6**
Mental & Emotional
Responsibility

Third Name
**6**
Spiritual
Responsibility

**6 + 6 + 6 = 18   Destiny — The Moon (Tarot Major Arcana)**

The number 6 represents family, duty, service, counseling, and most importantly *responsibility*. The true significance of the triple 6 is the importance of taking responsibility for personal physical actions, thoughts and feelings, and spiritual intent. We individually fulfill the prophecy of the 666 symbolism and proceed through the sixth level of initiation, represented by the Sphinx and Pyramid of Gizeh in the Egyptian initiation process. This process can be expanded from the personal to the planetary level, pertaining not only to individuals, but to nations and the whole of humanity as well. It is our divine challenge to act responsibly toward our fellow human beings.

The Twin Suns of God were the first creation of God and had the energies of yin and yang within them. The AnteChrist was the Firstborn Sun, the Christ was the second. Neither energy was accepted by humanity on any large scale until Jesus took on the manifestation of the Christ. There had been individual Christs and AnteChrists before, but Jesus was the first with the ability to embody the enormous energies of the Christ energy in order that it could be introduced to the mass consciousness. That did not guarantee that it would be understood or accepted, but did provide a way for the Christ energy to be grounded as it had never been before. Now is the opportunity for the other Twin Sun's energy (that of the AnteChrist) to be grounded as well in humanity's mass consciousness through many representatives. Once the Twin Sun energy of the AnteChrist has been established for 2,000 years, there will be a merger of the Twin Suns into One Sun and those souls still present on Earth will become the True Suns of God, the Christ/AnteChrist made One.

Spiritual twins like John the Baptist and Jesus, and Romulus and Remus (the first emperors of Rome) have existed since the advent of human life on this planet. It is a symbiotic relationship, as represented by the yin and yang symbol. The two energies combined create the whole. Out of fear, humanity has tried to separate the two Suns in their consciousness. It is time now to bring awareness of both Suns into the consciousness of all who are able to comprehend it. Those who cannot will continue to revolve around the Christ Sun and will remain blinded by fear to the Twin Sun of the AnteChrist whose energy is actually sustaining them as well.

The AnteChrist energy is about recognizing all that is buried in the darkness of human consciousness. Humanity must expose the darkness to the light of the Twin Suns so that all may know themselves as they really are with no illusions. Those who would keep humanity imprisoned in darkness seek to maintain power over humanity. As long as humanity has the ability to acknowledge only the Christ Star of the Twin Suns, it shall remain unconscious and unaware. Those who awaken to the AnteChrist Consciousness will bask in the binary star consciousness of The Christ/AnteChrist. Only then will they be able to view the face of God, for they shall be truly awake. In the future, many souls will act as the host for the AnteChrist Sun. There will be individuals who will spread the rays of the Christ and the AnteChrist. This light will overpower some and they will continue to reject the AnteChrist. Some will reject both Star energies. Those who thirst to be fully awake will soak up the rays of the AnteChrist spectrum of light. When one absorbs the light spectrums of both the Christ and AnteChrist, true higher consciousness is reached.

To accept only the Christ Star is to be half awake spiritually. When the fear of the AnteChrist Star is replaced with understanding, the full light of both Suns will beam into each being and into the world. The Sun of Man must merge with the Sun of God for the prophecy to come to pass. Each soul has the potential to become the Sun of Man and the

Sun of God. The energy of the Sun of God alone has been used by humanity to war with itself for its mass consciousness cannot perceive the truth, that we are united in One Consciousness. It is through the grounding of the energy of the Sun of Man, the AnteChrist, that the understanding will eventually reach humanity that it is One. Through the grounding of the consciousness of God within each individual can come peace, harmony and the resolution of all problems.

The Sun of Man as an archetype is the enlightenment of the individual consciousness to truly know itself. The Sun of God represents mass consciousness aware of itself as it truly is through the unity of all people. The concept of the individual and the whole made One without the loss of identity of either is what the next 2,000 years is all about.

## DEVIL

The Devil does not exist today. It is an illusion. In my work with groups over the years, I have attempted to  dispell the negative connotation of words that have historically held threatening meaning. In my attempt to reveal the esoteric meaning of the name Santorini, part of the original landmass of Atlantis, I inadvertently discovered a remarkable association with "The Devil." At one time in Earth's history, during the civilization of Atlantis, the "Devil" was a revered office. Humanity has a deep-seated memory of the actions of one priest-king while he held this political/spiritual office, and this memory has lingered on the inner planes of consciousness for thousands of years. It is the fear generated by the memory of a terrible event gone unforgiven by humanity that has perpetuated the Devil myth.

Atlantis was a utopian society founded on high ideals similar to those upon which the United States was founded: democratic principles based upon equality, justice and the right to self-actualization. Prosperity was enjoyed by all its citizens due to its strong foundation of spiritual principles. The highest office of responsibility in Atlantis was called the Double Devil Seat. Dual in nature, this office held the powers of both spirituality and politics, similar to the power of the Pharaoh in ancient Egypt. Atlantis flourished as long as the office holder of the Double Devil Seat maintained a purity of intent and governed with a spirit of compassion. When the term of office ended a democratic election was held and a new Double Devil took the reins of office.

The physical seat of this national office was at Santorini Island in the present-day Greek Islands. I was astounded to find the Devil vibration occur twice in this name. The odds against this occurring in any one word are huge, leading me to conclude that it carried a tremendous significance. It represents a principle which I call the Double Devil.

| [Personality] | 28 | + | | | 38 | | |
|---|---|---|---|---|---|---|---|
| | 20 + 8 | | | 4 + | 22 + | 12 | |
| | **T   H   E** | | | **D   E** | **V   I** | **L** | |
| [Motivation] | 5 | | | 5 + | 9 | | |
| | 5 | | | 14 | | | |
| | | | | | | | |
| [Expression] | 33 | + | | | 52 | | = 85 |


| [Personality] | 33 | + | | | 52 | | = 85 |
|---|---|---|---|---|---|---|---|
| | 19 + | 14 | | 20 + | 18 + | 14 | |
| | **S   A   N** | | | **T   O   R   I   N   I** | | | |
| [Motivation] | 1 | + | | 15 + | 9 + | 9 | |
| | 34 | + | | | 33 | | |
| | | | | | | | |
| [Expression] | | | | | 85 | | |


Note that both the Personality of "Santorini" and the Expression of its second syllable, "torini" vibrate to that of "The Devil"—two manifestations of that vibration in one word! It is this double vibration that led me to conclude that Santorini represented the seat of power for Atlantis, which was corrupted by the actions of one individual. Those actions resulted in the island's destruction by a great earthquake, leaving only a small portion of its original landmass.

I concluded that if the governmental seat of Atlantis could vibrate to the Double Devil in its essence, then, at that time in history, the Devil must have been a positive energy. Humanity has since decided from information passed down from generation to generation that the Devil is a negative force and should be feared. It is important to understand that all words are neutral until belief, negative or positive, energizes them with meaning.

Atlantis prospered for centuries because the people practiced and manifested the highest spiritual ideals. For hundreds of years, the Double Devil Seat was occupied by a person of great integrity. This was an important trait, as the purpose of this high office was to serve the people. This office holder possessed unlimited powers as long as these powers were not corrupted or used for personal gain. The powers of the Double Devil were concentrated in a beautiful crystal, an icon similar in significance to the biblical Ark of the Covenant. This crystal carried great power from the inner planes and was to be used for the benefit of the people. An analysis of the phrases "The Ark of the Covenant" and "The Devil of the World" reveals they bear identical energies of Expression. This shared characteristic is a reflection that in the language of the subconscious they represent the same principle.

[Motivation]                                               [Personality]

$$20 + 8 \qquad\qquad = \quad 28$$
$$\textbf{T} \quad \textbf{H} \quad \textbf{E}$$
$$5 \quad = \qquad\qquad 5$$

$$18 + 11 \qquad\qquad = \quad 29$$
$$\textbf{A} \quad \textbf{R} \quad \textbf{K}$$
$$1 \quad = \qquad\qquad 1$$

$$6 \qquad\qquad = \quad 6$$
$$\textbf{O} \quad \textbf{F}$$
$$15 \quad = \quad 15$$

$$20 + 8 \qquad\qquad = \quad 28$$
$$\textbf{T} \quad \textbf{H} \quad \textbf{E}$$
$$5 \quad = \qquad\qquad 5$$

$$3 \quad + \quad 22 \quad + \quad 14 \quad + \quad 14 + 20 \quad = \quad \underline{+73}$$
$$\textbf{C} \quad \textbf{O} \quad \textbf{V} \quad \textbf{E} \quad \textbf{N} \quad \textbf{A} \quad \textbf{N} \quad \textbf{T}$$
$$\underline{+21} \quad = \quad 15 \quad + \quad 5 \quad + \quad 1$$

|  |  |  |
|---|---|---|
|  |  | [Expression] |
| *47* | + | **164 = *211*** |
| [Motivation] |  | [Personality] |

```
                              20 +8                      =   28
                              T   H   E
        5   =                     5
                          4  +  22  +  12               =   38
                          D   E   V   I   L
       14   =                 5  +  9
                                   6                     =    6
       15   =                 O   F
                                  15
                              20 + 8                     =   28
                              T  H   E
        5   =                     5
                          23  +  18 +12 +4              =   +57
                          W   O   R   L   D
      +15   =                 15

         54                        +                    157  =  211
                                                            [Expression]


    19  +  14  =  33         19 +20   +   18      =   57
    S   U   N                S   T   A   R                    [1•57]
       21        + 21            1
                   54
```

The number 211 (the Expression of both phrases) represents Earth power—the power to create for the benefit of all. Recognizing that the Devil represents past lifetimes, the fact that the two expressions share the same Expression of energies indicates that they are closely related, and in the sense that they represent the two polarities that must be integrated—karmic past-lifetime debts and the power associated with God consciousness—they are. We must overcome the past—our past-lifetimes—to fully become our promised future God-selves, which is how our covenant is fulfilled.

Note that "Star" and "Sun" carry the same vibration as the Personality and Motivation, respectively, of the phrase, "The Devil of the World." This is another example of the hidden energies that are symbolized in the Book of Revelation. These energies were deliberately placed in the language of the Revelation text with the intention of sending a subconscious message to the reader. Recall that the Star and Sun cards of the Tarot major arcana represent positive principles and conditions. The Star represents meditation, inspiration, hope, contentment and abundance; while the Sun is an expression of regeneration and renewal, success, health, pleasure, and wholeness. It is not difficult, given these examples, to believe that the author(s) of the Book of Revelation knew and worked with the ancient science of symbolic language and used it to convey a deeper meaning than could be perceived by the uninitiated.

The office holder of the Double Devil Seat possessed unlimited powers until and unless that power was misused. Centuries of prosperity and high spiritual ideals were enjoyed by the Atlantean people under the guidance of benign and selfless leadership. All this came to an end when a new leader was chosen who did not possess the purity of intent of his predecessors. He began to experiment with the awesome power with which he had been endowed. His power was activated merely by thought, and he was tempted by the possibilities that were available to him. This errant leader began to experiment with the powers of the Atlantean crystal. At the same time, the emphasis was moving from an equality between the male and female polarities to a more male-dominant focus. The leader's motivation began to be dominated by a desire for self-aggrandizement at the expense of his altruistic mission to serve the Atlantean people.

The spiritual masters saw the degradation of the Atlantean society and moved the secrets that were stored in the Atlantean archives to three primary locations: Egypt, Bimini, and the Yucatan. According to Edgar Cayce, this move was made just prior to the destruction of Atlantis.

The corruption of the power of the Double Devil Seat resulted in the destruction of the most advanced civilization that had ever existed on the planet. Stored in the planetary subconscious memory bank, the Akashic Records, is the horrific memory of the fall of this great civilization at the hands of the Double Devil. This memory survives in the subconscious of each individual even today. The fear that is associated with the concept of the Devil is the residual effect of humanity's inability to forgive the individual responsible for the collapse of a beautiful and highly evolved society.

To illustrate the concept of transcendence of the Devil prototype leading to the attainment of the Messiah energy within ourselves we can numerologically analyze the terms, "The Devil's Seat" and "The New Messiah." Again, this is a representation of the two polarities which must be integrated. We must overcome the "Devil" — past lifetimes — to become the "Messiah" — our Christ-conscious selves.

```
     28        +              57            +          39          =   124
  20 + 8            4  +  22  +  12 + 19        19    +   20
   T   H   E        D    E    V    I   L' S         S    E    A    T
       5   +        5    +  9                        5 + 1          =   +25
                                                                       149
```

```
     28        +        37        +              59             =   124
  20+ 8            14   +   23     13  +  19+19   +        8
   T   H   E        N    E    W     M    E    S    S    I    A    H
       5   +        5         +      5   +   9+ 1               =   +25
                                                                    149
```

The above example reflects the principle of the Antechrist coming before the Christ. To become the New Messiah within, we must sit on our own Devil's Seat — overcome our accrued past-live karma. Each individual is destined to eventually reach their own unique attainment of messiahship by confronting and overcoming the personal Devil's Seat — facing karma from past lifetimes through the mirror of people, circumstances and conditions which have been brought into this lifetime as our teachers, and evolving to the higher consciousness of the Christed self. In reality there is no Devil with which to contend, only the karmic lessons of our own creation in previous lifetimes. By conquering our past, our Devil's Seat, we can emerge as the avatar we are in reality, the New Messiah.

It bears repeating: the Devil does not exist today. This term has evolved to represent a level of spiritual initiation that each initiate must face before progressing to another level of spirituality.

```
     28       +           18            +            38        =  84
  20 + 8            4    +    2 + 12          4   +  22   +   12
   T   H   E        D    O    U    B    L    E    D    E    V    I    L
       5   +       15+ 21   +       5    +        5   +   9         = +60
                                                                     144
```

(60 = The # of the word in flesh)     (144 = lower power of 144,000)

Note that the Expression of the phrase "The Double Devil" is the same numerical vibration as the one hundred forty-four thousand spoken of in the following Revelation passage:

> *And they sung as it were a new song before the throne, and before the four beasts, and the elders: and no man could learn that song but the hundred* and *forty* and *four thousand, which were redeemed from the earth.*

> Rev. 14:3

Recall the number 144,000 is also an important one in the structure of the Great Pyramid. The vibration of this number is physically represented in the number of casing stones that were polished so brightly they could be seen as far away as Israel. The symbolism is fairly obvious. The 144,000 are illumined souls (of all religions and nations) which are destined to redeem the earth.

Now, let's take a look at some important biblical names which represent transcendence of the fear of the Devil. The number we are interested in for Table1this analysis is 15, corresponding to the letter "O", the vibration of the 15th major arcana card of the Tarot — the Devil:

**L O R D**       **G O D**       **J O H N**
  *15*              *15*              *15*


**M E S S I A H**
  5  +  9 + 1   = *15*


## *ARCHANGELS:*

**S  A R I  E L**         **M I  C H  A E L**
1 + 9 + 5   = *15*    9 +   1 + 5  = *15*


**G  A  B  R  I  E  L**
1  +  9 + 5   = *15*

## ANGELS OF JUSTICE:

| Z | A | D | K | I | E | L | | R | A | Z | I | E | L |
|---|---|---|---|---|---|---|---|---|---|---|---|---|---|
| 1 | | + | | 9 + 5 | | = 15 | | 1 | + | | 9 + 5 | | = 15 |

| Z | A | P | H | K | I | E | L |
|---|---|---|---|---|---|---|---|
| 1 | | + | | | 9 + 5 | | = 15 |

| J | A | P | H | K | I | E | L |
|---|---|---|---|---|---|---|---|
| 1 | | + | | | 9 + 5 | | = 15 |

Each of these powerful words represent some of the highest spiritual energies that exist. The letter "O", a vowel, in the words "God" and "John" represents the Motivation of these words. The remainder of those listed above achieve the same Motivational numerical vibration through the sum of their vowels. Why does this same numerical energy appear repeatedly unless it has very important significance? The relationship between numbers and symbols were the ancient foundation of language in ancient Egypt. If the number 15, the energy of the Devil, has such a negative connotation, why do these highly revered words have the essence of its energy in their construction?

The underlying principle I have been attempting to communicate in this book is: *to become, one must overcome.* To overcome the Devil, ("Lived" spelled backwards) one must overcome the personal karma (the law of cause and effect) from past lifetimes. Even highly powerful vibrations like God (representing accumulated mass karma from all dimensions) and the Messiah (representing the individual I Am essence expressing on the universal level of Christ Consciousness) face past lifetimes dealing with their own Devil (representing accumulated past-life karma).

The vibration of the number 15 introduced aeons ago in Egypt is that of individuality and freedom leading to ultimate responsibility on every level of existence. This energy has manifested as residual issues from past lives, or as effects resulting from what we eat, what we say, what we think and how we feel.

Our experiences with our parents, our spouse and others with whom we have a relationship mirror those which we created in other lifetimes. Our spousal relationship is a mirror of our male-female polarity. When a marriage ends in divorce, the lessons presented by that particular individual are over and we move on to other relationships which will offer new lessons.

This principle applies to all interpersonal relationships: parental, sibling, marriage, employer, and any other significant relationship in which we participate. The Devil, that frightening demon which we fear so much, is in reality ourselves who, in the past, created the conditions and situations we must confront in the present. So, what of our redemption? Our great redeemer is forgiveness. We have been forgiven on the inner planes, and now it is time to forgive ourselves. How do we accomplish this great task? How does one begin to forgive him/herself and what is the measure of its accomplishment? Forgiveness by forever giving is the answer. The success of our forgiveness is revealed in the extent of our giving. The Devil of our past lifetimes can be transcended by practicing philanthropy in whatever way possible.

To rid ourselves of the fear that has dominated our civilization through religious beliefs, we must take an objective view of the source of the original writings of the text of the Bible. We are an educated and sophisticated people who has come along way in our understanding of the universe and the truth of our existence. It is time to let go of outmoded beliefs which only serve to hold us back from making the next leap in our evolution. It is time to perceive truth as it is, not what has been handed down to us through centuries of manipulation by theological authorities.

I propose a simple remedy for the negatively charged connotation of the Devil. View the word Devil for what it actually is — accrued past-life karma. This subconcious past-life accumulation in the Akasha of physical, mental, emotional and spiritual karmic energy applies to individual as well as universal experience. The individual and the organization, whether it be a business, church or nation, need to resolve this residual energy. The solution I propose is this: forgiveness of our past and application of the principle of unconditional love and service to all, regardless of nationality, color or creed.

In conclusion, I will quote Paul Carus, who so eloquently wrote:

*Truth is no longer what the Church teaches, or what some infallible man may deem wise to proclaim; nor is it what appears to me as true, or to you as true; but it is that which according to methodical critique has been proved to be objectively true, i.e., so proved that everybody who investigates it will find it to be so.*

*Objective truth...is the highest, the most reliable and the most valuable revelation of God...Faith in the objective authority of truth is the next step in the religious evolution of mankind. We stand now at the threshold of the third period* [in our civilization's development] *which will be...positive, constructive, practical* [as opposed to negative, revolutionising, theorising].[15]

With Truth as our ally, we will achieve our ultimate potential by overcoming our belief in the negative.

# 7

## ARMAGEDDON

*...when you come to the end of one time and the
beginning of a new one, it's a period of tremendous
pain and turmoil. The threat we feel, and everybody
feels — well, there is this notion of Armageddon
coming, you know.*

Joseph Campbell
*The Power of Myth*[1]

THE WORD ARMAGEDDON makes its first appearance in the written
word in the Book of Revelation in Chapter 16, Verse 16. It can be said
with a great deal of certainty that the writer(s) of Revelation drew upon
their own personal experience and knowledge as do all writers. For that
reason, it is logical to assume that Armageddon is a derivation of either
a place name or an event known to the author(s). In this case we needn't
look very hard for proof as the evidence is in plain view. The historical
Armageddon is the Plain of Megiddo, a place in Israel of many battles
that has had such a prominent place in history that it bears names from
several different cultures. The Greeks called it Esdraelon and in
Hebrew it is known as Har-Mageddon, which translates to "mountain
of Megiddo." It is certainly not difficult to see how the Armageddon
of Revelation was inspired by the Hebrew place name Har-Mageddon.
This place has become so synonymous with the concept of terrible
battles that the name Armageddon became the personification of the
"Great Battle" and was used symbolically in the Revelation text to
describe the ending of a major age in planetary history.

The difference of opinion regarding the meaning of Armageddon is due to the various perspectives of its interpreters. Many feel Revelation was written in language operating on the conscious level of expression and therefore are trying to interpret the passages literally. As previously stated, the entire 22 chapters were written on the subconscious level and intended to be interpreted symbolically. If we numerologically analyze the Revelation verse in which Armageddon appears, we find that the word "Armageddon" carries the vibration of a positive principle also carried by three famous birthdates in planetary history.

> *And they assembled them at the place which is*
> *called in the Hebrew tongue Armageddon.*
> > Rev. 16:16

### Revelation 16:16 (16+16) = 32

- The birthdate of the USA, July 4, 1776, has a Destiny of 32 (7 + 4 + 1 + 7 + 7 + 6 = 32)
- The birthdate of Thomas Jefferson, April 13, 1743, has a Destiny of 32 (4 + 13 + 1 + 7 + 4 + 3 = 32)
- The birthdate of Abraham Lincoln, February 12, 1809, has a Destiny of 32 (2 + 12 + 1 + 8 + 0 + 9 = 32)

The number 32 is an expression of the concept of communication from the feminine nature resulting in a new type of freedom. The significance of this number is that the empowerment of the feminine principle was encoded into the Book of Revelation as a goal for humanity to achieve, and that the births of the United States, Thomas Jefferson and Abraham Lincoln reflect this same principle; in other words, Jefferson and Lincoln had a destiny to assist in the United States' achievement of its destiny, to re-empower the feminine and establish freedom for all people.

In the presence of such astute company, numerologically speaking, it is difficult to understand how the term "Armageddon" can be anything but positive. To obtain further understanding about this word's esoteric meaning let's break it down, beginning with the first syllable:

$$18 + 13 \quad = \quad 31$$
$$\textbf{A} \quad \textbf{R} \quad \textbf{M} \quad \textbf{A}$$
$$1 \quad + \quad 1 \quad = \quad \underline{+2}$$
$$\textit{33}$$

The natural Expression (33) of the syllable "Arma" indicates that it is destined to serve as a prototype for others to emulate. This is one of the highest expressions of service on the earth plane and represents a great concern for the welfare of the masses. It also indicates the achievement of greater harmony on all levels of manifestation; responsiveness to the needs of all people; service to mankind with no limitations; accumulation and assimilation of advanced knowledge and wisdom; sacrifice for the overall betterment of the world with the objective of relieving the suffering of humanity on earth; and mastery of the ability to project "the Light of the world."

Now let's look at the second syllable:

$$7 \quad + \quad 4 + 4 \quad + \quad 14 \quad = \quad 29$$
$$\textbf{G} \quad \textbf{E} \quad \textbf{D} \quad \textbf{D} \quad \textbf{O} \quad \textbf{N}$$
$$5 \quad + \quad 15 \quad = \quad \underline{+20}$$
$$\textbf{49}$$

The number 49 symbolizes the capstone of the pyramid of Gizeh. The all-seeing eye on the back of the dollar bill is also representative of the number 49 vibration and is the highest degree of human motivation attainable on the earth plane. The Founding Fathers established the pyramid and all-seeing eye as the auspicious symbol of the United States of America (the Great Seal), and eventually, under Franklin D. Roosevelt, this symbolism was placed on the one dollar bill, the most commonly circulated currency of exchange.

Taking a look at the entire word, we find that Armageddon has a Motivation of 22:

$$18 + 13 \quad + \quad 7 \quad + \quad 4 + 4 \quad + \quad 14 \quad = \quad \textbf{\textit{60}} \text{ (the Word)}$$
$$\textbf{A} \quad \textbf{R} \quad \textbf{M} \quad \textbf{A} \quad \textbf{G} \quad \textbf{E} \quad \textbf{D} \quad \textbf{D} \quad \textbf{O} \quad \textbf{N}$$
$$1 \quad + \quad 1 \quad + \quad 5 \quad + \quad 15 \quad = \quad \underline{\textbf{+22}}\text{(the MasterBuilder)}$$
$$\textit{82}$$

(Organization of Feminine Leadership)

The number 22 represents: practical idealism, combining visionary talents with the added ability to put ideals into practice; practical genius; the physical creator of the future and the changer of the course of history; mastery of the material with the benefit of all humanity as the goal; philanthropy; a universal and international sphere of influence in government, finance, science and culture.

If we look at the Personality of "Armageddon," its outer form, we find that it carries the same vibration as the Expression of the "Word":

$$23 \ + \ 18+4 \ = \ 45$$
$$\textbf{W} \quad \textbf{O} \quad \textbf{R} \quad \textbf{D}$$
$$15 \qquad\qquad = \ \underline{+15}$$
$$\textbf{60} \ [Expression]$$

To sum up its general meaning, Armageddon represents the Master Builder of the Word in all earthly experience. Eventually, all people on earth will be positively transformed by the power of the word Armageddon.

Another expression of Armageddon is the rising of Kundalini in the individual. According to the Indian sage, Gopi Krishna, in his book *Kundalini: The Evolutionary Energy in Man*, "Kundalini represents the cosmic vital energy lying dormant in the human body" and its awakening is "a marvelous transformation of the nervous system and the brain, resulting in the manifestation of a superior type of consciousness, which will be the common inheritance of man in the distant future." Gopi Krishna, himself having experienced the rising of Kundalini, repeatedly stated that the "awakening of Kundalini is a perfectly natural biological phenomenon of an uncommon kind" and could be experienced by anyone. This awakening will be experienced by everyone at some time in humanity's evolution enabling the human "to transcend the existing boundaries of the mind and acquire a state of consciousness far above that which is the normal heritage of [humanity] at present." He also stated that the motivating force behind all of our advancements in civilization and spiritual and intellectual thought is Kundalini.[2]

The recent emergence of spiritual and human potential subjects in entertainment indicates that we are on the threshold of a major breakthrough in our spiritual awareness. It has been demonstrated that when humanity is ready for an advancement in consciousness, events and ideas emerge into the sociological milieu which assist in initiating the society into its new capacity. The recent movie *Phenomenon* demonstrates this beautifully. John Travolta's character, George Malley, an ordinary man of average intelligence begins to demonstrate superhuman abilities and intelligence as a result of an octopus-like tumor that is stimulating previously unused parts of his brain. What the film demonstrates is the idea that we humans have latent abilities which are lying dormant because we have not yet had that initiatory experience, our own stimulus to awaken the unused portions of the brain. I believe Kundalini is that stimulus.

Gopi Krishna believed it was evident that humanity was on the verge of this Kundalini awakening. He saw a change in human consciousness, which he knew would be attributed to the "change of times, to modernity, to progress, to freedom, to liberal education" and other factors, but which he knew to be the result of the rising of Kundalini. He also felt "completely sure" that his predictions about the awakening of Kundalini in all humans will begin to occur "before the end of this century and mainly in the centuries to come."[3] This is what Armageddon is all about, not a great battle that will result in terrible destruction on planet Earth, but a revolution in consciousness resulting in the evolution of a new human.

Collectively, humanity will make great strides in its social structure and systems as a result in the rising of its consciousness. This collective of humans is the Group Avatar. An avatar is a teacher of spiritual wisdom, one who operates above the earth ("Ava" — above; "Tara" — the Earth), and everyone has within them this potential. This principle is expressed in Revelation 16:18:

> *And there were voices, and thunders, and lightenings: and there was a great earthquake, such as was not since men were upon the earth, so mighty an earthquake, and so great.*
>
> Rev. 16:18

A numerological analysis of key parts of this verse demonstrates the higher energies represented within it and the relationship to the avatar principle.

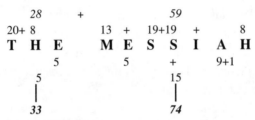

```
        45                                    74 (Messiah)
7 + 18    +    20          18 + 20 + 8 + 17    +    11
G   R   E   A   T      E   A   R   T   H   Q   U   A   K   E
        5 + 1              5 + 1       +       21 + 1  +   5
        6                             33 (The)
        |
        51 (Michael)


                        36
            13  +   3 + 8    +    12
            M   I   C   H   A   E   L
                9      +    1 + 5
                        15
                        |
                        51


            28      +              59
        20 + 8          13  +  19 + 19   +     8
        T   H   E      M   E   S   S   I   A   H
            5              5       +       9 + 1
        5                          15
        |                          |
        33                         74
```

(Highest degree of Masonry)

As we examine the numbers associated with the expression of the word "Great" we see that it is equal to the Expression of "Michael." Michael is an energy embodying Light and Love and overlights many individuals on the earth plane today. This is what I refer to as the Group Avatar energy.

The Group Avatar is the achievement of Christ Consciousness by many individuals and represents the Second Coming foretold and anticipated by the Christian world. While many people are expecting a single individual to return to earth as the Messiah, I have come to believe that this return is a potential return of the messianic vibration within each individual human. There will be many Messiahs, and their power combined will manifest the Love and Wisdom of God, the Creator.

The result of this Group Avatar activation is a greatly enhanced power of the healing force to assist in easing the world's karmic burden and elevate the consciousness of all humanity. This will require the unification of the world's spiritual philosophies, not in the sense that they form a new religion but that they work within their own diverse traditions in a cooperative spirit to achieve world peace. The need for unity is evident everywhere on earth, from the growing fields of Africa to the ice fields of the lands of the northern sun.

As the Group Avatar grows through the awakening of Christ Consciousness within more people, the light energy grows, increasing exponentially. The spiritual Hierarchy uses this light to break up areas of negative energy—anywhere people are oppressed and suffering, or are denied their divinely given right to freedom—that has been created by wrong thinking. This unified light energy is connected to the Central Sun, the God force, and carries out the universal plan to restore the original plan on earth, that of freedom and a spirit of sister/ brotherhood among people.

The work of the Group Avatar has begun to emerge as more and more people are directing their energies toward caring for their fellow human beings. This is evident in the many projects and efforts made both by individuals and governments to end the suffering of people caused by oppression and tyranny, and philanthropic programs directed toward alleviating poverty and hunger.

Humanity has been guided by its spiritual brethren throughout history, and the plan for the establishment of the Group Avatar is part of that guidance. The blueprint for the new group consciousness was given to the earth plane in the form of the Constitution of the United States of America. Certain Masters had incarnated during the historical period in which the young democracy, the New Israel, was established in the New World. The Founding Fathers served as emissaries of the spiritual Hierarchy for the purpose of the establishment of a government model that would ensure peace and freedom for the planet's inhabitants.

The Christ energy was originally introduced during the 3 years of Jesus' ministry. His teachings of 2,000 years ago were intended to show how light and love could be made manifest on the earth. Unfortunately, during that dark period of history, a humanity desperate for relief from wars and oppression venerated the bringer of these spiritual laws rather than the laws themselves — they worshiped the messenger instead of the message. The myth of a single Christ/ Messianic figure who will return to save humanity must be dispelled for humanity to redeem itself and it will only do so if it recognizes its own responsibility for changing present conditions on earth. The return of the Christ energy in the form of the Group Avatar will be the salvation of our species.

In the year 1831, it became apparent that the karmic debt incurred in the 1770's and 80's for the failed power test (and other tests, including the slavery issue) had come due. A date was selected in 1831 that had the perfect vibration to resolve the US karmic debt, November 11, 1831. This debt could be resolved at the planetary level beginning on this date, with its resolution occurring at the final Armageddon, the Gulf War, in 1991.

In Numerological analysis, a date is broken down both in terms of its numerical constituents and in terms of various combinations of those constituents. One such technique shows the progression or the maturing of the energies represented by that date. The results of this analysis technique are called "Pinnacles" and represent a range in years in which the energies mature, culminating in an event, which usually occurs within a year or two after the end of the period.

**Pinnacle #4—60** (11 + 49)
**(1878 - 1913)**
(World War I began in 1914)

**Pinnacle #3—82** (22 + 60)
**(1869 - 1877)**
(Reconstruction of the South)

(11 + *11*) **Pinnacle #1—22**              **Pinnacle #2—60** (*11* + 49)
       **(1831 - 1858)**                      **(1860-1868)**
   (Processing of Slavery Issue                  (Civil War)
      on Inner and Outer levels)

**11**       +       *11*       +       **49** (18+31)   =   **71** (Thoth)

*Cycle 1* **(2)**  +  *Cycle 2* **(2)**  +  *Cycle 3***(13/4)*   =   *Destiny #*
**(1831-1858)**    **(1859-1885)**      **(1886-1913)**

**Challenge:**   Cycle 3 - (Cycle 2 - Cycle 1) = **4** - (**2** - **2**) = **2**
(A challenge of **2** represents an inability to express the feminine.)

The single-digit analysis of the date, November 11, 1831, yields the number **224**, the numerological equivalent of the Spear of Longinus. The Spear of Longinus was given to the Centurion Gaius Cassius by Julius Caesar as a token of appreciation for his service. Gaius Cassius used this Spear to pierce the side of Christ after the crucifixion. Because blood flowed from the wound (the body doesn't bleed after death) a greatly moved Gaius converted to Christianity and The Spear became a symbol of immortality and sacred power. There is a great and long history to The Spear of Longinus, also known as The Spear of Destiny, which is covered in detail in the Epilogue. For our purposes here, suffice it to say that it originated in the higher planes and became an instrument for fulfilment of the Hierarchy's plan for Earth.

This energy was introduced on the earth plane by Thoth, evidenced by the fact that the "Destiny" of this date is equivalent to the vibration of Thoth. When the date is broken down by subtracting the difference between the $1^{st}$ and $2^{nd}$ cycles from the third, we find that the "Challenge" for the date is 2, symbolizing an inability to express and empower the feminine in earthly matters.

$$
\begin{array}{cccccccccl}
18+13 & + & 7 & + & 4+4 & + & 14 & = & \textbf{60} & \text{(Word)} \\
\textbf{A} & \textbf{R} \; \textbf{M} & \textbf{A} & \textbf{G} & \textbf{E} & \textbf{D} \; \textbf{D} & \textbf{O} & & \textbf{N} & \\
1 & + & 1 & + & 5 & + & 15 & = & +\underline{\textbf{22}} & \text{(Master Builder)} \\
& & & & & & & & 82 & \text{(Beginning of the} \\
& & & & & & & & & \text{organization of} \\
& & & & & & & & & \text{feminine} \\
& & & & & & & & & \text{empowerment)}
\end{array}
$$

All four pinnacle numbers for the date 11-11-1831 are reflected in the numerological components of the word Armageddon (60 + 22 = 82). This is no coincidence. The significance of this correlation is that we have already fought the battle of Armageddon that has been prophesied since ancient times, represented by the date which marked the beginning of the inner conflict experienced by the United States as the slavery issue.

If we carefully analyze the progression or maturing of this 11-11-1831 birthdate, some interesting patterns emerge. The second pinnacle begins on 11-11-1860, which corresponds with the beginning of the United States Civil War. The entire first life cycle (81 years) of the 11-11-1831 ends in 1913 and in 1914 the first World War began. The second cycle (81 years) of 11-11-1831 ends in 1993, two years after the second battle of Armageddon, the Gulf War. Armageddon, both as an event and as a word, has been misinterpreted throughout history. An analysis of the word Armageddon reveals that it really means the Master Builder (22) of the Word (60) leading to the advent of organization (8) of feminine empowerment (2).

Because we haven't nurtured the feminine within us, this has manifested as the neglect of the physical female (women and the environment) on the world stage in the practice of commerce, religion and politics. The maturation of this process—freeing our inner woman to take her place in the balance of power—arrives just in time for the official beginning of the feminine millennium, the year 2000 (the 1000th power of the feminine vibration).

As the primary agent in the Civil War conflict, Abraham Lincoln was charged with the responsibility for bringing the vibration of freedom and equality for all to the physical plane. Comparing the analysis of Abraham Lincoln's key aspects to that of the word Armageddon reveals some striking results:

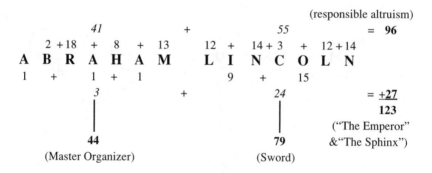

At a key point during the Civil War, Abraham Lincoln delivered his famous Gettysburg Address in an effort to strengthen the Union's resolve in bringing the bloody conflict to an end and to reiterate his— and the Union's—position. Lincoln understood the power of language and chose the language of his speech to evoke a desired response on subconscious levels. The phrase "Four score and seven years ago" is reminiscent of references to time in the Bible. Why didn't he just say "Eighty seven years ago our forefathers brought forth..."? If we numerologically analyze the phrase "Four score and seven years ago" we can answer that question.

|  |  | 6 | + | 18 |  | = | 24 |
|---|---|---|---|---|---|---|---|
|  |  | **F** | **O** | **U** | **R** |  |  |
| *36* | = |  | 15+ | 21 |  |  |  |
|  |  | 19+ 3 | + | 18 |  | = | 40 |
|  |  | **S** | **C** | **O** | **R** | **E** |  |
| *20* | = | 15 | + | 5 |  |  |  |
|  |  | 14 | + | 4 |  | = | 18 |
|  |  | **A** | **N** | **D** |  |  |  |
| *1* | = | 1 |  |  |  |  |  |
|  |  | 19 | + | 22 | + 14 | = | 55 |
|  |  | **S** | **E** | **V** | **E** | **N** |  |
| *10* | = | 5 | + | 5 |  |  |  |
|  |  | 25 |  | + | 18+ 19 | = | 62 |
|  |  | **Y** | **E** | **A** | **R** | **S** |  |
| *6* | = | 5 +1 |  |  |  |  |  |
|  |  | 7 |  |  |  | = | +7 |
|  |  | **A** | **G** | **O** |  |  |  |
| *+16* | = | 1 | + | 15 |  |  |  |
| *89* |  |  |  |  |  |  | *206* |

Triple digit analysis in numerology reveals energies that operate on the higher planes. In this case, the number 206 is the outer expression of "God." The number 89 is a reflection of Psalm 89 in the Bible, also known as the Davidic Covenant. The following verses from Psalm 89 are representative of the covenant of David:

> *I have made a covenant with my chosen, I have sworn unto David my servant,*
> *Thy seed will I establish for ever, and build up thy throne to all generations. Selah.*
> *And the heavens shall praise thy wonders, O Lord: thy faithfulness also in the congregation of the saints.*
> *For who in the heaven can be compared unto the Lord?* Who *among the sons of the mighty can be likened unto the Lord? ...*
>
> Psalm 89:3-6

> *Thou hast a mighty arm: strong is thy hand,* and *high is thy right hand.*

*Justice and judgment* are *the habitation of thy
throne: mercy and truth shall go before thy face.*

*Blessed* is *the people that know the joyful sound:
they shall walk, O Lord, in the light of thy
countenance.*

*In thy name shall they rejoice all the day: and in
thy righteousness shall they be exalted.*

*For thou* art *the glory of their strength: and in thy
favour our horn shall be exalted.*

*For the Lord is our defence; and the Holy of One
Israel* is *our king.*

*Then thou spakest in vision to thy holy one, and
saidst, I have laid help upon* one that is *mighty; I have
exalted* one *chosen out of the people.*

*I have found David my servant; with my holy oil
have I anointed him:*

*With whom my hand shall be established: mine
arm also shall strengthen him...*

Psalm  89: 13-21


*Also I will make him* my *first-born, higher than
the kings of the earth.*

*My mercy will I keep for him for evermore, and my
covenant shall stand fast with him.*

*His seed also will I make* to endure *for ever, and
his throne as the days of heaven.*

Psalm 89: 27-29


In his eloquent speech Abraham Lincoln invoked the energies of
the Davidic Covenant and the power of God to assist in the healing of
the North/South conflict. Whether he did so intentionally or by divine
inspiration we cannot know, but it is clear that Lincoln's Gettysburg
Address was used as an instrument to bring the vibration of higher
energies into the earth plane.

The energies of Armageddon and the date 11-11-1831 are
remarkably synchronous. This is indicative of the fact that
Armageddon has already occurred, at a time when it was most needed,
in 1831. The responsibility for laying the foundation for the future

freedom of humanity was an awesome task. It had to be given to one who could execute two momentous duties simultaneously. Specifically, they are:

1. To preserve freedom on planet Earth for the present time, the 1800's, and for future times when our understanding of freedom as a principle will have matured.

2. To be in the "hot seat" of the US Presidency during the Civil War, charged with the repayment of the karmic debt incurred by the Founding Fathers by not "practicing what they preached."

Whether Lincoln was a walk-in or had a "Sinai experience" as Moses did is unclear, however, he fulfilled his secret destiny to preserve freedom for all by championing freedom during the most difficult period in United States history.

The power of belief cannot be overstated. Humanity's collective belief regarding Armageddon manifested as the Gulf War in the early 1990's which symbolically represented the Great Battle. If we study the component parts of the Armageddon prophecy, we find striking parallels between the Gulf War and the prophesied battle of Armageddon. The common elements include Israel as one of the major players in this collective conflict and the United Nations Army, composed of the fighting divisions of many nations. The truth of the matter is that we didn't have to fight the Gulf War in Iraq. The power of the collective belief in a physical manifestation of Armageddon brought the event into the physical plane, manifesting a false prophecy.

The original Revelation text was intended to bear a very different meaning from what has been generally accepted, and it is important to understand that as we were able to manifest the Great Battle, we also have the ability to manifest the higher principles represented in it through the power of our beliefs. That future manifestation of Revelation prophecy will be expressed in the worldwide organization of women leading to their taking major positions of leadership. This new reality will become more evident around the year 2000. The misconceptions associated with the Armageddon myth will be replaced once and for all with the truth that any prediction of the future can be circumvented by a positive projection of love, light and concerted effort toward unity among religions, nations and peoples.

The conception of the Group Avatar began on November 11, 1949, at a little-known event that occurred at Mt. Shasta in the presence of 22 spiritual leaders. The former national leader of the Coptic Fellowship of America, Hamid Bey, was present at that event, about which he often spoke. The following account is representative of his description of the experience:

> At 11:00 a.m. on November 11, 1949, in a remote, isolated area on Mt. Shasta, California, an historical event took place. (This event had so impressed Hamid Bey that he conducted a special meeting on or near November 11 of each year until his passing on July 16th, 1976.) The days and events leading up to the November 11, 1949, date were extraordinary.
>
> The awe-inspiring event began on November 9 when Hamid Bey was in Chicago delivering a lecture. As he finished his speech he was handed a telegram. It stated he was to take a flight to San Francisco and that his reservation had been booked for 1:00 the following morning. His original plans had been to fly to Los Angeles to attend the International Peace Conference, but he chose to follow his intuition and take the flight to San Francisco.
>
> As the plane approached the Rocky Mountains there was heavy cloud cover and a hard rain was falling. When the flight reached its destination, both the San Francisco and Oakland airports were closed because of another powerful rainstorm. Early in the morning of November 10, the plane landed at Redding, California, near Mt. Shasta, a place of high spiritual energy for thousands of years. As Hamid deplaned in Redding, a stranger approached him and asked him if he was Hamid Bey. Upon receiving confirmation of his identity, the man took Hamid to a

*car wherein there sat three other men who had arrived under similar circumstances and, unbeknownst to Hamid, on the same flight.*

*Hamid asked, "What's this all about?" To which the stranger replied, "Do not be concerned that you were unable to land in San Francisco." Intuitively Hamid was satisfied with the response and the four men and their mysterious chauffer found a hotel in Redding, where they booked a room for the night. Even at this point, the four men had no idea why they had been brought to this small town in northern California.*

*The next morning, November 11th, each man was given a pack and all were taken in a jeep to a certain secluded glen on Mt. Shasta. At this point they were joined by 18 other individuals who had, not coincidentally, stayed at the same hotel the previous night. Each of these individuals was a representative from a different country and different spiritual philosophy. This group of spiritual leaders walked a considerable distance and were finally told to stop and put down all of their personal supplies in a prescribed position and manner which marked out an elongated half-moon shape. They were then asked to wait. At exactly 11:00 a.m. two male babies were presented to the 22 witnesses. Shortly thereafter a tremendous air pressure was felt which pushed over trees and vegetation, followed by the landing of a UFO about a quarter mile away.*

*While seated in this half-moon formation the 22 witnesses were told that what they had witnessed represented the birth of two highly evolved souls (twin male babies) who would play major roles in the future leadership of this earth.*[4]

A detailed explanation of the true significance of the November 11, 1949, event is needed to fully comprehend the momentous opportunity its occurrence affords humanity. This event was not only the birth of two male babies but represented the birth of a potential prototype to which an individual should seek to aspire.

These two highly evolved souls will be greatly involved in the fulfillment of the plan for world unity and permanent world peace as was prophesied 2,000 years ago. The unification of the Twelve Tribes of Israel is a symbol which represents the concept of unity through diversity. This symbol serves as the prototype for international unity that will become manifest bringing about cooperation and harmony on every level of earthly expression. These efforts are occurring today as the network of light grows stronger with the awakening of more people.

Numerology is a magnificent tool with which to explore the meaning of events; simple to use and understand, and precise in its interpretation. It is a system which breaks down language into numbers which have specific meaning, and has a further application to dates of specific events. The significance of an event can be determined by analyzing its date. To understand the importance of the birth of the twins under the extraordinary circumstances described above, let's analyze the date and time of that event.

| Month | Day | Hour | | |
|---|---|---|---|---|
| 11  + | 11 | +  11:00 a.m | = | 33 |

The two male babies are represented by the double 1's, as the number one represents male energy. The sums of the double 1's (2+2+2) added equal 6, which represents the Sixth Root Race. The Sixth Root Race is symbolized by the Aquarian Age and refers to the acceptance of more responsibility in the context of a humanitarian focus. In contrast, the Age which is just passing, the Piscean Age, represents the Fifth Root Race and symbolized expansion of freedom through spiritual orientation.

An examination of the significance of the number 33, a master number in Numerology, gives us further understanding about the importance of the birth of the twin males on Mt. Shasta. The number 33 represents:

- A destiny to serve as a prototype for others to emulate
- The highest expression of service on the earth plane
- Great concern for welfare of the masses

- Greater harmony on all levels of manifestation
- Service to humanity with no limitations
- Assimilation of advanced knowledge and wisdom
- An attraction to institutions and organizations involved with education, health and counseling-related fields of service
- Sacrifice for the overall betterment of the world
- A primary aim to relieve the suffering of humanity on earth
- Mastery of the ability to project "the Light of the World"

The analysis of the number 11 gives provides even greater understanding of the November 11, 1949 event.

- The name "Jesus" vibrates to the energy of the number 11.
- The 11th hour is considered the purest hour of the day. In Egyptian philosophy, the 11th hour is when the human body casts its smallest shadow.
- Masons are taught that the number 11 is the most important number because of the symbolism inherent in the two upright figures: "within of 2 units (equilibrium) one may come into the possession of all things."
- The number 11 symbolizes the messenger bringing to humanity"glad tidings of great joy."
- Ancient wisdom represents the powers of the number 11 as: In my grasp are all things held in perfect equilibrium, I bind all opposites together, each to its complement."
- Brotherhood and unity as expressed by the phrase, "The world is my home and to do good is my religion." The composition of the group of 22 witnesses to the Mt. Shasta event is representative of this concept. Each of the 22 spiritual leaders hailed from a different nation.

The combination of the month and day (11th month, 11th day) is an expression of the number 22 vibration. The number 22 represents expanded consciousness, the ability to operate on a planetary level of awareness, high ideals, and achievement on an international and universal scale. Its ultimate potential is reflected in the following:

- Practical idealism; the combining of visionary talents with the organizational ability to manifest enlightened reforms for the benefit of all humanity
- The physical creator of the future; the changer of the course of history
- The master builder with the benefit of all humanity as the goal
- Philanthropy
- Universal and international
- The power to organize and establish large, all-encompassing institutions

If we think of the monumental significance of this planetary event in terms of the birth of higher consciousness for the benefit of the planet, we can understand the reasons for the twin birth occurring at this particular time. The twin birth represents on a symbolic level the prototype for humanity to emulate.

To sum up the previous discussion, the November 11, 1949, event symbolized the birth of a prototype for the evolving human. He/she thinks in universal terms, and dreams of world peace and harmony possessing the ability to manifest hopes and achieve goals. He/she is attracted to large causes and seeks to bring about the unity of nations, and possesses the ability to unite people to bring about international cooperation and goodwill. He/she also possesses the ability to put into practice the highest visionary ideals. This is the prototype of the highest form of service to humankind.

It is remarkable that within the Book of Revelation, written nearly 2,000 years ago, exists a prophecy of the November 11, 1949, Mt. Shasta event. This prophecy is encoded within the phrase "Hebrew tongue" and spoken in the language of the subconscious. Using the wisdom of the Mystery School tradition in our technique of analysis we can decode the prophecy. If we add the word Armageddon to the phrase "Hebrew tongue" (see above analysis) and analyze it numerologically, we find that it correlates to the date, November 11, 1949:

- The sum of the Personalities of "Hebrew," "tongue"

and "Armageddon" (51+41+60) is 152
- The sum of the Motivations of these same three words (10+41+22) is 73
- The sum of the Personalities and Motivations of these three words results in a composite Expression (152+73) which is **225**
- Breaking down the date 11/11/1949 we arrive at the same numerical relationship:

| 1 1 | 1 1 | 1 9 4 9 |
|:---:|:---:|:---:|
| 1+1=2 | 1+1=2 | 1+9+4+9=23=5 |
| 2 | 2 | 5 |

To further validate this relationship, a thoughtful examination of Revelation 16:16 reveals that this prophecy is fulfilled by the occurrence of the event on Mt. Shasta.

> *And they assembled them at the place which is called in the Hebrew tongue Armageddon.*

The Personality of Armageddon, as stated earlier, vibrates to the energy of the number 60, which is also the Expression of the "Word." This vibration represents the conception of a new positive message for humanity in the body of a diversified Group Avatar, aptly represented by the 22 leaders who were present at the twin birth.

If we examine the words "Hebrew tongue" we find a strong relationship between these words and Michael, Maitreya Buddha, Lord, and the word Armageddon itself.

```
          51                        34      +      7    = 41
 8  +  2 +18  +  23          20  +  14        7
 H  E  B  R  E  W            T   O  N      G   U   E
    5      +   5                +15            21 + 5  = ±41
       +10                                     +26        82
       61/7                        49          33
```

$$12 \; + \; 18+4 \; = \; 34$$

**L    O    R    D**

$$15$$

$$\underline{+15}$$

$$\mathbf{49}$$

A complex relationship exists between these words on various levels of numerological derivation. The following is a list of the more significant relationships between these key words and phrases:

- The Personality of *Hebrew* is the same as the Expression of *Michael*—51 (see p. 100 for the analysis of *Michael*).
- The Personality of the second syllable of *Tongue*,"gue," is the vibration of illumined intellect—7.
- The Motivation of "gue" is the same as the Expression of *God*— 26.
- The Expression of "gue" is the same as the Expression of *the*—33 (see analysis on p. 100).
- The Expression of the first syllable of *Tongue*,"Ton," is the same as the Expression of *Lord*—49. In other words, *Tongue* is another way of saying "The Lord."
- The sum of the Personalities of *Hebrew* and *Tongue* is equal to the vibration of *Maitreya Buddha*—92; and last,but not least,
- The composite Expression (the sum of the Personalities of "Ton" and "gue" added to the sum of the Motivations for these syllables) equals 82, the Expression of the word Armageddon.

This is no coincidence. The author(s) of the Book of Revelation intentionally chose the words that would convey the subconscious message they wanted to preserve for future generations in the scriptures. The Group Avatar was conceived on November 11, 1949. The symbol of many Christs represents the world's many religions and nations. This Group Avatar will be birthed as individuals from all spiritual traditions acquire Christ Consciousness and fulfill the destiny of the Second Coming. If Christ was born in Bethlehem but not in me, his birth was in vain.

The Sixth Root Race prototype can be visualized as the image of a person whose eyes are directed upward to the clouds for supreme inspiration, while the feet are grounded in the earthly plane. This is the symbol of one who can integrate higher wisdom and organizational administration, while at the same time maintaining an awareness of human needs, both individual and group. This prototype has the highest ethical standards, and has achieved material and spiritual mastery. It represents altruism and the power to accomplish the building of a new world and a new consciousness.

We belong to a new humanity born again beyond personality, beyond soul, born again to a Universal Awareness. We should not be concerned with creating a new religion. The new message is one of unity, planetary sister/brotherhood and opportunity for all. We are presently in the transitional period between two dispensations. We are at the end of the old Piscean age and not quite ready for the new energies of the Aquarian. This is why the present age partakes of both the old and the new — a clinging to tradition and a yearning for greater enlightenment - a literal and symbolic pre-dawning. The eyes of the former centers of ancient civilizations are turning toward the West where the world awaits the beginning of a new dispensation and a new civilization of the Sixth Root Race.

A civilization is always based on a strong universal philosophy of Truth, for a strong productive center of civilization cannot survive without a steadfast belief in the Divine. In this new civilization, centered in the United States of America, the New Israel, we shall see a truer, more positively oriented schooling for the young, and a wider, greater understanding of the Divine by all social classes. A harmonious welding of the religious and scientific communities into one great philosophy of mutual understanding and respect for the principles of each will occur, bringing together the wonders of laboratories and the Truths of the Cosmos. All humanity will enjoy a new life guided by a greater mind.

In the United States, more than anywhere else on this earth plane, are blended together all races and nationalities of the earth. Out of this blend shall spring the highly evolved Sixth Root Race, man and woman of tomorrow, a race that by its universally strong faith in the supreme wisdom shall create a civilization of equality like none that has ever existed before on this planet.

# Timeline for Initiation of the Group Christ Office
## (The New Messiah)
### beginning November 11, 1949

**Numerological analysis of date:** **11** + *11* + **68** (19 + 49)

| | | |
|---|---|---|
| *1995 - 2030* | **CAPSTONE**<br>**79**<br>*The Sword* | 11 + 68 = 79 |
| *1986 - 1994* | **KING'S CHAMBER**<br>**101**<br>*Personality of the New Messiah* | [11 + *11*] + [*11* + 68] = 101 |
| *1976 - 1986* | **QUEEN'S CHAMBER**<br>**79**<br>*The Sword* | *11* + 68 = 79 |
| *1949 - 1976* | **THE GRAND GALLERY**<br>**22**<br>*Master Builder* | 11 + *11* = 22 |

**THE MIDDLE PILLAR**
**194**
*Individual Covenant*

*101* + *79* + *11* + *3* = **194**

[King's Chamber + Capstone + Day of Month + Challenge]

## Calculation of the Challenge for 11/11/1949:

| 11 | + | 11 | + | 68 |
|---|---|---|---|---|
| 2 | | 2 | | 14/5 |

*(5 - 2) - (2 - 2)* = *3* (Communication)

# 8

# THE FOUR HORSEMEN OF THE APOCALYPSE

THE FOUR HORSEMEN of the Apocalypse are generally regarded as ominous figures, the harbingers of destruction. This interpretation is the result of a strictly literal translation of symbolism in the Book of Revelation. To avoid the misunderstanding that results from this method of interpretation we must return to our premise of interpreting Revelation in the light of what we know about the esoteric meanings of language. This last book of the Bible was not written to be interpreted on a conscious, literal level. As has been previously established, I believe the subconscious language of the Mystery Schools teachings was the language in which Revelation was written. With that in mind, let's take a fresh look at the symbology of the Four Horsemen.

The Four Horsemen as positive symbols correspond to four of Jesus' closest disciples: John, Thomas, Peter and Judas. On a personal level, these four disciples represent our four bodies which are represented by the Four Horses: the Spiritual Body, the Mental Body, the Emotional Body, and the Physical Body. Symbolically we each have our own four disciples, physically manifesting as people in our lives, and spiritually representing our four bodies. The influences cast upon Jesus' life by John, Thomas, Peter and Judas can be summed up as follows:

- **John**: (White Horse/Spiritual Body) He was always there for Jesus, regardless of how difficult matters became or uncomfortable for John or Jesus. John was the disciple on whom Jesus could always rely.
- **Thomas**: (Gray Horse/Mental Body) He played the devil's

advocate. He challenged Jesus' decisions on an intellectual level.

- **Peter**: (Red Horse/Emotional Body) A powerful ally, Peter remained at Jesus' side until there was a crisis. He was the disciple that was there for Jesus as long as things went well.
- **Judas**: (Black Horse/Physical Body) He was an apparent ally and was proficient at handling money. He was the disciple that betrayed Jesus when Jesus needed him most.

In our own lives we also have our personal John, Thomas, Peter and Judas. The people with whom we have close relationships fill the roles of these four disciples, and we, in turn, represent one or more of these disciple archetypes in the lives of others. Much as they served Jesus, our own four disciples serve us. As indicated above, each of our four bodies also correspond to one of these roles.

- John is your buddy, someone in whom you can confide, and may be your marriage partner or significant other. John is always there for you, through any crisis. This is the spiritual body which is always with us.
- Thomas is your intellectual "policeman," the person who questions your decision-making and challenges you to reexamine your ideas. This is the mental body, causing us to question our beliefs.
- Peter is a powerful, dynamic ally as long as the going is good. If there is any kind of crisis, Peter will desert you. This is our emotional body, over which we have mastery until we face a crisis.
- Judas is your betrayer. The key to handling him is in how you treat him when he betrays you. This is our physical body, which betrays us, and we must learn to nurture the physical body to overcome its limitations.

On a personal level, then, these four archetypes represent the symbolism of the Four Horsemen.

The Four Horsemen of the Apocalypse appear in Chapter 6 of Revelation. As stated earlier, the number 6 refers to responsibility. In this case it is the care & responsibility of our four bodies which we bear when we incarnate. To gain further insight into their importance and significance in our lives, we examine the symbolism as it relates to our four bodies: the physical, mental, emotional and spiritual.

### I. Spiritual Body (the White Horse) — the First Beast

*And I saw, and behold a white horse. And he that*
*sat on him had a bow, and a crown was given unto him*
*and he went forth conquering and to conquer.*

Rev. 6:2

This white horse we ride is our multi-level spiritual body. White denotes purity. Most of this verse has obvious positive connotations with the exception of the word "conquering." As an example of the coded meaning of "conquering" we can make an intriguing comparison between it and "Abraham Lincoln."

$$
\begin{array}{ccccccc}
& & & & & & \text{(Independence)} \\
3 & + & 14+17 & + & 18 & + & 14+7 & = & 73/1 \\
\mathbf{C} & \mathbf{O} & \mathbf{N\ Q} & \mathbf{U} & \mathbf{E\ R} & \mathbf{I} & \mathbf{N\ G} \\
15 & & +\ 21+5 & + & 9 & & & = \underline{+50/5}\ \text{(freedom)} \\
& & & & & & & \mathbf{123/6}
\end{array}
$$

$$
\begin{array}{cccccccc}
& 41 & & & + & & 55 & & = 96/6 \\
2+18 & + & 8 & + & 13 & & 12 & + & 14+3 & + & 12+14 \\
\mathbf{A\ B} & \mathbf{R} & \mathbf{A} & \mathbf{H} & \mathbf{A\ M} & & \mathbf{L} & \mathbf{I} & \mathbf{N} & \mathbf{C} & \mathbf{O}\ \mathbf{L}\ \mathbf{N} \\
1 & + & 1 & + & 1 & & 9 & & + & 15 \\
& 3 & & & + & & 24 & & & = \underline{+27/9} \\
& & & & & & & & & \mathbf{123/6}
\end{array}
$$

The number 123 appears again and again in important symbolic images in archaeology, mysticism and in the Revelation text. It represents the spiritual power transferred from the hiercharical position to empower the common person. The Christ is not someone coming to save you. If you accept the responsibility for the power made available to you, you will save yourself. The following are further examples of the significance of the 123 vibration:

$$20 + 8 \quad + \quad 19 + 16 + 8 \quad + \quad 14 + 24 = 109$$

**T H E     S P H I N X**

(Ancient Egyptian monument)

$$5 \quad + \qquad\qquad 9 \qquad\qquad = \quad \underline{+14}$$
$$123$$

$$20 + 8 \quad + \quad 13 + 16 \quad + \quad 18 \quad + \quad 18 = 93$$

**T H E     E M P E R O R**

(Egyptian Tarot card)

$$5 \quad + \quad 5 \quad + \qquad 5 \quad + \quad 15 \qquad = \quad \underline{+30}$$
$$123$$

The foregoing examples can be further translated to mean the following, as relates to the vibration of the number 123:

CONQUERING — Spiritual action
ABRAHAM LINCOLN — Famous leader/human rights advocate
THE SPHINX — Ancient spiritual monument
THE EMPEROR — Ancient title of authority

These four apparently unrelated subjects each have their own unique expression of the energy of 123. Feeding the hungry, healing the sick, and housing the homeless — these are goals that represent the idealism and practicality of those who aspire to serve humanity. Abraham Lincoln, as a symbol of leadership, was in a position of power to accomplish the above-stated objectives. The Sphinx sits directly in front of the doorway to the Pyramid, symbolizing the sun, a cosmic source of power. According to the Edgar Cayce readings, the power sources from Atlantis are stored in a time-capsule under the right paw of the Sphinx. The Emperor Tarot card of the Major Arcana certainly represents power and was the title of ultimate political authority in ancient times.

The word "conquering" in Revelation 6:2 describes the action of the first beast riding a white horse (the spiritual body). The authority is in our spiritual motive, our power to pray, our power to visualize a positive impact of our own life upon others. We have the ability as common people to make the earth a better place to live by being shepherds to everyone we contact. The charitable act of donating money to organizations that can feed the hungry, heal the sick, and house the homeless is one such action. Another obvious choice is to use our minds positively to create positive conditions in our environment and use our words to encourage and uplift at every opportunity life provides. This is truly "conquering," and from a practical perspective places the word "conquering" in the same context as Lincoln, the Emperor and the Sphinx.

## II. Emotional Body (the Red Horse) — the Second Beast

*And there went out another horse that was red:*
*and power was given to him that sat thereon to take*
*peace from the earth, and that they should kill one*
*another: and there was given unto him a great sword.*
                                                    Rev. 6:4

Although the word "kill" obviously has a negative connotation, examining it in the light of numerological analysis we can see the positive meaning intended by this passage. "Kill" possesses the same vibrational energy as the word "Abraham," the energy of the Master Organizer.

$$11 \quad + \quad 12 + 12 \quad = \quad 35$$
$$\textbf{K} \quad \textbf{I} \quad \textbf{L} \quad \textbf{L}$$
$$9 \qquad\qquad\qquad \underline{+9}$$

**44**  (Master Organizer; Biblically, the
vibration of Abraham, the father
of many nations)

$$2 + \quad 18 \quad + \quad 8 \quad + \quad 13 \quad = \quad 41$$
$$\textbf{A} \quad \textbf{B} \quad \textbf{R} \quad \textbf{A} \quad \textbf{H} \quad \textbf{A} \quad \textbf{M}$$
$$1 \quad + \qquad\quad 1 \quad + \quad 1 \qquad\quad = \quad \underline{+3}$$
$$\textbf{44}$$

On a related note, if we analyze the energies of Abraham's designation as the "Father of many nations" we find a relationship to the famed Spear of Longinus, the spear that was used to pierce the side of Christ at his crucifixion.

```
              6    +   20 + 8  +   18              =    52
              F    A    T   H   E   R
        6 =        1        +   5
                   6                              =     6
              O  F
       15 =   15
              13   +   14 + 25                    =    52
              M    A    N   Y
        1 =        1
              14   +   20      +  14 + 19         =    +67
   92  {      N    A    T   I   O   N   S
(Buddha)  +25 =     1   +    9 + 15


              47                    +                177 =   224
      (Merging of Heart & Mind)          (Individual Christ Consciousness)



              20 + 8                             =    28
              T   H   E
        5 =           5
              19 + 16  +   18                     =    53
              S   P    E   A   R
        6 =            5 + 1
                       6                          =     6
              O  F
       15 =   15
              12   +   14 + 7  +   14   +   19   =    +66
              L    O    N   G   I   N   U   S
      +45 =        15    +    9   +   21


              71                      +              153 =   224
```

For the present, it is sufficient to understand that Abraham as the "Father of many nations" represents the divine principle of leadership and that the word "kill" as it is used in the context of Revelation 6:4 is a higher-plane expression of that same energy.

The Master Organizer is one who devises the Great Plan in accordance with hierarchical vision so that it may be implemented on the practical level. This is the higher application of the emotional principle, the solution to issues of a emotional nature from an elevated perspective.

The following steps are positive ways to approach the solution to any problem arising on an emotional level:

A.  *Depersonalize the problem.*
    Think of the problem as belonging to someone else.
    You will then get a different perspective for you have
    taken yourself out of the "center of the storm." The
    mind is freer to find a creative solution when it is not
    encumbered by ownership of the issue.

B.  *Don't try to solve a problem in the evening.*
    In the evening your mind is tired as you have led a
    mentally active life all day and your mind is cluttered
    with the day's events, inhibiting clarity and deep
    thinking.

C.  *Before going to sleep, give your problem to your sub
    conscious mind.*
    If you totally dismiss the problem from your conscious
    mind releasing it to the subconscious, you not only
    allow yourself the luxury of a restful night's sleep, but
    you permit the natural solution to emerge from your
    inner source of wisdom.

D.  *Don't try to solve a problem from an emotional view
    point.*
    It is unwise to make decisions based on emotion, for
    emotions often cloud an issue and disregard its other
    important aspects—namely the mental, physical and
    spiritual. It is a rare person who can successfully
    resolve problems through a strictly emotional approach.

E.  *Meditation.*
    Meditation is an important tool in transcending the
    immediate pressures of your problem. By clearing your
    mind of your concerns and releasing them, the solution
    comes more easily because there is nothing blocking its real-
    ization. The technique you use is up to you, and you
    may want to include a mantra and chanting to further

enhance the process.

F. *Concentration.*

Once you have cleared your mind through meditation or a similar method, and you have released the issue to your subconscious mind, it is time that you focus all your attention on the specific problem. If the problem is of a serious nature, you may have to repeat the process at another time.

To develop emotional control, it is necessary to acquire the habit of reacting in a constructive manner to every event that occurs in your life. Demonstrate calmness whenever you have the chance. This is simply a matter of utilizing the pathways which lead to your constructive emotions. You cannot prevent difficult events from happening, but you can control your reactions to them. Smile when things happen which arouse destructive emotions and say, as Abraham Lincoln did, "This, too, shall pass."

A person who has his emotions under control is self-confident. And by this I mean he operates from the positive pole of the emotional spectrum. He is able to resist the influence of anyone or any condition which could foster a negative emotion. This is not to say that emotion should be suppressed. Unexpressed emotion is the source of disease, because it creates an imbalance in the life force. Rather, finding a constructive outlet for emotion, whether positive or negative, will help maintain a healthy body and mind. The positive pole of emotion may be the forerunner of enthusiasm, of a sparkling magnetic personality which always attracts, while a person who is constantly withdrawing within himself repels, in spite of the fact that essentially the same energy is being expressed, albeit from the negative pole.

The quality of your life is influenced by the emotions you generate. Do not let yourself be controlled by emotions. It is by adopting a positive emotional posture that we can gain self-confidence and remain separate from a negatively charged environment. If you are in a place where the vibrations are positive you will likewise be influenced in a positive manner. The choice is yours to make.

Each of us will become master of our life and destiny when we have learned to govern our emotions, for we are then properly channeling the power of Spirit that enlivens our souls. Men like Moses, Socrates and Jesus had emotional control and were not governed by tradition and rules. They kept their minds clear, availing themselves of the light of spiritual wisdom and freedom from the bonds of personality. Spirit is beyond personality and the source of the true essence of the individual. In order to live with integrity and empowerment it is important to subdue the ego and listen to the small voice within. By following these principles we can achieve our goal of mastering the Red Horse of Revelation, the emotional body.

### III. Physical Body (the Black Horse) — the Third Beast

*And when he had opened the third seal, I heard the third beast say, come and see. And I beheld, and lo a black horse; and he that sat on him had a pair of balances in his hand.*

Rev. 6:5

Have you ever analyzed how much attention your physical body demands? How it clamors to be fed when it is hungry? How it complains when too warm or too cold? Always, the physical body lets you know in no uncertain terms when it suffers any discomfort. The physical body should be fed, clothed, and made as comfortable as possible. After all, it is the vehicle of the soul.

In absolute consciousness we are spiritual entities. In transitory consciousness we are ego, carried by the body. It is true that we gain in mental stature through knowledge and wisdom so that our ego, from a microcosmic state of consciousness, will eventually come to be part of the macrocosmic state of consciousness.

But what about our body? As the third member of the Holy Family of Creation it should not be neglected. In every moment of transitory consciousness God functions through us. If the instrument of expression (the body) is not in a healthy condition, or is neglected, it can inhibit the creative expression of God, resulting in a diminished expression of Spirit.

If God is perfect, it must follow that when the manifestation is imperfect it is because of man's limited consciousness and lack of endeavor and faith in the power possessed by man himself to create a harmonious, healthful life. It is, therefore, necessary to take care of the physical body from a physical viewpoint, through nutrition, exercise and breathing. The physical body could not function as it does were it not for consciousness. The consciousness of man in its expression goes through a process of change but its original state—Universal Consciousness—never changes.

There are two forces at work within the human form, electricity and magnetism. The energy of the physical body is therefore electromagnetic. This electromagnetic energy produces multiple frequencies because every part of the physical body produces a different vibrational frequency. However, each part of the physical body is an integral part of a greater whole—the human organism. Anytime a part of the body is removed, not only are cells destroyed, but the body's electromagnetic field is altered. This field is generated by consciousness and when damaged or unbalanced it ultimately results in disease in the physical body.

The human body has two centers from which it receives and transmits energy—The Mental Center, situated in the crown, and the Physical Center, located in the Solar Plexus. Depending upon the focus of attention by the Mental Center, the physical body can be influenced positively or negatively.

The Physical Center is nourished when you eat and digest food. The energy contained in the food is released and becomes energy for fueling your physical body. The muscles which power the physical body are composed of cells which have the ability to contract when stimulated by a nerve. An electrochemical reaction occurs with the glucose stored in the muscle, which causes a release of energy. While your digestive process releases that energy, your consciousness can command and direct it for good or ill. It is up to you to direct it toward a positive use or a negative one.

When the discharging of a battery exceeds the charging, the battery will die. The same is true of the physical body—when the quantity of negative energy produced exceeds the positive for any reason, the life span of that physical body is shortened. If this imbalance continues for a long enough period of time, the physical body will of necessity deteriorate and die. However, the physical body can be recharged by the mind, and the mind in turn is recharged by contacting the God-source, or Spirit, through prayer, inspiration or meditation.

Maintenance of a healthy body requires a balance of positive and negative expression of energy.

Researchers have determined that the human body is capable of sustaining itself for well over 100 years. It is not unheard of even in this day and age for people to live to be 140 years old. Dr. Joel D. Wallach, 1991 Nobel Prize for Medicine nominee, states in his audio program "Dead Doctors Don't Lie" that we have a genetic potential for longevity to live to 120 to 140 years, and, in fact, people do routinely live to be well into their hundreds. The oldest known living person in relatively recent history was a Chinese man named Dr. Li who lived to 256 years old. Dr. Wallach attributes long life to proper nutrition and blames a shortened life span on nutritional deficiency.

The human body is a remarkably adaptable organism. Provided with the correct ratio of diet to exercise it can have a long and healthy lifespan. Exercise is essential for good blood circulation, which performs the function of clearing away the dead cells to be expelled by the eliminative organs. Exercise also helps maintain physical strength and stamina enabling the body to respond positively to stress.

The importance of maintaining the physical body in good health cannot be overstated. It is, after all, the instrument through which the soul and Spirit operate. Diet and exercise are important parts to achieving good health, a vital aspect of the mastery of the Black Horse —the physical body.

### IV. Mental Body (Pale Horse) — the Fourth Beast

*And I looked, and behold a pale horse: and his name that sat on him was Death, and Hell followed with him. And power was given unto them over the fourth part of the earth, to kill with sword, and with hunger, and with death, and with the beasts of the earth.*

Rev. 6:8

Interpreted in the light of numerological symbolism, this would read as follows:

*I am perceiving a new state of mind, embodied in
a renewed Christ-conscious form. This change is to be
followed with accelerated mental powers. My life will
become more balanced, equally dedicated to work
and play, with a new energy of heart and mind not
experienced before. The ultimate result of this
transformation is the 33rd degree of consciousness
where I will perceive all Earth life with my all-seeing
inner eye.*

The foregoing interpretation includes the occult meanings of
"Death," "Hell," "hunger," and "kill with a sword". Below are the
numerological analyses of these words, showing how words carry
hidden meaning, and how they were used to encode higher teachings in
the text of Revelation:

$$
\begin{array}{llll}
4 & + & 20 + 8 & = & 32 \\
D & E \quad A & T \quad H & \\
5 + 1 & & & = & +6 \\
& & & & 38
\end{array}
\qquad
\begin{array}{llll}
8 & + & 12 + 12 & = & 32 \\
H & E & L \quad L & \\
5 & & & & +5 \\
& & & & 37
\end{array}
$$

**32** – Communication from our feminine nature
**6** – Independence and freedom leading to responsibility
**38** – Communication of organizational power
**37** – Balance of the introvert and extrovert

$$
\begin{array}{lllllll}
8 & + & 14 + 7 & + & 18 & = & 47 \\
H & U & N \quad G & E & R & \\
21 & + & 5 & & & = & +26 \\
& & & & & & 83
\end{array}
$$

**7**— Energy of the heart  and mind
**26**— God
**83**— The communicative expansion of organization

```
        11  +  12+ 12          =  35
         K   I   L   L
  9  =       9
        23  +  20 + 8          =  51
         W   I   T   H
  9  =       9

         A
  1  =    1
        19 + 23  +  18+ 4      =  +64
         S   W   O   R   D
 +15  =      15

  34             +              150   =  184
```

**150**—10th power of responsibility
**34**— practicality of communications
**184**— Individual power to communicate

I do not accept the generally accepted definition of Hell. In my opinion, the ancient concept of Heaven and Hell as opposites was instituted by a religious despot to control and dominate his people. If his followers agreed with his ideas they were going to Heaven, if not, these non-compliant members of his flock were going to Hell. It is time now to discard this outmoded idea. The occult meanings are revealed in the above and in examples elsewhere in this book to assist in the effort to accomplish this task.

The Pale Horse is the intellect. Although the brain is composed of approximately 14 billion cells, only a relatively small number of these cells are in active use. The remainder are dormant, awaiting development, to be put into action. The number of activated brain cells varies with the individual and can be increased by exercising this sophisticated organ. Science has discovered that we can increase our brain power via the activities of reading, thinking and studying.

The brain governs the nervous system which conducts electrical impulses along the neural pathways in the body. Sensory impulses are sent to the brain, which returns responsive impulses as a reaction to the stimulus.

Nerves are composed of millions of elongated cells. To a great extent, they are involuntary, responding to stimuli automatically without the mind's conscious awareness. If the body is in a healthful condition and the energy is properly directed, such communication is effected in a fraction of a second. An unhealthy body has a diminished response to stimuli of all kinds.

As the human species evolves, each successive generation activates more brain cells. The people of 1,000 years hence will be able to accomplish things we only dream of today because their brains will have evolved to a higher level of functioning. This process is ongoing, and eventually humankind will achieve the apex of the evolutionary process and a complete activation of all 14 billion brain cells.

The strength of the brain is dependent upon its usage. As stated earlier, exercising the brain through mental and intellectual activities, such as reading, studying and problem-solving helps activate new brain cells. As the vehicle of the mind, a higher-functioning brain allows for greater expression by the mind, and a greater capacity to master the Pale Horse, the Mental body.

Who would have thought this lengthy discussion about care of the self could be stimulated by an examination of the Four Horsemen of the Apocalypse of Revelation? The lens of Numerology provides us with the insight to do so. If we understand the fact that the mystic language of Numerology was the key with which the Book of Revelation was written, it is an easy thing to understand the symbolism as it relates to ourselves. In this case, the Four Horsemen verses are an admonishment to take care of our four bodies, the health of which is of supreme importance to a long and fulfilling life.

# 9

## WORLD CHANGES

*woman brings man to balance,*
*brings the world to justice and truth.*[1]

THE SUBJECT OF world changes has been receiving a great deal of attention as so much has been prophesied about events that are to occur as we enter a new millennium. This is not a new phenomenon by any means. Every one thousand years a whole rash of millennial prophecies are reported as the human psyche anticipates the birth of a new era in human life on this planet. New interpretations of biblical prophecy emerge in tandem with new visions from contemporary seers. Add to this the fuel of increasingly frequent natural catastrophes and you have a fertile seedbed for the incubation of "millennial fever."

Of the more compelling prophetic offerings, one that holds a great deal of promise is a code recently discovered in the Bible by Dr. Eliyahu Rips, an Israeli mathematician. Dr. Rips' discovery has passed the stringent tests of peer review and confirmation by a high-level code breaker in the U.S. National Security Agency. The code is only found in the Hebrew version of the Bible but has been found to be highly accurate in describing events that have occurred and, more importantly, will occur, if the prophecies are fulfilled. The details of the code itself are complicated, but in simple terms it consists of a "skip-sequencing" method of locating letters to find a hidden word or words. This code was discovered with a computer program written specifically for this task and has revealed 3000-year-old prophecies that have been fulfilled, such as the assassination of Yitzhak Rabin, the elections of President Clinton and Prime Minister Netanyahu, the

Oklahoma City bombing, as well as the Kobe, Japan earthquake. The code also has revealed that we can prevent such devastating events as a world-wide holocaust for within a key section of the Hebrew text it gives the phrase, "Will you change" in conjunction with the words, "Holocaust of Israel" and "You delayed," as well as the years 1996 and 2000. Author Drosnin believes that these encodings reflect probabilities that exist and that the outcome, whether positive or negative, depends upon our own actions.[2] As the code is further studied, I would hope that the researchers would focus upon positive events to give people the opportunity to see what our other options are and how we can prevent further global destruction and turmoil.

Other sources of prophecy also focus on the negative, although there are those which focus on the positive, also. It all depends upon where the attention is focused. After all, prophecy is merely the prediction of a *possible* event and not set in stone. From where do prophecies come? Prophets, ancient and modern, acquire their visions in various means from the great data bank of the Cosmos, the Akashic Records, or what Jung called the collective unconscious. What is often not understood, however, is that what they are perceiving are probabilities which exist in a sort of existential limbo, an alternate universe where events only emerge into our physical reality if the conditions are right. In other words, the likelihood of an event occurring depends upon certain conditions being met, and those conditions are the result of decisions and choices we make individually and collectively. Therefore, if we understand that our choices determine the reality we experience, we can change the nature of our future experience by altering the nature of our choices. If we choose to live together in peace, accept all people as our sisters and brothers, honor the earth, and work together to make the world a better place for all people, we can avert the disastrous events that have been prophesied.

Some of our most illustrious prophets have said the same thing. Nostradamus, Edgar Cayce, and the Hopi prophecies, in spite of the fact that they have seen tremendous destruction in their visions, have all stated that we can avert these disasters by changing our behavior and priorities. All have called for a more spiritual focus to counteract the negative effects of our past actions. After all, this is the purpose of prophecy, to give humanity a chance to alter its future. Three principles of prophecy are the foundation for this statement:

1. A negative prophecy fulfilled is a prophecy failed.
2. Any event that has not yet happened can be prevented.
3. Achieving a positive end result is the true purpose of prophecy.

To provide a basis for this discussion we will take a look at some of the prophecies of Nostradamus, Cayce and Hamid Bey and how they stack up against each other. So much has been said by others with regard to devastating world changes that we need say no more about it, and such a discussion would be antithetical to the book's intent. What follows is a sampler of some of the more benign predictions that have been made by our three exemplary seers. Even so, I recognize that there are many others deserving of mention, both contemporary and ancient, which have contributed to the great body of prophetic material.

## NOSTRADAMUS

The mysterious prophecies of Nostradamus were first published in 1555 as his *Centuries* and have been the object of a great deal of debate and conjecture ever since. In an attempt to avoid the persecution so rampant during the Inquisition, Nostradamus concealed his prophetic messages in four-line verses called quatrains using the language of the subconscious, a sort of secret code of his own design which included the use of anagrams, astrological references, and alchemical and Kabalistic symbolism. Born to Jewish parents, he was raised a Roman Catholic, as conversion was forced on the Jews in France during that time. Even so, he was raised by his grandfather who undoubtedly taught him about the mysteries of the Kabala. He was trained as a physician, which at that time included the study of astrology, and was well known for his emphasis on hygiene in the practice of medicine. Nostradamus achieved fame for his cure for the Black Death plague in the 16th century.[3]

Of the many researchers who have studied and attempted to translate Nostradamus' enigmatic quatrains, one stands out as not only having the most intriguing and unusual approach to the work but undoubtedly has the most accurate interpretation. This researcher is Dolores Cannon, who utilized a kind of hypnotic regression to send her subjects (she worked with twelve over the course of her research) through time to speak with Nostradamus as he worked in his study. This connection was evidently sought out by Nostradamus as well, as he often would seek connection with "the spirits" through his method of scrying the future. He was able in this way to communicate by providing answers to the questions Cannon would pose. Nostradamus and Cannon were both possessed by a compelling sense of urgency about humanity's future, which no doubt was the magnet that attracted them to each other.

Of Nostradamus' prophecies for our present and future, there are several which we can readily identify with specific events. One is the eroding of the spiritual essence of Christianity as a religion, as referred to in the following quatrain:

> *The law of the Sun contending with Venus,*
> *appropriating the spirit of prophecy:*
> *Neither the one nor the other will be understood*
> *The law of the great Messiah retained through the*
> *Sun.*
>
> Century 5-53

According to the interpretation revealed through Cannon's subject, this quatrain "refers to the development of Christianity. It shows how Christianity lost its spirit."[4]  Nostradamus evidently foresaw how the Church's tampering with Biblical text has had a subconscious effect on people, causing them to lose their conviction regarding Church doctrine, following it only because they have been raised to do so. Christianity's loss of spirit is a symptom of the negativity which permeates its doctrines, a common malady of most religions, according to Nostradamus.

Nostradamus understood that his prophecies represented probabilities which he had perceived and that they could be averted if humanity channeled its energy into positive directions. He wanted us to avoid the catastrophic events which he foresaw. Perhaps we have succeeded in doing so to some extent, because he had made one prophecy which he translated for Dolores Cannon (her work with Nostradamus took place in 1987) which very specifically predicted that the United States' President elected in 1988 would be a man with dark hair in his late 50's who would not survive his term of office.[5] Michael Dukakis lost his bid for the presidency in 1988 to George Bush, who, as we know, survived his tenure. It is entirely likely that other prophecies have been averted as well.

Other predictions made by the great French seer include earth changes and the rise to power of women, such as is described in the following quatrain:

> *The faint voice of a woman is heard under the holy*
> *ground.*
> *Human flame shines for the divine voice.*
> *It will cause the earth to be stained with the blood of*
> *celibates*
> *and destroy the holy temples for the wicked.*
>
> Century 4-24

This quatrain describes the collapse of religious and financial institutions and the "unleashing of the female energies of the universe."[6] While the scene it describes has a frightening context when interpreted literally, its character softens when we understand it to be allegorical. The positive message of this prophecy is the empowerment of the feminine and one to which humanity can look forward.

Nostradamus was an astrologer, and many of his prophecies contain astrological references. This has caused confusion for most researchers who are not well-versed in astrological symbolism. Dolores Cannon went to trained astrologers to obtain assistance in understanding the specific timing of events identified by Nostradamus with astrological references. One quatrain in particular with such references had caught her attention because it had received a great deal of attention from other researchers of Nostradamus' prophecies. The following quatrain has been incorrectly translated by many who do not understand the astrological material within it:

> *Saturn in the bull, Jupiter in water, Mars in the arrow*
> *The sixth of February brings death,*
> *Those of Tardigne so great a breach at Bruges,*
> *That the barbarian chief will die at Ponteroso.*
>
> Century 8-49

Other interpreters have translated the first line of this quatrain as: "Saturn in Taurus, Jupiter in Aquarius, Mars in Sagittarius," but as any astrologer knows, Aquarius is an air sign and so Jupiter must be in either Pisces, Cancer or Scorpio, which makes a big difference in terms of placing a date. Cannon consulted with astrologer Mark Lerner, publisher of a monthly astrological magazine, who gave his interpretation of the preceding quatrain, wherein he placed the timing as February 6, 2002, and suggested that the energies acting at the time indicated by the quatrain could be referring to the peaceful resolution of our planet's nuclear "problem."[7] Another astrologer with whom Cannon consulted felt that Nostradamus worded many of his quatrains to include the possibility of several different outcomes, which any student of astrology knows is a basic characteristic of astrological interpretation. Each symbol or energy represented by the zodiacal signs, planets, houses and their various relationships with each other possess many possibilities. It is up to the individual to decide how to use or misuse the energies with which he or she has to work, and it is the individual who determines the outcome, consciously or not.

Most interpreters of the prophecies of Nostradamus focus on his quatrains relating to devastating earth changes and those portending war. Nostradamus had much more to say about changes to come at the dawn of the twenty-first century, however, and much of it is positive, promising a better life for humankind. Manuela Dunn Mascetti and Peter Lorie examine a great number of the seer's quatrains relating to the influence of the feminine on our future in *Nostradamus: Prophecies for Women*. They write: "The most interesting and exciting aspect of Nostradamus' prophecies concern the advent of a new social order is that the different 'energy' of womankind appears to impinge on different aspects of life...It is not simply that we see a change from patriarchal to matriarchal values, but a change in the balance of power, so to speak, which brings about a completely new vision of how life can function."[8]

We will examine some of these quatrains as interpreted by Mascetti and Lorie with an eye toward the impact of the feminine on late 20th century society. There is a strikingly frequent number of references to the United States' influence and involvement in these prophecies. The following quatrain is an example:

*New law to occupy the new land* [America]
*Towards Syria, Judea and Palestine:*
*The great barbarian empire of men to decay,*
*Before the Moon completes its cycle.*

Century 3:97

Mascetti and Lorie interpret this quatrain to mean the following:

*A new law will emerge in the new world of*
*America, at a time when Syria, Judea and Palestine*
*are significant: The great barbarian patriarchy that*
*men have created will decay during the time that the*
*feminine spirit is completing its cycle.*[9]

Mascetti and Lorie also saw in the quatrains evidence that "Nostradamus foresaw democracy as a force in human affairs which would supercede the autocratic monarchies of his day," and that eventually through this democratic model, there would emerge a growing feminine influence causing a dramatic change in the socio-cultural balance of power. In fact, they consider the prediction of a "critical mass of female power" at the close of this century to be a message of paramount importance in the quatrains. The authors also state that the changes that will result from the woman's rise to power will be difficult in some respects, but humanity will benefit and that the heart will symbolize the character of the change.[10] The following quatrain expresses the effects of the empowerment of the feminine in very clear terms:

*Oh vast Rome, your ruin approaches,*
*Not your walls, but your lifeblood and substance:*
*Someone with a sharp tongue will make a dent in you,*
*Harsh chains will be around it all.*

Century 10:65

The most encouraging aspect of Mascetti and Lorie's interpretation of the "feminine" quatrains is that they see a trend away

from the domination/competition approach to solving world problems
and toward a cooperative approach. The patriarchal tendency toward
control has created a legacy which no thinking person should want to
leave his or her children. This is not to say that society will return to the
long-gone matriarchal social model, but that the pendulum has swung
from the feminine to the masculine pole and is swinging back toward
the feminine ultimately to settle at the balance point between the two.
This is the model for true equality between the sexes, a cooperative
partnership.

Mascetti and Lorie see a by-product of the emergence of feminine
power as an ending of fear:

> *One of the most important transforming powers of*
> *the women's movement, which is of great value to the*
> *future, is the ability to end fear.*
>
> *If there is one aspect of the patriarchal system that*
> *has done the greatest damage, it is the engendering of*
> *an almost inherent fearfulness within us all...*[11]

People seem to prefer to hear about the prophecies which predict a
devastating and frightening future. Perhaps this tendency arises from
our fear-induced conditioning, as spoken of by Mascetti and Lorie in
the previous quote. It is evident that fear sells, if the increasing
attention to apocalyptic prophecies in the media can be used as a
measure. Books on predictions of traumatic, continent-altering earth
changes have proliferated, accompanied by dramatic representations
on television of future-world scenarios based upon prophecy.

It is time to recognize prophecy for what it is, an impression of the
probabilities that exist for a place and time, not an unalterable fate that
must be endured. Nostradamus gave us many positive prophecies
along with the negative. We can choose to focus our energy on the kind
of future we want to have rather than accept with resignation those we
dread as inevitable. By embracing all people in a spirit of sister/
brotherhood and honoring the earth as the mother of us all we can
create the kind of earth where we can thrive in peace.

## EDGAR CAYCE

Another famous prophet who has astounded people with the accuracy and depth of his prophetic material was Edgar Cayce. Cayce was born in 1877 in Kentucky, and as early as the age of six he had already begun to display powers of clairvoyance. When it was discovered that he could give accurate medical diagnoses and remedies for healing, he began to work with doctors in his local area to help them in treating their patients. It didn't take long for the word to reach other parts of the country and soon he was being sought out by people from across the nation.[12]

Cayce's method was to recline on a couch and relax himself into trance. For several years his abilities were used only for medical purposes to assist in diagnosis and treatment, but then in 1923 a man by the name of Arthur Lammers began to ask questions of a more universal nature. His questions leaned more toward the philosophical than the practical and touched on the very basis of human life. This was when Cayce began to talk about reincarnation, a shocking subject for Cayce's family, who were deeply devoted Christians. This idea of reincarnation was completely foreign to their beliefs. The readings took on a new character and thus began his "Life Readings," which he continued to give until 1944.[13] Fortunately, all of his readings (over 14,000) were recorded and preserved allowing researchers a valuable resource and the opportunity to evaluate and validate or refute their accuracybased upon historical events.

The Association for Research and Enlightenment is responsible for maintaining the Cayce material and conducting research in the field of parapsychology in general. Regarding the subject of earth changes, a variety of opinions exist within the membership of the A.R.E. as to the interpretation of Cayce's prophecies. Some feel that events that were predicted did not occur when Cayce said they would (although timing is still a matter of debate) and therefore constitute unfulfilled prophecy. Others point to Cayce's own explanation that these events can be avoided if humanity gets its act together, leading to the conclusion that events that haven't occurred at their prophesied time have been averted by an awakening in humanity.[14] Many of the Cayce readings of the future concern earth changes and include devastating events that alter the face of the planet in dramatic ways. Others have chosen to focus on these prophecies and I leave the reader to refer to that material for the specifics of the prophecies. My intent is to emphasize the predictions which relate to positive changes that are looming on the horizon, for these are the events which I feel most people want to experience. By giving energy to the positive outcomes we can manifest them in our reality.

Significantly, Cayce gave several prophecies which we will have the opportunity in the near future to gauge for ourselves as to their accuracy. These pertain to the year 1998 and offer us some added insight regarding the evolution of humanity. One of his prophecies predicts his own return to physical form in the year 1998. Another relates to the "restoration of phosphorus" in humanity. Cayce stated that phosphorus will be restored as an element of the human body as a medium through which one can develop awareness of spiritual consciousness. He also states that the sun's activity and its cycle through "the various spheres of activity" will bring about gradual changes (rather than cataclysmic) in the earth during this period.[15] Clearly, this is a more benign prophecy in terms of the changes we are about to experience.

Another revelation for the year 1998 is the beginning of recognition of the emerging Aquarian Age and Cayce also prophesied that this is the year of the return of the Messiah.[16]  If we follow our previously established theory that the return of the Messiah is the activation of Christ Consciousness within many, rather than a single individual, this would be the year of the activation of the Group Avatar. As the human body changes to include an increase of phosphorus content, we will become aware of our divinity and relationship to Universal Consciousness, which in turn will enable us to understand the meaning and significance of the dawning Aquarian Age where the Group Avatar will create a new earth.


## HAMID BEY

Hamid Bey was a spiritual Master who received his training into the Coptic tradition in a temple in Egypt between the ages of six and eighteen. He emigrated to America in the 1920's to establish the Coptic Fellowship in America, traveling and lecturing throughout the country, eventually to become highly respected within the metaphysical and spiritual community. As an initiate, he had learned the art of suspended animation where he could slow down his heart to a nearly negligible rate and had also demonstrated the gift of prophecy.[17] These prophecies he recorded within his many self-published "lessons," which now reside in the archives of the Coptic Fellowship of America.

Before his death in 1976, Bey predicted that humanity will discard their traditions based upon superstition and follow the inner teacher that is the individual spark of the Divine within each person. He said that there will be a new universal message of hope and truth which will be embraced by the masses and that there will emerge a multitude of Messianic figures who will embody the Buddhic/Christ Consciousness.

Bey stated that a new civilization will emerge with the United States as its center wherein there will be a more idealistic schooling for the young and a deeper understanding of the Divine by humanity at large, and there will be a merging of scientific and religious thought into a single philosophy. A uniting of the disciplines of science and religion, endowing each with the strengths of the other, will result in a science with soul and conscience — one that cannot be corrupted or misused.

Another of Hamid Bey's predictions relates to fear. He saw the banishment of fear and the emergence of Love and Truth and a resurgence of conscious spirituality. As a result of the new spiritual consciousness, Bey predicted the emergence of a new race of people on the earth. This new race will be primarily concerned with the welfare of humanity and maintaining harmony among nations and peoples. He stated that there have been four previous ages in human development and that we now stand on the threshold of the fifth age, to be followed by another, the last. These six ages of humanity he describes as follows:

*First Age* — The Age of Brute Strength when the human had limited cognitive ability. The brain was not yet fully developed and was concerned primarily with fulfilling instinctive needs: food, shelter and procreation

*Second Age* — The Age of Mind and Philosophy when the human became aware of the heavens and was conscious of its mental powers. Instinct was still a strong factor influencing behavior, but a rudimentary religious and philosophical consciousness began to take shape. The beginning of superconsciousness.

***Third Age*** — The Age of Religious Darkness when a regression occurred in the development of consciousness. Overemphasis on religious dogma; a manic obsession with sinfulness and repentance. The foundation of ethical standards came out of this era.

***Fourth Age*** — The Age of Machinery when the desire to attain material success grew out of a reaction to the "have-not, do-not" previous age. An overemphasis on the material threatens to leave society devoid of spirit.

***Fifth Age*** — The Age of Energy when the intellectual prowess and inventiveness of humanity will yield great discoveries in understanding the nature of energy and how it can be harnessed technologically and in medicine to benefit humanity.

We are presently in the Fifth Age and will continue to enjoy technological advances in the area of the understanding of energy. The Sixth Age is prophesied by Bey to be an era when we will have overcome the limitations of our present physical existence. The Sixth Age bears a striking resemblance to the prophesied future as seen by Nostradamus and Edgar Cayce where the feminine comes into power and the human body increases its phosphorus content to illuminate the human mind:

***Sixth Age*** — The Age of Cosmic Consciousness when humanity will have surpassed its previous cognitive abilities to harness the power of the mind to resolve the old problems and achieve a sustainable peace among nations. A new kind of religious philosophy which satisfies the soul and banishes fear will emerge to foster the development of individual Christ Consciousness.

It is clear that there are many prophecies for a bright future. We can choose to focus our attention on those that portend doom and destruction, or we can recognize that our future is of our own creation and choose to give energy to those that hold promise for the earth and the human race. Fear sells, but harmony and peace are the conditions which nourish and sustain us. Hamid Bey believed that one day all nations and peoples would unite behind the banner of cooperation and embrace the ideals of democracy and freedom. All three prophets saw the United States at the forefront in this movement toward global harmony and the restoration of the feminine to its rightful place as a guiding force. This is the legacy we should strive to leave our children for it will foster our evolution, leading us ever closer to the goal of achieving a higher state of consciousness where we recognize the divine within all of us.

# 10

## CREATING A NEW WORLD

NONE OF THE information I have shared in this book is of value unless it can be put to practical use. In this chapter we will explore the power of the Word and of thought as tools of manifestation. Each of us is a co-creator with the Supreme Creator whether we realize it or not. We create for good or ill by the nature of our thoughts, words and deeds. Every person has the capacity to change the world. All it takes is intentional effort to manifest the world we desire. If each of us, with proper intent and motivation, takes responsibility for the nature and quality of our thoughts, and the proper care of the little piece of earth over which we have stewardship, we could eliminate the negativity, fear and degradation that presently exist on the planet. If each of us chose to care for our fellow human beings who are less fortunate than ourselves in a spirit of philanthropy we could eliminate suffering and want among the human family. These are realistic and achievable goals.

A simple, daily regimen of meditation, prayer, and practical action in whatever form suits you — volunteerism, environmental activism, or other humanitarian endeavor — is all that is required to create the world you want. It does require discipline and the willingness to encourage others to do the same, for manifestation works best when the participants are great in number. This is the calling which the Group Avatar hears. Every person on the planet who responds to the inner desire to serve in some fashion is a part of this group of world servers, and the contribution of each is as significant as that of the collective.

If you are reading this book, you are part of this group, whether conscious of it or not. The fact that you were drawn to its message is evidence enough. One need not be conscious of his/her mission to be able to fulfil it on the physical plane. There are many servers who would scoff at the idea that they are carrying out a plamŒ evised by an unseen spiritual board of directors designed to help the planet transition to its next level on its evolutionary journey. Even so, this does not diminish the contribution they make. And in truth, knowledge of one's part in the plan is only a secondary consideration; carrying it out is the primary goal.

That goal and the means by which it can be achieved is the subject which will be addressed in this chapter. To this end, we need to discuss the basic tool of manifestation available to everyone, thought. Everything that exists, or has ever existed, began as thought. The creation of the universe began as a thought in the mind of the Creator. On earth, the first being to create by thought was Thoth. Even his name evokes the power of thought — Thot(h). According to the *Dictionary of All Scriptures and Myths* Thoth "was the incarnated Thought, the living Word...the divine intelligence which at the creation uttered the words which resulted in the formation of the world. He was self-produced, and was lord of earth, air, sea, and sky; he was the scribe of the gods, and the inventor of all arts and sciences."[1]

Alice Bailey wrote of the Power of the Word or "the Word of Power" (AUM) wherein she described the Logos, or Creative Source, which created our solar system. From this Word are derived countless other words all of which are credited with the creation of the planet and the "five kingdoms of nature": 1) the Mineral; 2) the Vegetable; 3) the Animal; 4) the Human; and 5) the Spiritual. It is an awesome creative power which the "Word" possesses. Bailey describes the origin and power of the Word as follows:

[1] *All the words of Power are rooted in the Great Word committed to the Solar Logos at the dawn of manifesttion.*

[2] *All the words of Power are permutations or expansions of the three basic sounds, and increase in length as the planes are involved, until the sentences and speech of the finite unit, man, in their myriad differentiations are arrived at.*

[3] *Therefore, on the path of return, speech becomes ever*

*more brief, words are more sparingly used, and the time
eventually comes when the adept employs formulas of
words only as required to carry out specific purposes
along two lines —*

    *a. Definite creative processes*

    *b. Specific direction of energy*

    *This, of course, on the planes in the three worlds.*

[4] *The aspirant, therefore, has mainly three things to do
when preparing for initiation —*

    *a. To control every activity of his threefold lower
nature (physical, astral and mental)*

    *b. To control his speech every minute of every
day...[This] refers to the controlled use of words
to effect certain ends*

[5] *Every Word...affects the deva kingdoms, and hence the
form-building aspects of manifestation. No sound is
ever made without producing a corresponding response
in deva substance, and driving multitudes of tiny lives
to take specific forms...The majority of human beings as
yet build unconsciously, and the form constructed is
either of a beneficent or maleficent agency.*[2]

A basic understanding of the power that words and, by extension,
thoughts have on the spiritual and mental planes is necessary before we
can begin to understand how this can impact our physical lives. All
events which occur on the physical plane have their start in the higher
(spiritual, mental, emotional) planes. This is a basic principle of
manifestation and the reason why our beliefs create our reality. They
have their beginning in the subtler realms, where a seed is planted by
a thought, emotion, or spoken word. From there they grow as they are
given energy by repetition of the thought, emotion or word, and
eventually become manifest as physical events. As Bailey stated, most
people create unconsciously, and a great deal of damage and
unnecessary trauma has been created by people creating unconsciously.
Bailey wrote about this very subject more than 75 years ago. Imagine
what a different world we would have if people had taken her wisdom
to heart at the time of her writing. We can do something now to change
our future if we so choose. This is a very simple discipline which

anyone can practice, with a little conscious effort.

I stress the power of thought as it is important for us to understand as we stand at the threshold of a new millennium and the beginning of a new era, the Aquarian Age. Thoth is an appropriate symbol for this age for it is a mental age. Representing that higher mind available to everyone who strives for it, Thoth is a symbol of the common person striving for the attainment of uncommon goals. In the course of this striving, the individual accepts the responsibilities of what I term "The Thoth Seat." It is from here that the creative power of thought is executed, and it is with this power that we can recreate the world.

Imagine, if you will, a visual representation of the "Thoth Seat." This Thoth Seat is flanked on each side by two sets of eleven symbolic pillars; those on the right represent the superconscious (masculine), and those on the left, the subconscious (feminine). Located within the Sphinx temple which sits adjacent to the Sphinx itself are the physical representations of these two sets of eleven pillars. The individual occupying this Seat integrates the masculine and feminine energies from the higher planes to implement creative power. The Thoth Seat is available and attainable for anyone who seeks and strives for it. The aspirants are not perfect, yet strive for perfection. They are common people who aspire to uncommon goals. The following table represents the energies acting within the "Thoth Seat":

| T | H | O | T | H |
|---|---|---|---|---|
| Right Hand | Right Foot | Alpha-Omega | Left Hand | Left Foot |
| Willpower | Masculine foundation | Responsible intellect | Love | Feminine foundation |
| Masculine | Strength | Creating a New World | Feminine | Practicality |
| Conscious | Creative Power | Thought projection | Subconscious | Inspired creativity |
| Discernment | Charisma | Mental Ark of the Covenant | Equality achieved | Worldly responsibility |
| Objectivity | | Power of Prayer | Resolution | |

The past & future of the Spiritual Unity of Nations

The rising sun over the Great Pyramid of Gizeh

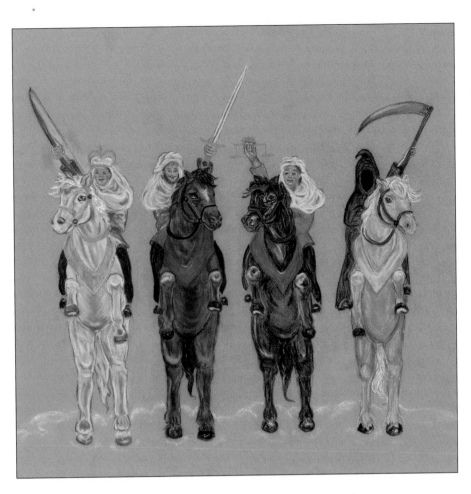

The Four Horsemen of the Apocalypse

Master Hamid Bey, founder of the Coptic Fellowship

The group avatar sword piercing SUN consciousness

Archangel Michael holding inner world power of the
black rose and the sword

The advent of feminine leadership

Mother Mary acknowledging feminine &
masculine equality

As an example of the power and meaning of "The Thoth Seat," it is interesting to note that this expression shares the energies of "The New Messiah" and "The Double-Headed Eagle," which is a symbol of the 33rd degree of the Masonic Order. I mention this because to the Masons the 33rd degree represents mastership. This relationship can be graphically demonstrated by a numerological analysis of the phrases "The Thoth Seat," "The New Messiah," and "The Double-Headed Eagle."

```
      28        +          96          +          39      = 123
20 + 8          20 + 8  +  20 + 8       19 +          20
T   H   E       T   H   O   T   H       S   E   A   T
        5 +                 15          +   5   +   1   = +26 (God)
                                                         149


      28        +      37      +                59            = 124
20+ 8           14 +   23       13 +  19+19  +      8
T   H   E       N   E   W       M   E   S   S   I   A   H
        5 +         5           +   5   +   9 + 1       = +25
                                                         149


                20 + 8                      =      28
                T   H   E
        5 =           5
                4       +   2 + 12          =      18
                D   O   U   B   L   E   -
        41 =        15 + 21      +   5
                8       +   4   +   4       =      16
                H   E   A   D   E   D
        11 =        5 + 1   +   5
                        7 + 12              =      +19
                E   A   G   L   E
        +11 =   5 + 1   +   5

        68                      +              81    =    149
```

Taking our discussion of creation back in time to the origin of the earth, according to Alice Bailey, the development of sentient life on Earth was supervised by Sanat Kumara, a higher spiritual being whose home was Venus. Sanat Kumara came to Earth during the time of the

Lemurian civilization eighteen million years ago, and represents the Planetary Logos in matters of the mental plane and the ego. Sanat Kumara is expressly concerned with the principle of beauty in any form and rules over the planetary Hierarchy, working with the mental activities of meditation and visualization, and manifesting through the power of "enunciated sound."[3]

Bailey calls Sanat Kumara the One Initiator, and as such he is charged with the transference of power which occurs in the initiation of a World Teacher (ie., Jesus Christ, Buddha). The means by which this transference is made is through the Rod of Initiation (the One Rod), of which there are several in our solar system. The One Rod for Earth is charged by the Lord of the World and given to the initiate who is to become a World Teacher, and is produced during times when certain work must be performed on the Earth plane. This very esoteric description of the initiation of the World Teacher is significant for it describes higher-plane activity that occurs when the World Teacher (Messiah) makes his/her appearance. The "Rods" can be thought of as a symbol of power, which have the additional function of influencing those with whom the initiate comes in contact, "thus inspiring them to increased activity and service for the race."[4] In other words, by mere association with one who has accepted the mantle of World Service, others follow suit. This is the power of the Group Avatar.

To continue with Bailey's description, the specific One Rod of Sanat Kumara is recharged for each new World Teacher, which occurs a total of seven times for the planet. This charging is electrical in nature. There are two primary forces of energy in the universe, electrical and magnetic, and these forces work together in creation.

In my study of Revelation, I found certain numbers kept reappearing in my numerological analysis of the text. One of these was the number 120, the numerological equivalent of Sanat Kumara and Archangel Michael. This is significant because the corresponding symbols representing this energy are electrical and magnetic; what I term the Left Hand and the Right Hand:

|          Left Hand           |          Right Hand          |
| :--------------------------: | :--------------------------: |
| Sanat Kumara                 | Archangel Michael            |
| Electric                     | Magnetic                     |
| Feminine                     | Masculine                    |
| Subconscious                 | Conscious                    |
| Feeling Nature               | Will                         |

These are all elements of the two polarities which are represented by the symbol of the Yin/Yang, or the two halves that compose the whole. It is upon the higher (inner) planes where manifestation begins, and the whole of creation must be integrated in order for manifestation to occur. Bailey wrote, "all physical plane organization— governmental, religious, or cultural—is the working out of inner forces and causes, and, before they definitely appear in physical manifestation, a focalization...of these influences and energies takes place on etheric levels."[5] We must integrate the masculine and the feminine on the inner planes of existence before we can integrate them in the physical.

This process was begun in 1949 at Mount Shasta, California. The event that occurred on November 11, 1949 (discussed in Chapter 7), was the seed event (the birth of a Messiah) for the 48-year cycle which culminated in the present-day births of the many Messiahs, the Group Avatar. Every nine years is a culmination of a cycle. This cycle which was begun on 11/11/49 reached culmination in 1958, 1967, 1976, 1985 and 1994. The year following a date of culmination is the beginning of a new cycle. The year 1995 was such a year and on November 11, 1995, the energy that was birthed on 11/11/49 matured. It is no coincidence that this was also the date of the fulfillment of the Mayan prophecies.

Another number which reappears over and over is the number 151. This number correlates to the energies represented by the following:

- Jesus Christ
- The Pipecarrier
- Lord of Hosts
- Mount Shasta
- Holy Spirit
- The Embodiment of Michael
- The 151st Psalm (the Davidic Covenant)

These principles were birthed on the physical plane on December 25, 1995. Christmas Day 1995 was one of a succession of Christmases leading to the advent of the new millennium beginning in the year 2000. Each Christmas day in the decade of the 1990's symbolizes a different aspect of the return of Christ in the form of an awakening in consciousness in humanity. The following complex analysis illustrates how the date, 12/25/1995, represents the energy of the number 151.

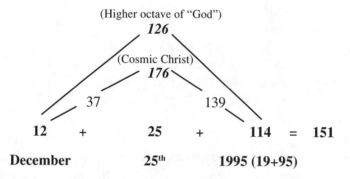

There is little question that, in numerological terms, the dates 11/11/49 and 12/25/95 have a significant relationship. Esoterically, they represent the birth and maturation of the Group Avatar, the birthing within many people of the Messiah principle, one which is not reserved for those of high office or of earthly greatness, but for the common person who strives to accomplish great goals.

The little-known Psalm 151 is a poignant example of the promise that the humble and most common can arise to greatness through the God-given power of Christ Consciousness:

## Psalm 151

Smaller was I than my brothers
and the youngest of the sons of my father,
So he made me shepherd of his flock
and ruler over his kids.

My hands have made an instrument
and my fingers a lyre;

And (so) have I rendered glory to the Lord,
thought I, within my soul
The mountains do not witness to him,
nor do the hills proclaim;
The trees have cherished my words
and the flock my works.

For who can proclaim and who can bespeak
and who can recount the deeds of the Lord?
Everything has God seen,
everything has he heard and he has heeded.

He sent his prophet to annoint me,
Samuel to make me great;
My brother went out to meet him,
handsome of figure and appearance.

Though they were tall of stature
and handsome by their hair,
The Lord God chose
them not.

But he sent and took me from behind the flock
and annointed me with holy oil,
And he made me leader of his people
and ruler over the sons of his covenant.

For the plan of the Hierarchy to be realized, it is imperative that the idea of male superiority be extinguished and the feminine be returned to her rightful place alongside the masculine as the co-creative principle. The year 2000 marks the beginning of the feminine millennium. The belief in a vengeful male God will be replaced with a "kinder, gentler" image of a supreme divine intelligence which nurtures all Creation. The present dominant concept of a male Creator harkens back to prehistory when early humans sought to explain the source of various phenomena of which they had no understanding. Their limited perception gave mysterious meaning to things which we take for granted today: the motion of the moon around the earth, the changing patterns of the constellations in the night sky, and the changing of the seasons, to name a few. To this early human mind a god with human attributes was reassuring and logical, and the nature of human relationships became the model for explaining humanity's relationship with the Divine. Hence, the idea of God as a father figure arose. The father principle continued to be a major aspect in various religious philosophies and eventually came into use by initiates of the Mysteries as a tool to invoke higher plane assistance in response to a crisis.

At the age of 12, Jesus traveled to Egypt accompanied by John the Baptist (Jesus' symbolic Christ twin). While in Egypt, Jesus was instructed by the Egyptian Masters in how to deal with crises. They gave Him a word to be spoken to invoke assistance from the higher realms. That word was "Father." The father principle is the domain of Archangel Michael, whose responsibility it is to assist the planet Earth on the inner planes during her current transition. Sanat Kumara's responsibility is related to the Mother principle and represents the other half of the creative impulse.

Jesus' greatest crisis obviously occurred on the cross when He was faced with transcending the physical, mental and emotional experience of crucifixion. In the act of crying out "Father," during His crucifixion, Jesus brought forth the power of the inner planes to assist Him in that transcendence. The energies symbolized by the word "Father" are evident when it is analyzed numerologically:

| | 26 (God) | | 26 (God) | | | 11 | 11 |
|---|---|---|---|---|---|---|---|
| 6 | + 20 | 8 | + 18 | | 7 | + 4 | |
| **F** | **A  T** | **H** | **E  R** | | **G** | **O  D** | |
| (Independence) **1** | | **5** (Freedom) | | | | 15 | |
| | | | | | | +15 | |
| | | | | | | 26 (God) | |

In Jesus' case, He called in the independence and freedom of God while on the Cross, to elevate His consciousness to overcome the challenge of physical crucifixion. According to the records of the Essene order, of which Jesus was a member, He lived through His experience on the cross and settled in Egypt where He lived until the age of 247. The years following His crucifixion He spent in service to the earth to assist in her evolution, albeit in a less public manner than during His ministry. Jesus attained the number 11 position of Egyptian

Mastership, which had never been attained before on earth.

In later times, when members of the religious patriarchy had finally accepted that Jesus was the chosen Messiah of the Piscean Age, they began to analyze and interpret Jesus' life, including the words He uttered on the cross during His crucifixion. Because they didn't understand the esoteric meaning of language they took the name "Father" as its literal interpretation and attributed "Father" to the energy of God. It is the misapplication of the basic teachings of the Mystery Schools regarding the power of language—and thought especially—that has kept humanity from realizing how our words and thoughts are creating the world in which we live.

It should be clear by now that the average person is an integral factor in world and earth events. This is an important statement as there is a difference in meaning between the "world" and the "Earth." The world is the cumulative effect of the ideas, emotions, goals and ambitions of the five billion individuals residing on the planet. The Earth is the physical body of the planet. The world can be thought of as the mind of the planet. The thoughts of these five billion individuals both individually and collectively impact the well-being of the Earth.

Meditation is the key to effecting positive changes for the planet. It is a discipline that should be practiced as fervently as many do prayer. Prayer is talking to God; meditation is listening to God. So many people are eager to tell God what it is that they want, but they give little thought to listening to what God might have to say to them. Many are the benefits of regularly practiced meditation. They include:

1. Relaxation—better sleep, less anxiety
2. Stress reduction—rapid recovery from stress, lower blood pressure
3. Stamina—higher alertness level, increased resistance to fatigue
4. Confidence—stronger will-power, greater self-confidence
5. Mental clarity—rapid assimilation of information, more creative problem solving
6. Empathy—feeling more "in tune" with others, better ability to relate with others
7. Spiritual growth—an expanding sense of wholeness, a

renewed sense of purpose and meaning in life, an
increasing access to the intuitive and other higher levels
of mind

8.    Inner peace—the happiness associated with a healthy,
balanced life, the sense of well-being built on contact
with one's essential nature

    Hamid Bey, former spiritual leader of Coptic International, had
this to say about the importance of meditation:

> *Meditation is the process of the mind in which we
> find our innermost self, our individual spiritual
> center. Meditation is often spoken of as "going into
> the Silence," to quietly and serenely enter a higher
> state of consciousness by quieting the mind, sweeping
> from it all but one idea so that the full force of
> consciousness can be opened to receive guidance
> upon one thought. This means reasoning must stop
> because as long as reason is working, the mind cannot
> hear the soul. This requires exiting from the limitation
> of Nature into the infinite world of the Spirit— into the
> limitless realm of God. Therefore, by meditation an
> entirely different attitude and an entirely different
> world can be found by not allowing the inception of
> negative thoughts. The control of the seeds of thought
> can be attained, just as shape can be given to the
> character of a child, when the child is grown, the mind
> cannot be bent so easily.*
>
> *As the mind expands through meditation, it
> becomes a reflection of the Spirit of God, then one can
> find liberation from limited thinking. The potential of
> deeper understanding and the basis of peaceful
> communication and experience may be gained, for the
> purpose of meditation is to attain the vision of Truth...*
>
> *Meditation is different from concentration in that
> meditation is a withdrawal from all exterior concepts.
> It is the cessation of your conscious thinking, thus you
> cease remembering about anything. It is like going*

*into a state of nothingness and in that state you receive a recharging of energy. This period of mental and physical solitude must be experienced by every individual. No one can express in words how it feels for every individual has a different experience in that state...*

*By going into meditation, you can proceed with this investigation and learn something about yourself which no one else can tell you. By delving into abstract ideas, the mysterious fields of the mental world can be tapped. New ideas can be brought forth and made available for the benefit of the whole world. While ideas brought forth will not be wholly new, they will be new to the world. We must never lose sight of the fact that "there is nothing new under the sun."*

*When you have established your center in God through meditation, the power of God will flow into you in greater portion because during this particular period your conscious reasoning is in a state of relaxation, in spiritual receptivity. If you want to become God-like, you must become gods first. You must become conscious of God before you can be Christ conscious. The spiritual master that we seek is the invisible core of our being— the "I" of each one of us which relates to the spiritual world.*

*There is an inner part of man which must become known to man's mind. The correlation of man's intellect and ability with that inner part is most important. When man wants something he directs his energy toward achieving that which he had been concentrating upon. In meditation you cross the threshold of the invisible, cosmic world. You do not make this crossing with your senses or with your intellect. It takes the key of faith to open the door. Meditation is taking refuge in Christ—de-personalized consciousness. You depart from yourself as a personality because your mind and body are tired and want to find refuge in Christ, just as wild animals want to find a refuge where they cannot be hunted. In other words, it could be called a state of Nirvana or a heavenly state. By practice you gradually go a little deeper which is very necessary.*

*We need to pay greater attention to our spiritual training, unfoldment and to show more of our humble self in terms of truer friendship, love and compassion. This can be done by practicing transcendental meditation in order to exit from outer awareness and become more acquainted with the inner self. Do not go into meditation because you do not feel well or because you want something. Meditation is not for begging. Meditation is for the purpose of blending your mind, your soul, your thoughts, with Cosmic Consciousness. Such contact is only possible when you have purified your mind. Then you ingress into the world of power...*

Through the power of prayer and creative visualization, we can unite in peace, for the healing of the races, for the healing of the nations. What follows is a selection of meditations, prayers and devotions to be used to assist those interested in the practice of healing the earth, and world. These are merely suggestions and I encourage the reader to use whatever method feels appropriate in service to the planet and humanity. The important thing is to practice with the proper intent and purity of motivation and to do it daily. A few minutes a day is all it takes to change the world.

## *Robe of Light Meditation*

1.  *In meditation, envision yourself clothed in a robe of Light.*
2.  *Ask for the highest good to result from your meditative action.*
3.  *Ask for the atomic powers of the proton, electron and neutron to become activated within you.*
4.  *Visualize a huge light enveloping each continent one by*

*one. Then visualize a trap door opening under each continent and all the negative thoughts collected in the akashic record of each continent falling out through the bottom of the continent. Picture in your mind's eye these millions of negative thoughtforms collected into a huge dark ball. Finally perceive a collective group taking this accumulated sphere of negative thoughtforms into the Sun for cleansing purposes.*

I believe in the power of prayer to bring about world peace. An inspiring example of the power of prayer is the story of Jim Goure. Jim served as a Naval Commander following the close of World War II after which he was appointed Senior Executive Officer in the Atomic Energy Commission. Due to Jim's exposure to classified information, he was acutely aware that the potential for nuclear or conventional war was great. His deep desire to prevent such an occurrence and to work for positive change on the planet led him to take an early retirement and move his family to Black Mountain, North Carolina, where he, his wife Diana, and their eight children devoted their lives to prayer.

Eventually, others learned of the Goures' commitment to praying for peace and of Jim's spiritual insights, and sought him out for guidance. The Goures' following grew and the prayers evolved to include not only world peace, but the economy, energy, the environment, communications, organizations, and world religions.

In 1976, Jim and Diane founded "United Research," an organization dedicated to promoting personal and planetary change through the power of prayer. So many people were drawn to the Goures' home that in 1979 they built the Light Center to accommodate their numbers. Over the years, United Research has expanded its outreach programs to include international prayer missions and has traveled to 50 nations on six continents.

Now deceased, Jim Goure lives on through his vision which has been carried forth by his successors at United Research, who continue to promote world peace, a powerful example of the power of prayer to move people to effect change in the world. United Research operates from the Light Center's beautiful geodesic dome set on land situated among the tranquil woods of the North Carolina mountains and graced by a mountain stream. The entire area serves as an enormous meditation garden and due to year after year of prayer, an energy of quietude overlays the site. From this vantage point United Research is able to carry out its mission to help people become citizens of Light so they may carry the energy of Light back into the world to fulfill Jim Goure's mission.

The following prayer is distributed by United Research as part of their outreach program. For information about programs and facilities, write or call the Light Center at P.O. Box 1146, Black Mountain, NC 28711, (704) 669-6845.

## *Effective Prayer*

- *I release all of my past, my negativities, my fears, my human relationships, my inner self, my future, my human desires and my judging to the Light.*

  Our highest potential is limited only by ourselves. The first step in becoming effective is to release all of the things which hold us back.

- *I am a Light being.*

  We have thought negatively about ourselves far too long. The time has come to change that, and so we affirm the truth that "I am a really great person," or "I am a being of "Light and Love."

- *I radiate the Light from my Light Center througout my being.*

  By radiating the Light from your solar plexus (or Light Center) throughout your being, you begin to change every cell and every part of your being. Where there is Light, there can be no darkness.

- *I radiate the Light from my Light Center to everyone.*

  The first three steps concentrate on self. Here you begin to help others. Radiating the Light from your Light Center to everyone begins to affect everyone's Light Center and to bring about an important happening in your life from helping others.

- *I radiate the Light from my Light Center to everything.*

  When you radiate the Light from your Light Center

to the mineral, plant, animal and angelic kingdoms, you help theses kingdoms fulfill their work which helps you in return.

- *I am in a bubble of Light and only Light can come to me and only Light can be here.*
  There are over five billion people on Planet Earth now. Most are thinking negative thoughts and having negative emotions. These affect you and protection from this is imperative. This is the purpose of the bubble of Light.

- *Thank you God for everything, for everyone and for me.*
  Being thankful for others and for all that exists is very important to our spiritual growth. Many of us, however, never remember to be thankful for ourselves. It is very important to say, "Thank you, God, for me."[6]

Visualization is another helpful technique for ameliorating the negative effects of misguided energy on the planet. The following visualization can be utilized toward this goal:

> *Create an image of a large pyramid of light over the Earth. Inside the pyramid, envision world leaders of all nations, religions, and philosophies—as well as economic, financial and political—sitting in a large circle holding hands (symbolizing unity and goodwill for all peoples). Maintain this image until you feel a sense of unity among them. Acknowledge the feelings of goodwill and watch those present disperse with a renewed sense of purpose. Gradually allow your consciousness to return to its normal state of being.*

A simple, yet effective visualization for projecting light is a powerful tool when applied with the proper intent. Darkness is simply the absence of light. Therefore, that which is of the darkness disappears when sufficient light is generated and sent forth. The first fiat of creation, "Let there be light," is a powerful mantra for the accomplishment of this goal. The magnitude of the light that is generated by many people projecting light to the planet is awe-inspiring. Stand firm in the realization of the bright light that comes to you; be in the vanguard of projecting new light and know that love enfolds you, and that the plan is being fulfilled.

Another powerful meditation for manifestation is the following:

*Center and ground yourself in whatever manner suits you. Then amplify your thoughts by visualizing a pyramid of light and funneling your thoughts through it. Pass these thoughts through several such pyramids until you see your chosen thoughtform growing as it passes through each successive pyramid. When the thoughtform has expanded to your satisfaction, send it out through your third eye. Repeated practice of this procedure for your desired thoughtform will manifest in the physical, if the motive and intent are pure; in other words, "for the highest good of all concerned."*

The following simple technique was given to me almost twenty years ago in a healing seminar:

*Imagine the Earth as an intelligent, conscious being (as she is). Visualize the brain of the Earth and place it over your head as if it were a helmet. Use your mind to think like the Earth Mother would if she was trying to improve Earth's conditions. Then use your inner sight to imagine the problems of Earth being solved—the clearing of hostile and fearful emotions from war-torn areas, the reversal of pollution, the healing of degraded land, water and air. Then visualize the Earth as it looks from space, appearing in pristine condition, with clear blue seas, green continents and a sparkling atmosphere.*

# World Light and Love Projection

*I put the mineral kingdom in light and love.*
*I put the vegetable kingdom in light and love.*
*I put the animal kingdom in light and love.*
*I put my family in light and love.*
*I put my city in light and love.*
*I put my state in light and love.*
*I put my country in light and love.*
*I put the North American continent in light and love.*
*I put the South American continent in light and love.*
*I put the Asian continent in light and love.*
*I put the European continent in light and love.*
*I put the African continent in light and love.*
*I put the Australian continent in light and love.*
*I put the Polar Regions in light and love.*
*I put all other lands and peoples in light and love.*
*I put Planet Earth in light and love.*
*I put all other planets of existence in light and love.*

A daily practice of one or more of these methods will have a profound effect on the planet and our lives. The mind is a powerful force when allowed to express in its fullest capacity. Even when it is not it can have a profound effect on personal well-being. Illness and disease are the products of fear. Disease, or dis-ease, has its beginnings on the higher planes of existence. Disease doesn't manifest physically until it has existed for a period of time in the mental, emotional and spiritual bodies. Fear is the stimulus for the "dis-ease" on the higher planes. Negative thinking feeds it and helps it grow, while positive thinking is the powerful antidote.

Negatively charged thoughts reach beyond the boundary of the individual body and affect the environment around it as well as everything in that environment. Positive thoughts have the same effect. Fortunately, we can choose the kind of environment in which we live. The mind that can "fear" itself into disease can also heal itself into wellness. By focusing on the positive principles of love, service, sharing and good will we can strengthen our bond with Universal Intelligence and create a world of peace and harmony.

The importance of preserving and strengthening our bond with the Universal Intelligence cannot be overstated, for it is this bond which nurtures our existence and evolutionary growth. The means by which we can achieve this stronger bond is through positive worship—eliminating the fear from our spiritual traditions and replacing that fear with a sense of oneness. The time has come to supplant superstitious religious fears with spiritual reasoning. Our world needs a new paradigm that reflects the sister/brotherhood of humanity. People must receive intellectual food from those in the pulpit. When people beg for the bread of enlightenment and are instead handed the stone of fear, they suffer from spiritual malnourishment. Any spiritual philosophy which fosters fear, distrust and hatred is directly antithetical to Universal Truth. The miseries of humanity are self-inflicted. The kindest thing a religion can do for humanity is to teach the existence of an Eternal Wisdom, a spark which dwells in every human's consciousness, empowering each of us as the powerful creators which we in truth are.

By projecting the goals of world peace and healing every day, we assist the many levels of consciousness on the higher planes in creating a better world in which to live. A daily devotion to achieving these goals is needed to sustain the creative energy of thought. Our collective mental visualization can be a catalyst for the manifestation of a new world where peace and harmony prevail.

*Have a vision not clouded by fear.*
Cherokee saying

# CONCLUSION

# THE SPIRITUAL UNITY OF NATIONS

*In today's highly interdependent world, individuals and nations can no longer resolve many of their problems by themselves. We need one another. We must therefore develop a sense of universal responsibility...It is our collective and individual responsibility to protect and nurture the global family, to support its weaker members, and to preserve and tend to the environment in which we all live.*[1]

His Holiness the Dalai Lama

WE PRESENTLY LIVE at a critical turning point in Earth's history. People in every nation on the planet have felt the pull toward a spiritual unification of the human family and have responded to the call from Spirit by establishing groups devoted to the promotion of planetary peace. The primary thesis of my book originates in the premise that humanity must rid itself of a belief in negativity and its companion, fear, if we are to ever realize our dream of peace. Fear is the bane of civilization. It breeds intolerance, adversity and separatism. It closes our minds to the truth and blinds us to a greater reality. And the only way we will conquer our fear is to openly examine its source. The examination of one of the most pervasive and long-standing sources of the fear myth has been the thrust of this book, and one for which I feel a compelling sense of purpose.

Casting fear aside is only the first step, however. In order for us, as a species, to continue to grow and evolve we must band together and pool our collective resources—physical, financial and spiritual—to solve the world's problems. We must come to regard ourselves as one people. We can no longer afford an "Us versus Them" approach to international relationships. This way of thinking has been the source of the degradation of the environment, the oppression of people, overpopulation, and the obvious, war. I have said that the coming millennium will bring the New Messiah, the Group Avatar, to earth. It is this entry of the Christ energy into our reality that will transport us to a greater reality where all will live in cooperation and harmony. We are all potential avatars. We all carry within us the stuff of which Messiahs are made.

There can never be a real peace on earth until humanity is united in its ideals and sense of purpose toward the goal of equality and freedom for all people without regard to gender, race, spiritual belief or nationality. Due to its inherent intent to promote the virtues of love and goodwill among people, the spiritual organization or religious institution is the logical vehicle by which this goal can be achieved. It was with this in mind that the Spiritual Unity of Nations was formed, an organization whose goal it is to create a body of leaders from all spiritual and peace-advocating traditions to promote and foster spiritual unity among all people in the pursuit of world peace.

The universe is governed by basic spiritual principles which are the creation of the Source or Supreme Being. The plan for the Spiritual Unity of Nations, as for any great spiritual endeavor conceived by humanity, originated in the higher planes. For such a plan to be implemented on the material, or third-dimensional plane, it must be perceived and acted upon by someone who is receptive to the impulses from the subtler realms. There have been many adepts throughout history who have heard the call from Spirit, and many more who are awaiting their awakening to fulfill their part of the plan. Alice Bailey called the source of this higher plan the Hierarchy. The work of the Hierarchy of the planet involves the development of self consciousness in all beings, the development of consciousness in the lower three kingdoms (mineral, vegetable and animal), and the implementation of the will of the Planetary Logos. The will of the Planetary Logos is primarily concerned with promoting and fostering the spirit of sister/ brotherhood in humanity.[2] This spirit has begun to seep into the consciousness of many individuals and will soon reach a critical mass.

The Spiritual Unity of Nations was conceived by the Hierarchy to achieve the goals of peace and harmony on earth. A unifying spirit of love, understanding and tolerance must be developed and grown within humanity to carry out this plan, for which the objectives are three-fold:

1. Political—to develop and establish international consciousness in which it is recognized that all are members of the human family and have basic human rights as their birthright.
2. Religious—to establish a better world-wide understanding and consciousness of the nature of the subjective realms and tolerance among philosophies.
3. Scientific—to coordinate the activities of those in the scientific community to share scientific discoveries for the benefit of all humanity.

This plan for spiritual unification does not imply forfeiture of personal religious affiliation, rather it seeks to bring together people of different faiths in a spirit of tolerance and cooperation for the purpose of creating a better world in which to live.

All of the great illumined teachers who have come to the planet— Buddha, Krishna, Jesus, Mohammed, to name a few—have taught the basic principles which are embodied by the Spiritual Unity of Nations. This guiding principle is a unifying love that embraces all philosophies and can be invoked with the following prayer:

> *Oh, Light of God,*
> *Illumine our minds —*
> *Oh, Love of God,*
> *Fill our hearts —*
> *Oh, Power of God,*
> *Direct our will —*
> *Let Light, Love, Power enlighten humanity.*

The major influence of the emerging Aquarian Age is the awakening of humanity to its divinity and its place in the universe. This awakening has been referred to as the attainment of Christ Consciousness, but it has seeds in all traditions for it results from the activity of Light on human consciousness. Alice Bailey described the development of the human being as "a succession of expansions" in awareness, where consciousness progresses from a personality-centered, to a higher-self or soul-centered, and then to a spirit-centered focus until it reaches divinity.[3] This can be alternately described as "stages" of growth humanity is experiencing, and the evolution toward Christ Consciousness (the Christ return) is presently in its second stage, to be fully realized with the establishment of the Spiritual Unity of Nations.

When humanity reaches the end of its own capacity to solve its collective problems, it ultimately turns to the Source for answers. While science has made tremendous strides in its discoveries, these advancements have exacted a great price. While the benefits have been many, we all know the cost of the discovery of nuclear power. Scientific research is limited in that it is still conducted by humans with finite wisdom. A merging of spirituality and science could help alleviate the inadequacies of a purely scientific approach, and is, in fact, closer to reality today than ever before. Physicists are discovering the very truths that eastern mystics have espoused for thousands of years. They are offering theories of a holographic nature to the universe, the probability of parallel universes, and of the power of thought to affect the outcome of scientific experiments. Scientists are discovering that the Source of life is not found in a test tube, but in higher, divine law.

People are realizing that the state of human affairs cannot be separated from spiritual reality, and more importantly, that they cannot leave it "up to God." We must stop being spectators and become initiators for action. Humanity must have the courage and will to educate its youth to respect that the right human relations are vital to a peaceful world and then to give them the opportunity to pursue them. People need to talk about commonality rather than differences and boundaries. If spiritually oriented people became committed to the principle of unity and universal love, it would change the world. It is our responsibility to reverse the negativity and damage that has been done to our planet and our species for we have created it. Groups that are wishing and waiting for some extraterrestrial civilization to appear in their spaceships and save us from destruction—or expecting to be "raptured" to heaven—fail to realize this. It is up to us. And we must do it now. Christ said it nearly 2,000 years ago: "Now is the appointed time."

The United States is uniquely poised to begin this process. It is part of the heritage of America to promote the ideals of freedom and choice. This heritage goes to the heart and soul of America and was imprinted upon its spirit at the time of its founding by an illumined group of people who recognized the integral part that spirituality plays in human life. They intended this spirit to serve as the ideal to which other nations could aspire.

Ryoho Okawa, the Buddhist Master, writes in *The Laws of the Sun*:

> *If tens of thousands, or millions, of people all had a desire to create a Land of Buddha or Utopia on Earth, and if they all focused their will on the task, a beam of light would spring out of the Earth and this light would filter into the minds of others until the whole world became a happier place.*[4]

World Goodwill, an organization that was founded to assist in "establishing right human relations," speaks of the New Group of World Servers, or in our terms, the Group Avatar. These World Servers are described as:

> "[People who are] *serving humanity, and are, through the power of their response to the spiritual opportunity, tide and note, emerging out of every class, group, church, party, race and nation, and are therefore truly representative. They speak all languages; they embrace all religions, all sciences and all philosophies...[they] are so inclusive in their outlook and so wide in their interpretation of truth they are the hand of God in all happenings...*"[5]

These are the people who will change our world. We are seeing the influence of these visionaries as we search for peaceful solutions to our global problems. And their work is rooted in the ideal of unity.

People who are spiritually awake will be calling for unity in increasingly greater numbers as the new millennium approaches. And they will not be doing so as a single mind, but with the wonderful diversity that characterizes humankind. For it is not in creating identical entities that this great goal will be accomplished. The strength of our species is in its variety. Each tradition will work within its own system to promote peace through unity. These groups are like the rays of the sun, merely individual streams of light, but united they radiate the awesome power of a star. This is the vision of the Spiritual Unity of Nations.

The seed for the establishment of the Spiritual Unity of Nations (SUN) germinated within the mind of Coptic Fellowship International's founder, Hamid Bey, nearly 60 years ago. As I stated in an earlier chapter, Hamid Bey was trained in the ancient Mystery tradition in Egypt which he brought with him when he immigrated to the United States in the 1920's. These teachings became the foundation for Coptic Fellowship International. However, Bey's work in establishing the Coptic organization occupied so much of his time that he had to leave the development of SUN to Joseph Busby in Capetown, South Africa, which Joseph began in 1952.

The unexpected death of Hamid Bey in 1976 resulted in the transfer of the responsibility for establishing SUN in the United States to Bey's successor—myself. True to my charge and mission, SUN, in spite of its painfully slow birthing, was established as a non-profit organization on November 11, 1982.

The first SUN Conference was held in Chicago, Illinois in 1982 and showcased presenters dedicated to assisting those on the spiritual path. In 1983 and 1984 additional conferences were held again in Chicago, and then in 1985, Estes Park, Colorado hosted the conference which had changed its agenda to include audience participation rather than strictly lecture presentations. In subsequent years, SUN conferences were held in many cities around the nation.

In March 1984, SUN sponsored a tour to Egypt with the intention of linking East-West, inner-outer philosophies and wisdom, and then in September of that year SUN invited leaders of metaphysical and peace groups to join together in a World Unity Forum in Colorado Springs to seek ways to promote world unity. This first meeting saw the adoption of the motto "Dedicated to the Vision of the World as One Family" and provided the attending organizations the opportunity to become acquainted with each other.

The second Forum was held in January 1985 in North Carolina and it was here that the Forum's spiritual declaration of independence called "A Declaration for a United Humanity" was authored.

## A Declaration For A United Humanity

**WE**, *as members of humanity, recognize a potential on Planet Earth for a just Peace and Unity, a balance of health and abundance for all. This inspires us to know our Oneness and impels us to action, action to manifest a united humanity. We pledge our lives and dedicate ourselves to these basic truths:*

**WE AFFIRM** *there is Unity in the life force within all that is. This Unity includes all names and forms. All life forms are unique expressions of this Unity.*

**WE RECOGNIZE** *the place of each individual and Planet Earth in the unfolding Universe. To express this reality, we respect all life and we share life's abundance. We support opportunities for self fulfillment and freedom of expression for all.*

**WE RESOLVE AND DEDICATE** *ourselves to be an expression of unity at all times and in all places. Our Unity calls us to serve with love, compassion and understanding. Our oneness creates trust, harmony and peace and reflects the very nature of our being.*

**WE ACT** *for World Unity in the practice of these basic truths.*

Each successive Forum resulted in a greater sense of organization and refinement of the SUN organization. At subsequent Forums issues such as meeting format, membership, funding, project development and the establishment of a "Code of Ethics" were on the agenda.

## CODE OF ETHICS

*Recognition of the Light in all.*
*Respect for each being.*
*Respect for earth, air, and water.*
*Respect for plants and animals.*
*Respect for space and all life.*

At the last World Unity Forum in January 1988, it was decided by consensus that each group could best serve the vision as set forth in previous Forums by working in their respective organizations in the promotion of the vision of unity among all people, and the forum format was discontinued. This however, did not end SUN's work in the promotion of world unity and world peace.

Additional efforts included SUN's invitation to the 191 leaders of Earth's nations to attend the "Healing of the Nations" SUN Conference in West Palm Beach, Florida, in January 1990. As part of its educational initiative, SUN also sponsored a tour to Arthurian England and Rennes-Le-Chateau, France, with the intent to study the implications for synthesis of the past with the future in pursuit of global peace and unity. In 1992, a SUN Think Tank was established and met on two occasions with the intention of refocusing and expanding SUN's active role in the world. These efforts have been ongoing and presently SUN continues to explore new ideas and ways to promote world unity and peace at the practical level.[6]

The Spiritual Unity of Nations serves as an instrument for unity. The SUN serves other organizations with the sole objective of coming together in harmony for purposes of sharing perspectives of truth. This affords each participating group the opportuniy to broaden its perspective without sacrificing its individual mission and principles. The SUN ideology emphasizes the importance of diversity and personal choice:

1.  SUN encourages you to work within your own personally preferred church, religion, or metaphysical organization.
2.  SUN does not encourage you to "identify with" the SUN, but to identify with the Divine Principle.
3.  SUN does ot encourage you to be guided by dogma or an authoritative external source, rather by the living Divine Essence within.
4.  SUN encourages cooperative study of a broad range of philosophies and spiritual perspectives.
5.  SUN encourages you to apply what you believe to be truth within yourself.

Beyond these basic tenets, the SUN's creed states:

- *The Spiritual Unity of Nations believes that all humanity is created spiritually equal.*
- *The SUN strives to help each person learn to express through his or her life on earth the perfection he or she already possesses in spirit.*
- *The SUN recognizes each person's right to express his or her concept of the Creative Force of the Universe.*
- *The SUN seeks unity, harmony and love among all persons, peoples and nations.*
- *The SUN shall not dictate to any person, church, religion or philosophy any dogma or doctrine.*
- *The SUN accepts the differing practices and theologies of all religions and philosophies. The seeds of truth exist in all religions and philosophies. Though the paths are many, the ultimate goal is oneness.*
- *The SUN believes that it is each person's responsibility to use wisely the gifts of matter to achieve perfect balance with spirit.*
- *Through common purpose, we can transcend the limitations which hinder the spiritual unification of humanity.*
- *The Spiritual Unity of Nations is dedicated to world peace.*

In 1981, the apparition of the Virgin Mary appeared to three children in Medjugorje, Yugoslavia. She reportedly told them that in God there are no religions and no divisions between people, that men have made the divisions that exist. Therefore it is "men," humanity, which must remove those divisions. We must adopt a creed that transcends religion. Harold Sherman in his *The Green Man and His Return* advocated the following statement of faith which has universal and non-sectarian appeal and would well serve as a creed for all.

> *I Believe*
> *In One God, Father[Mother] of All—*
> *In One Humanity—Every [Hu]Man my Brother[Sister]!*
> *In One Common Freedom of Thought and Expression*
> *    —Established Among All Races and Nations!*
> *In One World—of Unity and Co-operation!*

*In One Purpose—Mutual Love and Understanding!*
*To the end that All May Attain One Great Goal in Life*
   *—Universal Peace and Happiness!*[7]

If the people of the world, without concern for ideological, racial, national or other differences, would come together with the guiding principle of "One World/One People" as their focus, such great things we could accomplish. This is the dream and the vision for which the Spiritual Unity of Nations stands. It is with the hope for unity among all people and a great reverence for our Creator and for my sisters and brothers on this planet Earth, that I dedicate this book.

# EPILOGUE

# THE SWORD AND THE SPEAR OF DESTINY

IN MY ANALYSIS of the chapters and verses of Revelation I discovered a common thread running throughout, a thread that would become apparent and then become almost invisible as if it was winking at me, teasing me to investigate further; a thread that I believe is an important, albeit subtle, feature of the Revelation message. This thread, represented by the cover illustration, relates to the concept of the Sword and the Holy Lance.

Throughout the Revelation text the word "Sword" and the numerological symbolism of the Sword keeps popping up. In addition, there are many phrases and images in this text which vibrate to the numbers 209 and 224, corresponding to the "Spear of Destiny" and the "Spear of Longinus," respectively. These two phrases are alternately referred to as the Holy Lance, and my research shows that they represent the same energy even though they have different numerological correspondences. The relationship between the "Sword" and the "Spear" was not at first clear until some literary sleuthing turned up a most intriguing story, which I recount below.

Another significant matter that came to my attention relates to the Kabalistic symbolism of the word "serpent," another word that appears frequently in Revelation. In the Hebrew Kabala, words are assigned a numerical value. The Hebrew word for "serpent" has a Kabalistic value of 358, which, when reduced numerologically equates to the number 7. It so happens that the number 7 is also the Kabalistic value of the Hebrew word for "sword." As if this weren't enough, the number 358 corresponds to the Kabalistic value of Messiah. This is too much of a coincidence for me to dismiss as mere happenstance. I believe that the significance of the Sword and Spear is a major theme deliberately woven into the Revelation story by its author(s). To further emphasize the importance of the Spear and Sword theme I offer here a brief history of the known facts regarding this pair of symbols.

The Spear of Longinus, as discussed in Chapter 7, was given to the Centurion Gaius Cassius by Julius Caesar who used it to pierce Christ's side after his lifeless body had been removed from the Cross. It became a symbol of divine power when it drew blood from the wound, and was subsequently handed down through history to many powerful leaders, both famous and infamous.

The Spear was passed down from Gaius Cassius to his descendants until it came into the possession of Emperor Maximian, who gave it to Emperor Constantine on the occasion of his marriage to Maximian's daughter. From there the Holy Lance passed into the possession of Attila the Hun, who, not understanding its power, eventually returned it to Rome. The Spear was then passed down through a succession of Roman Emperors until it became the property of the Frankish general Charles Martel. Charlemagne became the next owner of the Spear and he carried it throughout his military career. In the ninth century A.D., King Heinrich I (Henry the Fowler) held it in his possession until he gave it to the English King, Athelstan. From there the Spear was passed on to a series of German monarchs, including Barbarossa. For several centuries, he was the last in a long line of owners to have the Spear in his personal possession, for at his untimely death during a Turkish campaign, his companion crusaders known as the "Teutonic Knights" placed the lance in a secret place for safekeeping until it was eventually transferred to Vienna, where it ultimately found its way into the collection of the Hofburg Museum, remaining there until 1938.

The Spear of Destiny was originally part of a set, the other half of which was the Sword. The pair was created in 3061 B.C. by a metalsmith named Tubal-Cain, a descendant of the biblical Cain. The properties of the Spear and Sword were such that they could not be dulled, nor would they rust, and were said to endow the possessor with invincibility as long as they were carried together. The metal of which they were made is believed to have been from a meteorite containing a variety of metals, in other words it was an alloy, made up of iron, carbon, chromium, nickel, tungsten and various other metals, which gave the blades their strength and remarkable properties.

The two weapons remained together for 3000 years passing from hand to hand until they were discovered buried at Masada by the Roman general Pompey in 63 B.C., who presented them to Julius Caesar. As stated previously, Caesar gave the Spear to Gaius Cassius. The Sword he gave to Brutus, a decision which was to portent his undoing, for Brutus used it to strike Caesar down during his infamous assassination.

The history of the Spear of Destiny or Longinus is known well into the 20th century, but the lineage of the Sword has been less clear. It was eventually given to Aulus Plautius by Emperor Claudius in 43 A.D., and was then passed on to a commanding officer of the Roman legions in Britain, Ostorius Scapella. Scapella presented it to the Celtic Queen Cartimandua of the Brigantes, and the Sword eventually found its way into the hands of Queen Boudicca, Celtic Queen of the Iceni, in 65 A.D. From there the history of the sword's ownership is murky until we get to the late 5th century, where it surfaces again as the fabled sword Excalibur. If this assumption is correct, and it is most likely so, King Arthur was the last mortal to hold the physical Sword in his possession. From the time that Bedivere threw the Sword into the waters of the lake, it has remained in the possession of the Lady of the Lake, as no trace of the fabled Sword Excalibur has ever been found.[1] But the physical existence of both talismans of power is only part of their importance for they possess important symbolic significance as well. Many have symbolically held them—the biblical patriarch, Abraham—"The Father of Many Nations"—as well as Abraham Lincoln and Thomas Jefferson are among them—and at the present time this energy is held by many more.

Of the two, the Spear of Longinus has been much more prominent even in modern times. Adolph Hitler became obsessed with the power of the Spear when he was living in Vienna. Hitler was actively involved in the occult, his interest in which began during this time. After he rose to power, he was determined to obtain possession of the Holy Lance to endow himself with the invincibility the Spear promised. After Austria was annexed to Germany during World War II, Hitler finally realized his dream, although it was a short-lived victory, for as the legend states, in the hands of an evil master the Spear would only protect him until it passed from his possession.[2]

A copy of the Spear was fashioned by a Japanese craftsman at the behest of Himmler, who was also privy to knowledge of the Spear's legendary power. It was this Spear which was recovered by the American 45th Army Division in April 1945. The authentic Spear of Destiny had been secretly shipped to Antarctica along with other treasures of the Third Reich and buried in a subterranean cave in the spring of 1943. Wilhelm Bernhart, co-author of *Adolph Hitler and the Holy Lance*, was a member of the team assigned the task of hiding the Spear in its icy vault. He states that the Spear remained there until July 1979, when a team of four German Knights of the Secret Order of the Sacred Lance secretly led an expedition to Antarctica to recover the Spear and return it to Germany where it rests today at a secret location under 24-hour guard. Bernhart states that the mission of these Knights of the Order of the Sacred Lance is to work to secure world peace and they all share a devotion to Christianity and the institution of democratic ideals. I am hopeful that this is true, for enough blood has been shed in pursuit of the ultimate power represented by the Spear.[3]

History aside, the significance of the Spear of Longinus/Destiny and its original mate, the Sword, is clearly marked in Revelation scripture. The following Appendices provide more detailed analyses of the twenty-two chapters of the Book of Revelation, a thorough discussion of which would have proven unwieldy in the main text of the book. In them, you will see the Sword and the Spear of Longinus/Destiny emerge as participants in a carefully choreographed dance, which the author(s) of Revelation must have intended to be discerned by careful scholarship.

# *APPENDICES*

## APPENDIX *I*

## *The Magician*

In Revelation, Chapter 1 (The Magician of the Egyptian Tarot), the first individual mentioned is Jesus Christ, the greatest magician who ever lived. The prototype of Jesus Christ exists today on the etheric plane as an ideal for which each of us is to strive in our personal quest to achieve Christ Consciousness; to become the Magician who creates miracles for the benefit of others.

> *The Revelation of Jesus Christ, which God gave unto him, to shew unto his servants things which must shortly come to pass; and he sent and signified it by his angel unto his servant John.*

Rev. 1:1

The birth of the Christ Consciousness within the individual is the most powerful experience one can have. This is the first step toward the merging between the individualized spark and the Godhead. This important principle is reflected in two short phrases in this verse:

```
                                                      (Saint Michael)
       28        +                       86         =    114
    20 + 8          18  +  22  +  12  +  20  +       14
     T  H  E        R   E   V    E    L    A    T    I    O   N
           5   +     5  +   5  +  1  +   9 + 15   =   +40
                                                         154
                                              (The Christ Office)
                                              (Cosmic Christ)
       27        +                      112         =    139
     8  +  19      19  +  18+ 22  +  14+ 20+ 19
     H  I  S       S   E   R    V    A    N    T    S
        9      +     5  +   1                       =   +15
                                                         154
```

*And from Jesus Christ,* who is *the faithful witness,* and
*the first begotten of the dead, and the prince of the kings of
the earth. Unto him that loved us, and washed us from our
sins in his own blood.*

Rev. 1:5

```
                    14+  4                        =    18
              A    N    D
      1  =    1
              6+  18   +   13                     =    37
              F    R    O    M
     15  =              15
             10   +  19   +   19                  =    48
              J    E    S    U    S
     26  =         5   +   21
            3+8+18 + 19+20                         =   +68
              C    H    R    I    S    T
     +9  =              9
     51                +                    171   =   222
  (Michael)                        (Thoth, Moses) (Responsibility)
```

This phrase symbolizes the energies of Thoth and Moses merging with the
Michael energy resulting in the responsibility to emulate the principles
inherent within them. The prototype of Jesus Christ is to be the model for the
achievement of this goal.

The phrase "and the first begotten of the dead" must be analyzed as it does
not represent what it appears to at first glance.

The word "dead" symbolizes the principle of freedom and is a component
of the energies which are indicated by the Personality and Motivation of the
phrase, which are the principles of the illumined intellect and of the master
communicator, respectively. This is a statement of the important part freedom
plays in the attainment of the higher ideals of these principles.

```
              (Freedom)
                14+  4                                =    18
              A    N    D
      1    =   1
                20+  8                                =    28
              T    H    E
      5    =             5
                6    +   18+  19+  20                 =    63
              F    I    R    S    T
      9    =             9
                2    +   7    +   20+  20   +   14    =    63
              B    E    G    O    T    T    E    N
     25    =             5 +  15    +  5
                6                                     =    6
              O    F
     15    =   15
                20+  8                                =    28
              T    H    E
      5    =             5
                4    +        4                       =    +8
              D    E    A    D
     +6    =             5+   1
     66                                                    214
```

(Master communicator)                                (Illumined intellect)

*Saying, I am Alpha and Omega, the first and the last:*
*and, What thou seest, write in a book, and send* it *unto the*
*seven churches which are in Asia; unto Ephesus, and unto*
*Smyrna, and unto Pergamos, and unto Thyatira, and unto*
*Sardis, and unto Philadephia, and unto Laodicea.*

Rev. 1:11

This verse signifies the activation of the seven energy centers of the individual's light body. The seven churches are the seven chakras, corresponding to the seven churches listed in the verse:

| Personal Chakra | Church |
| --- | --- |
| Pineal (Crown) | Laodicea |
| Pituitary (Third Eye) | Philadelphia |
| Throat | Sardis |
| Heart | Thyatira |
| Solar Plexus | Pergamos |
| Navel | Smyrna |
| Root | Ephesus |

|  |  | 14 + 4 |  |  |  |  |  | = | 18 |
|  |  | **A** | **N** | **D** |  |  |  |  |  |
| 1 | = | 1 |  |  |  |  |  |  |  |
|  |  | 19 | + | 14 + 4 |  |  |  | = | 37 |
|  |  | **S** | **E** | **N** | **D** |  |  |  |  |
| 5 | = |  | 5 |  |  |  |  |  |  |
|  |  | 20 |  |  |  |  |  | = | 20 |
|  |  | **I** | **T** |  |  |  |  |  |  |
| 9 | = | 9 |  |  |  |  |  |  |  |
|  |  | 14 + 20 |  |  |  |  |  | = | 34 |
|  |  | **U** | **N** | **T** | **O** |  |  |  |  |
| 36 | = | 21 + 15 |  |  |  |  |  |  |  |
|  |  | 20 + 8 |  |  |  |  |  | = | 28 |
|  |  | **T** | **H** | **E** |  |  |  |  |  |
| 5 | = |  | 5 |  |  |  |  |  |  |
|  |  | 19 | + | 22 | + | 14 |  | = | 55 |
|  |  | **S** | **E** | **V** | **E** | **N** |  |  |  |
| 10 | = | 5 + 5 |  |  |  |  |  |  |  |
|  |  | 3 + 8 | + | 18 + 3 + | 8 | + | 19 | = | +59 |
|  |  | **C** | **H** | **U** | **R** | **C** | **H** | **E** | **S** |
| +26 | = |  | 21 | + | 5 |  |  |  |  |
| **92** |  |  | + |  |  |  |  |  | **251** |
| (Buddha) |  |  |  |  |  |  |  |  | (2nd octave of Michael) |

The Personality of the higher octave of the Michael energy is combined with the Motivation of Buddha in this verse. If we understand that these energies represent the higher consciousness available to all people, we can see how they relate to the activation of the chakras. The number seven is repeated throughout the first chapter of Revelation, indicating its importance to the spiritual aspirant.

# APPENDIX *II*

## *The High Priestess*

In Revelation Chapter 2 (The High Priestess), the opening verse, 2:1, speaks of "the seven stars in his right hand." This is a key phrase representing the Group Avatar energy.

> *Unto the angel of the church of Ephesus write; These*
> *things saith he that holdeth the seven stars in his right hand,*
> *who walketh in the midst of the seven golden candlesticks.*
>
> Rev. 2:1

The phrase "the seven stars" symbolizes "The Lord of the World," a collective consciousness resulting from many people on earth working to create a better world.

|  | 28 | + |  | 55 | + | 14 | + | 76 | = | 159 |
|---|---|---|---|---|---|---|---|---|---|---|
|  | 20+ 8 |  | 19 + | 22 + |  |  | 19+ 20 + | 18+ 19 |  |  |
| **T** | **H** | **E** | **S** | **E** | **V** | **E N** | **S** | **T A R** | **S** |  |
|  | 5 | + | 5 + | 5 |  | + |  | 1 | = | +16 |
|  |  |  |  |  |  |  | (Lord of the World) | **175** |

In Rev. 2:9 Satan (our Earth test) appears for the first time—to our feminine aspect, no less. Our feminine nature has long been dominated and controlled by a patriarchal social structure. We must risk exposing the vulnerable and compassionate feminine nature and forgive the masculine, represented by the right hand in Rev. 2:1, to rid ourselves of the Satan myth and the energy it has generated.

*I know thy works, and tribulation, and poverty, (but
thou art rich) and* I know *the blasphemy of them which say
they are Jews, and are not, but* are *the synagogue of Satan.*

Rev. 2:9

```
                    14+  4                                    =    18
                 A   N   D
      1  =    1                                          (Arthur, Pyramid)
                 20+ 18  +   2   +   12  +  20  +      14  =   86
(Master leader)  T   R   I   B   U   L   A   T   I   O   N
      55  =    9 + 21 +  1  + 9+15
                    14+  4                                    =    18
                 A   N   D
      1  =    1
                 16  +   22  +   18+ 20+ 25               =  +101
  121 {          P   O   V   E   R   T   Y
     +20  =    15 + 5
      77                         +                223    =   300
    (Christ)                                         (Communication to
          121 = The individualized "World"          the hundredth power)
```

The energies of Arthur, the Great Pyramid, the Master leader, Christ and
the power of the World on an individual level are all represented in this phrase.
This is symbolic of a great power which is available to the initiate to assist her/
him in empowering her/his feminine nature to achieve the goal of a better
world.

Verse 2:24 is important for it represents the energy of the Spear of
Longinus.

*But unto you I say, and unto the rest in Thyatira, as
many as have not this doctrine, and which have not known
the depths of Satan, as they speak; I will put upon you none
other burden.*

Rev. 2:24

$$14 + 20 \qquad = \quad 34$$

**U**    **N**    **T**    **O**

$$36 \quad = \quad 21 + 15$$

$$20 + 8 \qquad = \quad 28$$

**T**    **H**    **E**

$$5 \quad = \quad 5$$

$$18 \quad + \quad 19 + 20 \qquad = \quad 57$$

**R**    **E**    **S**    **T**

$$5 \quad = \quad 5$$

$$14 \qquad = \quad 14$$

**I**    **N**

$$9 \quad = \quad 9$$

$$20 + 8 + \; 25 \quad + \quad 20 \quad + \quad 18 \qquad = \quad \underline{+91}$$

**T**    **H**    **Y**    **A**    **T**    **I**    **R**    **A**

$$\underline{+11} \quad = \quad 1 + 9 + 1 \qquad \qquad \text{(Spear of Longinus)}$$

**66** (Master communicator)         ***224***

The Motivation of this phrase symbolizes a mastery of communication. Its Personality carries the energy of the Spear of Longinus, that instrument of destiny which was handed down to powerful leaders throughout history.

The phrase "the depths of Satan" is a symbolic representation for The Christ Office combined with ultimate altruism leading to the higher octave of the Horus (Egyptian god) energy as shown in the following analysis:

$$20 + 8 \qquad = \quad 28$$

**T**    **H**    **E**

$$5 \quad = \qquad\qquad 5$$

$$4 \quad + \quad 16 + 20 + 8 + \; 19 \quad = \quad 67$$

**D**    **E**    **P**    **T**    **H**    **S**

$$5 \quad = \quad 5$$

$$6 \qquad\qquad = \quad 6$$

**O**    **F**

$$15 \quad = \quad 15$$

$$19 \quad + \quad 20 \quad + \quad 14 \qquad = \quad \underline{+53}$$

**S**    **A**    **T**    **A**    **N**

$$\underline{+2} \quad = \qquad 1 \quad + \quad 1 \qquad \text{(Ultimate altruism)}$$

**27**        +        ***154***    =    ***181***

(The Christ Office)          (Higher octave of Horus")

The High Priestess card of the Tarot represents the taking on of responsibility, in this case for eliminating the negative connotation and fear associated with Satan.

# APPENDIX *III*

## *The Empress*

Revelation Chapter 3 relates to our personal communication from the heart, mind and throat. The Empress symbolizes our feminine expression of these forms of communication.

Rev. 3:12 symbolizes the result of our expression of our true selves through conquering our alter ego. This verse clearly characterizes the importance of expressing our real nature and the reward that results: success and happiness.

> *Him that overcometh will I make a pillar in the temple of my God, and he shall go no more out, and I will write upon him the name of my God, and the name of the city of my God,* which is *new Jerusalem, which cometh down out of heaven from my God, and* I will write upon him *my new name.*
>
> Rev. 3:12

The phrase "the name of my God" carries some powerful energies. The vibrations of Earth power, the Master Communicator, and the Holy Spirit (see discussion about the number 151 in Chapter 10) are all contained within these five words.

|  |  |  |  |  |  |  |  |  | (Earth Power) |
|---|---|---|---|---|---|---|---|---|---|
| 28 | + | 27 | + 6 | + 13 | + | 11 | = | **85** |  |
| 20+8 |  | 14 + 13 | 6 | 13 | 7 | + 4 |  |  |  |
| **T H E** |  | **N A M E** | **O F** | **M Y** | **G** | **O D** |  |  |  |
|  | 5 + | 1 + 5 | + 15 | + | 25 + | 15 | = | +*66* |  |
|  |  |  |  |  |  |  |  | *151* |  |

66 = Master Communicator                    (Holy Spirit)

Each individual is an aspect of the Holy Spirit. The significance of this expression in Revelation chapter 3 (number 3 symbolizes communication) is that the Holy Spirit is an integral part of the principle of the power to communicate on the earth plane, a feminine principle.

```
         23+ 8   +   3+  8                      =    42
         W   H   I    C   H
  9  =            9
                 19                             =    19
         I   S
  9  =   9
                 14  +  23                      =    37
         N   E   W
  5  =   5
                 28              44             =   +72
                 10  +  18  +    19  +  12  +  13
33 (The) {  J   E   R    U    S   A   L   E   M
 +32  =   5        +  21  +   1   +  5
                                +27
                             71 (Thoth, Moses)
 55                          +            170   =   225
                                              (11/11/49)
```

The phrase "which is new Jerusalem" is first introduced in this verse. This is a representation of The Thoth (Moses) energy which symbolizes the collective power of communication possessed by the Group Avatar.

> *Because thou sayest, I am rich, and increased with goods, and have need of nothing; and knowest not that thou art wretched, and miserable, and poor, and blind, and naked.*

Rev. 3:17

(Organization of the feminine
leading to leadership)

```
         18        +              64            =   82
         14+  4       13  +  19  +  18  +  2+  12
  A   N   D       M   I   S   E   R   A   B   L   E
  1           +       9   +  5   +  1   +      5   =  21 (World)
```

The phrase "and miserable" represents the principle of feminine organization resulting in leadership on a world level. This is the empowerment of women in an organizational sense to assume global leadership.

|  | 18 | + |  |  | 32 |  | = | *50* (Freedom) |
|--|----|---|--|--|----|--|---|----------------|
|  | 14+ 4 |  | 2+ | 12 | + | 14+ 4 |  |  |
| **A** | **N** | **D** | **B** | **L** | **I** | **N** | **D** |  |
| 1 |  | + |  |  | 9 |  | = | *+10* (New beginning) |
|  |  |  |  |  |  |  |  | *60* (Word) |

This phrase represents the principle of a new beginning of freedom resulting in a new expression of the Word, the creative principle.

|  |  |  |  | (Merging of Heart and Mind) |  |  |  |  |
|--|--|--|--|--|--|--|--|--|
|  | 18 | + |  |  | 29 |  | = | *47* |
|  | 14+ 4 |  | 14 | + | 11 | + | 4 |  |
| **A** | **N** | **D** | **N** | **A** | **K** | **E** | **D** | (Illumined |
| 1 |  | + |  | 1 | + | 5 |  | = _+7_ intellect) |
|  |  |  |  |  |  |  |  | *54* (Sun) |

The phrase "and naked" symbolizes the merging of the heart and mind combined with the Motivation of the illumined intellect to result in the manifestation of the energy of the Sun. This is a powerful combination of energies which reveal the true power (the life-giving power of the Sun) of conceiving from the heart *and* intellect together.

# APPENDIX *IV*

## *The Emperor*

Each of us possesses a three-fold nature which can be described as consisting of a masculine, a feminine, and a child aspect. The Emperor represents the masculine aspect of our nature. This "Emperor" or masculine aspect is depicted as seated on a throne in the Tarot. In Revelation Chapter 4 the "throne" is mentioned throughout, and its meaning and relationship to the word "Word" are derived as follows:

$$
\begin{array}{llll}
23 & + & 18+ \ 4 & = & 45 \\
\mathbf{W} & \mathbf{O} & \mathbf{R} \quad \mathbf{D} \\
15 & & & = & \underline{+15} \\
& & & & \mathbf{60} \ \text{(Word)}
\end{array}
$$

$$
\begin{array}{lllll}
20+ \ 8+ & 18 & + & 14 & = & \mathbf{60} \ \text{(Word)} \\
\mathbf{T} \quad \mathbf{H} & \mathbf{R} & \mathbf{O} & \mathbf{N} \quad \mathbf{E} & & \text{(Supportive Nature—} \\
& 15 & + & 5 & = & \underline{+20} \quad \text{motivation)} \\
& & & & \mathbf{80} \ \text{(Organization—natural} \\
& & & & \text{expression)}
\end{array}
$$

Expressing our "Word," our covenant, to fulfill our individual destiny is essential in this life. On the higher planes, fulfilling our destiny in this lifetime is the fulfillment of our Word in the largest sense of the word.

The Throne throughout history has symbolized regal power and control from a high position in government and/or religion. In Rev. Chapter 4, the personal issue is completing our personal destiny and doing what we came to earth to accomplish this lifetime.

> *And he that sat was to look upon like a jasper and as sardine stone: and* there was *a rainbow round about the throne, in sight like unto an emerald.*
>
> Rev. 4:3

|  | 23 |  |  | + |  |  | 63 |  |  |  | = 86 (Pyramid, |
|---|---|---|---|---|---|---|---|---|---|---|---|
| 12 | + | 11 |  |  | 10 | + | 19+ | 16 | + | 18 | Arthur) |
| **L** | **I** | **K** | **E** | **A** | **J** | **A** | **S** | **P** | **E** | **R** |  |
| 9+ | 5 |  | + | 1 | + | 1 | + |  | 5 |  | = +21 (World) |
|  |  |  |  |  |  |  |  |  |  |  | **107** |
|  |  |  |  |  |  |  |  |  |  |  | (The Messiah) |

This phrase represents the principles of the Pyramid and Arthur combined with the energy of the World to express the vibration of the Messiah. This is the application of power in selfless service for the benefit of all earth's inhabitants.

$$
\begin{array}{llll}
 & 14+ & 4 & = \quad 18 \\
\mathbf{A} & \mathbf{N} & \mathbf{D} & \\
1 = 1 & & & \\
\end{array}
$$

$$
\begin{array}{l}
\mathbf{A} \\
1 = 1 \\
\end{array}
$$

| 1 = | A | | | | | | |
|---|---|---|---|---|---|---|---|
|  | 19 | + | 18+ 4 | + | 14 | = | 55 |
|  | **S** | **A** | **R** **D** | **I** | **N** | **E** |  |
| 15 = |  | 1 | + | 9 | + 5 |  |  |
|  | 19+ | 20 | + | 14 |  | = | +53 |
|  | **S** | **T** | **O** | **N** | **E** |  |  |
| +20 = |  | 15 | + | 5 |  |  |  |
| **37** |  |  |  |  |  |  | **126** |
| (Gnostic Cross) |  |  |  |  |  | (Individualized God Consciousness) |  |

This phrase signifies the initiate with the Gnostic Cross, the stored reserves of past-lifetime experience, combined with the principle of God consciousness on an individual level—a symbolic representation of the act of remembering the true self.

> *And the first beast* was *like a lion, and the second beast*
> *like a calf and the third beast had a face of a man, and the*
> *fourth beast* was *like a flying eagle.*
>
> Rev. 4:7

The word "beast" appears again and again throughout the Book of Revelation and is almost always associated with the "shadow side" of the human psyche or other negative principle. A numerological analysis reveals a compelling subconscious meaning for this word.

```
2    +        19+ 20  =  41
B    E    A   S   T
5+   1             = + 6
                     47
```

41 = practicality & independence leading to new freedom
6 = independence & freedom leading to responsibility
47 = energy of heart & higher mind plus crown

In this context, "beast" means practicality and independence resulting in a new freedom combined with responsibility leading to a merging of the heart and mind. The corresponding meanings for the numbers 4 (Heart chakra) and 7 (Crown chakra) can be easily understood when we examine their association with the chakras. For a thorough discussion of the Beast and its relationship to the four bodies (physical, emotional, mental, and spiritual) see Chapter 8.

> *And the four beasts had each of them six wings about* them; *and they were full of eyes within: and they rest not day and night, saying, Holy, holy, holy, Lord God Almighty, which was, and is, and is to come.*
> Rev. 4:8

Verse 4:8 carries the energy of the number 48, the vibration of "Roundtable." This energy combined with the creative principle and the merging of the Heart and Mind results in the realization of the principle of equality through the act of creation from the heart and intellect.

```
                                    (Word)        (Creative principle)
     28        +       24      +       60              = 112
20+ 8              6 +    18   2     +  19+ 20+ 19
T   H   E        F   O   U   R      B   E   A   S   S
     5  +       15+ 21     +      5+ 1              = 47
                                    (Merging of Heart and Mind)
```

Rev. 4:8 states that the four Beasts had each of them six wings about them. Numerologically, the number six represents responsibility, therefore, the six wings around each of the Beasts represents responsibility, our responsibility for each of these natures or aspects of ourselves.

|  |  |  | 20+ | 8 | + | 25 |  |  | = | 53 |
|---|---|---|---|---|---|---|---|---|---|---|
| **51** { |  |  | **T** | **H** | **E** | **Y** |  |  | = | 53 |
| (Michael) | 5 | = |  |  | 5 |  |  |  |  |  |
|  |  |  | 23 | + | 18 |  |  |  | = | *41* |
|  |  |  | **W** | **E** | **R** | **E** |  |  |  |  |
|  | 10 | = |  | 5 | + | 5 |  |  |  |  |
|  |  |  | 6 | + | 12+ | 12 |  |  | = | *30* |
| **51** { |  |  | **F** | **U** | **L** | **L** |  |  |  |  |
| (Michael) | 21 | = |  | 21 |  |  |  |  |  |  |
|  |  |  | 6 |  |  |  |  |  | = | 6 |
|  |  |  | **O** | **F** |  |  |  |  |  |  |
|  | 15 | = | 15 |  |  |  |  |  |  |  |
|  |  |  | 25 + | 19 |  |  |  |  | = | *44* (Abraham, the Father |
| **54** { |  |  | **E** | **Y** | **E** | **S** |  |  |  | of many nations) |
| (Sun) | 10 | = | 5 | + | 5 |  |  |  |  |  |
|  |  |  | 23 | + | 20+ | 8 | + | 14 | = | +65 |
|  |  |  | **W** | **I** | **T** | **H** | **I** | **N** |  |  |
|  | +18 | = |  | 9 |  | + | 9 |  |  |  |
|  | **79** |  |  |  |  |  |  |  |  | **239** |
|  | (Sword) |  |  |  |  |  |  |  |  |  |

This is a powerful phrase. The double Michael energy represents a subconscious and superconscious power to contact the angelic realm in service to others. The Sun symbolizes the act of affirming our commitment to serve by radiating our energy outward to touch others. The end result is applying our power (Sword) to achieve the symbolic equivalent of Abraham's (the ancient Jewish patriarch) leadership—the right use of power to lead.

# APPENDIX V

## The Lovers

In the present-day Egyptian Tarot deck, The Hierophant is the #5 major arcana. I don't feel that this correspondence fits and, as stated earlier, it is the opinion of scholars of the Mysteries that the order of the original cards was rearranged. In my opinion, The Lovers, representing the five senses, diversity, change and variety, closely correlate with the definition of the number 5 in our present-day modern civilization. This is another reason why I believe that Revelation must be interpreted on a symbolic and subconscious level. Changes were made long ago in both the ancient Tarot and controversial Revelation verses by religious authorities in an effort to advance their own agenda.

Revelation Chapter 5 deals with the beginning of the opening of the seven seals—the seven energy centers—within the human auric field. The second verse raises this subject:

> *And I saw a strong angel proclaiming with a loud voice,*
> *Who is worthy to open the book, and to loose the seals*
> *thereof?*
>
> Rev. 5:2

The initiate is assisted in opening the seals (chakras) by the energies of Thoth/Moses (171) and the power of mastership reflected in the highest attainable degree of Masonry (33). Michael (51) and The Lord of the World (175) are also energies which act during this process. All this points to the higher-plane principles which are available to each individual who aspires to higher consciousness.

```
                    14+  4                    =    18
              A    N    D
   1    =    1


              I
   9    =    9
              19   +    23              =    42
             S    A    W
   1    =         1


              A
   1    =    1
              19+  20+  18   +    14+  7    =    78
             S    T    R    O    N    G
   15   =                   15
              14+  7    +    12        =    ±33
             A    N    G    E    L
   +6   =    1         +    5
   33
```

(Highest degree of Masonry)                     **171** (Thoth, Moses)


```
         16+  18   +    3+   12        +    13   +    14+  7    =    83
         P    R    O    C    L    A    I    M    I    N    G
34  =              15   +         1+   9    +    9
         23   +    20+  8                             =    51 (Michael)
         W    I    T    H
9   =              9


         A
1   =    1
         12        +    4                        =    16
         L    O    U    D
36  =              15+  21
         22        +    3                        =    ±25
         V    O    I    C    E
+29 =              15+  9    +    5
109                                              175
```

(Lord of the World)


The answer to the question posed in the second verse is given in the fifth:

> *And one of the elders saith unto me, Weep not: behold,*
> *the Lion of the tribe of Juda, the Root of David, hath*
> *prevailed to open the book, and to loose the seven seals*
> *thereof.*

Rev. 5:5

In this verse, the lion symbolizes the qualities of mind power to manifest what we desire in our lives.  Proper use of mind concentration awakens hidden powers for success in our lives.

"Juda" is an interesting term in this 5th verse since it represents the circle of life ever present in the earth condition.

$$
\begin{array}{llllll}
10 & + & 4 & = & \textbf{14} \text{ (Independence and practicality} \\
\textbf{J} & \textbf{U} & \textbf{D} & \textbf{A} & & \text{leading to new kind of freedom)} \\
& 21 & + & 1 & = & \underline{+22} \text{ (Master Builder)} \\
& & & & & \textbf{36} \text{ (Return)}
\end{array}
$$

The universal law of cause and effect is found neatly tucked away in this remarkable Revelation passage.  The circle, consisting of 360° (a higher power of 36) is a powerful and appropriate symbol.  It is often said that what goes around, comes around.  This is the significance of the energy of "return" in this verse.

In Revelation 5:6 the seven horns and seven eyes and the seven spirits of God are symbols for Christ Consciousness.

> *And I beheld, and, lo, in the midst of the throne and of the four beasts, and in the midst of the elders, stood a Lamb as it had been slain, having seven horns and seven eyes, which are the seven Spirits of God sent forth into all the earth.*

> Rev. 5:6

The number seven clearly symbolizes an important principle as it often appears in the fifth chapter.  The double seven — 77 — is the number of Christ and represents the seven male and seven female chakras.

$$
\begin{array}{llllll}
3+ & 8+ & 18 & + & 19+ \ 20 & = & 68 \\
\textbf{C} & \textbf{H} & \textbf{R} & \textbf{I} & \textbf{S} \quad \textbf{T} \\
& & & 9 & & & \underline{+9} \\
& & & & & & 77
\end{array}
$$

(the opening of seven male  & seven female
chakras —the seven horns & seven seals)

The numerical configuration of this verse, 5:6 (56), is also important for it is an expression of "Light."  Other energies which operate here are the vibrations of God, the Messiah, the Word, the "return" and the higher octave of Maitreya, all of which represent the influences of these principles upon the opening of the chakras.

|       |   |   | 14+ 4 |   |      |   | = | 18 |
|-------|---|---|-------|---|------|---|---|----|
|       |   | **A** | **N**   **D** |   |      |   |   |    |
| 1     | = | 1 |       |   |      |   |   |    |

|       |   | **I** |   |   |      |   | = |    |
|-------|---|---|---|---|------|---|---|----|
| 9     | = | 9 |   |   |      |   |   |    |

|        |   | 2 | + | 8 | + | 12+ 4 |   | = | **26** (God) |
|--------|---|---|---|---|---|-------|---|---|--------------|
|        |   | **B** | **E** | **H** | **E** | **L**  **D** |   |   |    |
| 10     | = | 5 | + | 5 |   |       |   |   |    |

|       |   |   | 14+ 4 |   | = | 18 |
|-------|---|---|-------|---|---|----|
|       |   | **A** | **N**   **D** |   |   |    |
| 1     | = | 1 |       |   |   |    |

|          |   | 12 |   | = | +12 |
|----------|---|----|---|---|-----|
|          |   | **L**  **O** |   |   |     |
| +15      | = | 15 |   |   |     |
| *36*     |   |    |   |   | **74** (Messiah) |

|       |   |   | 14 |   | = | 14 |
|-------|---|---|----|---|---|----|
|       |   | **I** | **N** |   |   |    |
| 9     | = | 9 |    |   |   |    |

|       |   | 20+ 8 |   |   | = | 28 |
|-------|---|-------|---|---|---|----|
|       |   | **T**   **H** | **E** |   |   |    |
| 5     | = |       | 5 |   |   |    |

|       |   | 13 | + | 4+ | 19+ | 20 | = | **56** (Light) |
|-------|---|----|---|----|-----|----|---|----------------|
|       |   | **M** | **I** | **D** | **S** | **T** |   |    |
| 9     | = |    | 9 |    |     |    |   |    |

|        |   | 6 |   | = | 6 |
|--------|---|---|---|---|---|
|        |   | **O** | **F** |   |   |
| 15     | = | 15 |   |   |   |

|       |   | 20+ 8 |   |   | = | 28 |
|-------|---|-------|---|---|---|----|
|       |   | **T**   **H** | **E** |   |   |    |
| 5     | = |       | 5 |   |   |    |

|       |   | 20+ | 8+ | 18 | + | 14 |   | = | +60 (Word) |
|-------|---|-----|----|----|---|----|---|---|------------|
|       |   | **T** | **H** | **R** | **O** | **N** | **E** |   |    |
| +20   | = |     |    |    | 15 | + | 5 |   |    |

| *255* = |   | 63 |   |   | + | *192* (Higher octave |
|---------|---|----|---|---|---|----------------------|
| (Feminine master leader) |   |    |   |   |   | of Maitreya) |

> *And I beheld, and I heard the voice of many angels*
> *round about the throne and the beasts and the elders: and*
> *the number of them was ten thousand times ten thousand,*
> *and thousands of thousands.*

Rev. 5:11

The word "thousands" represents a key principle in the Book of

Revelation. Numerological analysis reveals the energies which compose this principle.

| 20+ | 8 | + | | 19 | + | 14+ | 4+ | 19 | = | *84* (Authority) |
| T | H | O | U | S | A | N | D | S | | |
| | 15+ | 21 | + | | 1+ | 14+ | 4+ | 19 | = | *+37* (Cross) |
| | | | | | | | | | | *121* |

(The woman clothed with the Sun)

Every time the number 121 appears in Revelation, as it does here in the word "thousands," or in Rev. 12:1, where that verse describes the body (symbolising the Mother figure, Mary, Quan Yin and Isis) "clothed with the Sun," or as it appears in the name "Revelation" itself, an important point is being made. The Mother energy in any religion represents the birth of a new energy, a new purpose in life or the conception of a planetary miracle.

"Thousands of thousands" symbolizes the higher octave of Messiah combined with the energy of the Davidic Covenant (Psalm 89). Important component energies are also revealed when this phrase is analyzed.

|  | | 20+ | 8 | + | | 19 | + | 14+ | 4+ | 19 | = | *84* (Authority) |
| (Cross) | | T | H | O | U | S | A | N | D | S | | |
| *37* | = | | 15+ | 21 | + | | 1+ | 14+ | 4+ | 19 | | |
|  | | | | 6 | | | | | | | = | 6 |
|  | | O | F | | | | | | | | | |
| 15 | = | 15 | | | | | | | | | | |
|  | | 20+ | 8 | + | | 19 | + | 14+ | 4+ | 19 | = | *+84* (Authority) |
| (Cross) | | T | H | O | U | S | A | N | D | S | | |
| *+37* | = | | 15 + | 21 | + | 1 | | | | | | |
| *89* | | | | | | | | | | | | *174* |

(Davidic Covenant)                    (Higher octave of Messiah)

*Note: "Thousands" = 121(The woman clothed with the Sun) is repeated.*

*The expression of the word "of" = 21 (The World).*

The Davidic Covenant (Psalm 89:3&4) reads:

> *I have made a covenant with my chosen, I have sworn*
> *unto David my servant, Thy seed will I establish for ever,*
> *and build up thy throne to all generations. Selah.*

Symbolically, we are all modern-day Davids. Our goliaths appear to us in different forms and at various times during our lives. By slaying our Goliaths—outmoded thoughtforms and emotional patterns—we fulfill our individual covenant, our life's destiny. Chapter 5 of Revelation is about the attainment of freedom on all levels, resulting in the ultimate fulfillment.

# Appendix VI

## *The Hierophant*

Revelation Chapter 6 is such an important and heavily symbolic one that an entire chapter, Chapter 8, has been devoted to its symbolism, specifically the symbolism of the Four Horsemen. Duty, responsibility and service symbolized by the Hierophant are key principles represented in Revelation 6.

> *And I beheld when he had opened the sixth seal, and, lo,*
> *there was a great earthquake; and the sun became black as*
> *sackcloth of hair, and the moon became as blood.*

> Rev. 6:12

|  |  | 23+ | 8 | + | 14 |  |  | = | 45 |
|---|---|---|---|---|---|---|---|---|---|
|  |  | **W** | **H** | **E** | **N** |  |  |  |  |
| 5 | = |  |  | 5 |  |  |  |  |  |
|  |  | 8 |  |  |  |  |  | = | 8 |
|  |  | **H** | **E** |  |  |  |  |  |  |
| 5 | = |  | 5 |  |  |  |  |  |  |
|  |  | 8 | + | 4 |  |  |  | = | 12 |
|  |  | **H** | **A** | **D** |  |  |  |  |  |
| 1 | = |  | 1 |  |  |  |  |  |  |
|  |  | 16+ | 14 |  | + | 4 |  | = | 34 |
|  |  | **O** | **P** | **E** | **N** | **E** | **D** |  |  |
| 25 | = | 15 | + | 5 | + | 5 |  |  |  |
|  |  | 20+ | 8 |  |  |  |  | = | 28 |
|  |  | **T** | **H** | **E** |  |  |  |  |  |
| 5 | = |  | 5 |  |  |  |  |  |  |
|  |  | 19 | + | 24+ | 20+ | 8 |  | = | *71* (Thoth, Moses) |
|  |  | **S** | **I** | **X** | **T** | **H** |  |  |  |
| 9 | = |  | 9 |  |  |  |  |  |  |
|  |  | 19 |  | + | 12 |  |  | = | +31 |
|  |  | **S** | **E** | **A** | **L** |  |  |  |  |
| +6 | = | 5+ | 1 |  |  |  |  |  |  |
| *56* |  |  | + |  |  |  |  | 229 = | *285* |
| (Light) |  |  |  |  |  |  |  | (2nd octave of Earth Power) |

In Rev. 6:12 the principles of Thoth/Moses, "Light" and Christ are all encoded. These principles reflect the various vibrational aspects which are utilized as tools in the performance of responsible service.

The phrase "the moon became as blood" possesses the Personality of Christ Consciousness and the Motivation of Christ. It represents the taking of responsibility for one's life and experiences on all levels resulting in self-mastery.

```
                20+  8                       =    28
                 T   H   E
        5   =            5
                13     +  14               =    27
                 M   O   O   N
        30  =        15 + 15
                 2  +  3  +  13            =    18
                 B   E   C   A   M   E
        11  =        5  +  1  +  5
                19                          =    19
                 A   S
        1   =    1
                2+  12       +  4          =   +18
                 B   L   O   O   D
      +30   =        15+ 15        (Christ Consciousness)
       77 (Christ)                          110
```

*And the stars of heaven fell unto the earth, even as*
*a fig tree casteth her untimely figs, when she is shaken*
*of a mighty wind.*

Rev. 6:13

Rev. 6:13 is a very powerful verse as it deals with Earth power (physical) as well as representing the principle symbolized by the Spear of Longinus. These two energies combine to provide the initiate with the power to master the physical plane by employing the principle of the Sacred Lance, the spear used by Longinus to pierce the side of Christ which drew blood from his lifeless body.

```
        14+ 4                    =  18
         A   N   D
  1  =   1
        20+ 8                       =   28
         T   H   E
  5  =           5
        19+ 20  +   18+ 19         =   76
         S   T   A   R   S
  1  =           1
            6                       =   6
         O   F
 15  =   15
         8       +   22  +  14  =  44
         H   E   A   V   E   N
 11  =       5+  1   +   5
         6   +  12+ 12              =  30
         F   E   L   L
  5  =   5
        14+ 20                      =  34
         U   N   T   O
 36  =   21 + 15
        20+ 8                       =  28
         T   H   E
  5  =           5
        18+ 20+ 8                   =  +46
         E   A   R   T   H
 +6  =   5+1
  85                                    224
(Earth Power)                      (Spear of Longinus)
```

Each verse within the 6<sup>th</sup> chapter of Revelation (except for the last, the 17th), as well as a compelling number throughout the entire Book, begins with the word "and." This was not done without intent. The author(s) understood that this little word carries the energy of "Ra," the Egyptian Sun God, the Supreme Self.

```
        18  =  18              14+ 4  =  18
  R     A                 A    N   D
        1   =  +1          1           =  +1
               19                         19
```

I have an intuitive understanding that the repeated use of the word "and" is used to invoke the energy of Ra. It is likely that the word "and" has been used throughout history subsequent to the loss of common knowledge of the sacred language for purposes of keeping the energy and power of Ra alive on the physical plane. Its placement preceding another word would have the effect of lending greater power to that word. I believe this was intentional on the part of the author(s) of Revelation.

> *And said to the mountains and rocks, Fall on us, and hide us from the face of him that sitteth on the throne, and from the wrath of the Lamb.*
>
> Rev. 6:16

| | | | | | |
|---|---|---|---|---|---|
| | 6+ | 18 | + | 13 | = 37 |
| | **F** | **R** | **O** | **M** | |
| 15 = | | | 15 | | |
| | 20+ | 8 | | | = 28 |
| | **T** | **H** | **E** | | |
| 5 = | | | 5 | | |
| | 6 | + | 3 | | = 9 |
| | **F** | **A** | **C** | **E** | |
| 6 = | | 1 | + | 5 | |
| | | 6 | | | = 6 |
| | **O** | **F** | | | |
| 15 = | 15 | | | | |
| | 8 + 13 | | | | = <u>+*21*</u> (World) |
| | **H** | **I** | **M** | | |
| <u>+9</u> = | 9 | | | | |
| **50** | + | | | | **101** = *151* |

(Holy Spirit, Jesus Christ, etc.)

The energy of the Expression of 151 relates to the Holy Spirit, Michael embodiment, the Davidic Covenant and Jesus Christ, to name just a few of the important principles which are symbolized by this number. (See Chapter 10) These are all facets of this multi-dimensional vibration.

> *For the great day of his wrath is come; and who shall be able to stand?*
>
> Rev. 6:17

This final verse of Chapter 6 brings forth the Personality of the Lord of the World, the potential of everyone to create a world of peace and harmony, through a universal perspective.

|   |   |   |   |   |   |   |   |
|---|---|---|---|---|---|---|---|
|        | 23+ | 8   |     |       |     | =  | 31  |
|        | **W** | **H** | **O** |       |     |    |     |
| 15 =   |     | 15  |     |       |     |    |     |
|        | 19+ | 8   | +   | 12+   | 12  | =  | 51  |
|        | **S** | **H** | **A** | **L** | **L** |    |     |
| 1 =    |     | 1   |     |       |     |    |     |
|        | 2   |     |     |       |     | =  | 2   |
|        | **B** | **E** |     |       |     |    |     |
| 5 =    |     | 5   |     |       |     |    |     |
|        | 2+  | 12  |     |       |     | =  | 14  |
|        | **A** | **B** | **L** | **E** |     |    |     |
| 6 =    | 1   | + 5 |     |       |     |    |     |
|        | 20  |     |     |       |     | =  | 20  |
|        | **T** | **O** |     |       |     |    |     |
| 15 =   |     | 15  |     |       |     |    |     |
|        | 19+ | 20  | +   | 14+   | 4   | =  | +57 |
|        | **S** | **T** | **A** | **N** | **D** |    |     |
| +1 =   |     | 1   |     |       |     |    |     |
| 43     |     |     |     |       |     |    | *175* |

(Lord of the World)

# APPENDIX VII

## *The Chariot*

The seventh chapter of Revelation, corresponding to The Chariot of the Tarot, represents the illumined intellect. In the illustration on the 7th card of the Egyptian Tarot, a charioteer is holding the reigns of four horses. While Chapter 6 explores the nature of The Four Horses of the Apocalypse, Chapter 7 discusses the mastery of these four horses introduced in chapter 7. Seven is the vibration of the Higher Mind and acting from the perspective of the Higher Mind is required to master the four bodies (physical, mental, emotional and spiritual).

> *And after these things I saw four angels standing on the four corners of the earth, holding the four winds of the earth, that the wind should blow on the earth, upon the sea, nor on any tree.*

Rev. 7:1

```
                    14+  4                    =    18
              A    N    D
    1    =    1
                    6+   20   +    18         =    44
              A    F    T    E    R
    6    =    1         +    5
                    20+  8    +    19         =    47   (Merging of heart
              T    H    E    S    E                     & mind)
    10   =              5    +    5
                    20+8 + 14+7+19            =    +68
77 (Christ) {   T    H    I    N    G    S
    +9   =                   9
    26                                             177
   (God)                            (Higher octave of Christ)
```

The numerical configuration of verse 7:1 corresponds to that of Thoth and Moses (71). This is an example of how the simplest phrase can possess powerful energies. In this case, Rev. 7:1 represents the vibration of God and Christ Consciousness in an otherwise unremarkable set of words.

The ancients understood that the simplest words evoked the highest energies, as in the case of the word "things." A word in common use can bring into manifestation higher energies by virtue of the fact that it is spoken often. The symbolism of the four angels has multiple meanings:

1.  The practical, down-to-earth approach to life:   self-discipline, honesty and dependability.
2.  The illumined mind is more controlled and focused on the laws of successful living.
3.  The symbology of the four sides of the pyramid, representing high ideals from the astral and First Cause planes.
4.  The potential of energies of the Heart, the 4th chakra, and Mind, the 7th chakra—the lion (mind) lying down with the lamb (heart).

> *And I heard the number of these which were sealed:*
> *and there were sealed an hundred and forty and four*
> *thousand of all the tribes of the children of Israel.*
>
> Rev. 7:4

The numerical configuration of this verse, 7:4, represents "Messiah."

$$
\begin{array}{ccccccccc}
13 & + & 19+ & 19 & & + & 8 & = & 59 \\
\mathbf{M} & \mathbf{E} & \mathbf{S} & \mathbf{S} & \mathbf{I} & \mathbf{A} & \mathbf{H} & & \\
 & 5 & + & 9+ & 1 & & & = & \underline{+15} \\
 & & & & & & & & \mathbf{74}
\end{array}
$$

```
                14                              =   14
        A   N
  1  =  1
        8    +   14+  4+  18  +   4             =   48
        H   U   N   D   R   E   D
 26  =  21           +       5
                14+ 4                           =   18
        A   N   D
  1  =  1
        6    +   18+ 20+ 25                     =   69
        F   O   R   T   Y
 15  =  15
                14+ 4                           =   18
        A   N   D
  1  =  1
        6    +       18                         =   24
        F   O   U   R
 36  =          15+21
        20 + 8   +       19  +   14 + 4         =  +65
        T   H   O   U   S   A   N   D
+37  =          15+ 21  +   1
117                                                256
                                        (2nd octave of Light)
```

The number **256** is the energy of the second octave of "Light" and **117** is that of the higher power of "Star." In addition, 144 is the energy of Abraham in the Hebrew language. The number 144,000 is the number of the "chosen people," interpreted as the number of illumined people required for all people to be able to achieve global illumination.

> *Of the tribe of Juda* were *sealed twelve thousand. Of the tribe of Reuben* were *sealed twelve thousand. Of the tribe of Gad* were *sealed twelve thousand.*
>
> Rev. 7:5

Rev. 7:5 reduces numerologically to the number 13. The 13th letter of the Hebrew alphabet is *Mem*, representing the Mother mystery. This is the feminine principle of birth, death, sublimation and transfiguration. The Book of Revelation is keyed to the number 13, the completion of this feminine fourfold process. Of the three Hebrew Mother letters, Mem is the most significant and is ranked second in power only to the "1" of absolute unity. The glyph of the letter Mem is similar to that of the constellation of Aquarius, the shepherd in the sky pouring water bearing 13 stars onto earth.

$$19 \quad + \quad 12 \quad + \quad 4 \qquad = \quad 35$$

**S E A L E D**

$$11 \quad = \qquad 5+ \quad 1 \quad + \quad 5$$

$$20+ \quad 23 \quad + \quad 12+ \quad 22 \qquad = \quad 77$$

**T W E L V E**

$$10 \quad = \qquad 5 \quad + \quad 5$$

$$20+ \quad 8 \quad + \qquad 19 \quad + \quad 14+ \quad 4 \quad = \quad \underline{+65}$$

**T H O U S A N D**

$$\underline{+37} \quad = \qquad 15+ \quad 21 \quad + \quad 1$$

$$58/13 \qquad\qquad\qquad\qquad\qquad\qquad 177$$

(13ᵗʰ letter of Hebrew alphabet)          (Christ Consciousness)

*After this I beheld, and, lo, a great multitude, which no man could number, of all nations, and tribes and peoples, and tongues, stood before the throne, and before the lamb, clothed with white robes, and palms in their hands.*

Rev. 7:9

The number "79" is the energy of the Sword. If you subtract the "S" from the word "sword" the result is "word," and "S" is the 19th letter of the alphabet representing the Sun card of the major arcana.

The symbolism can be understood if we consider the sun's significance to us. Human beings have a basic need for sunshine. Many people suffer from depression if they are deprived of sunlight for too long, such as can happen in northern climates in the winter. The sun is the center of our solar system and the source of the energy that is required to sustain life.

$$14+ \quad 4 \qquad\qquad\qquad = \quad 18$$

**A N D**

$$1 \quad = \quad 1$$

$$16 \quad + \quad 12+ \quad 13+ \quad 19 \qquad = \quad 60 \ (\text{Word})$$

**P A L M S**

$$1 \quad = \quad 1$$

$$14 \qquad\qquad\qquad\qquad = \quad 14$$

**I N**

$$9 \qquad 9$$

$$20+ \quad 8 \quad + \qquad 18 \qquad = \quad 46$$

60 (Word) {     **T H E I R**

$$14 \quad = \quad 5+9$$

$$8 \quad + \quad 14+ \quad 4+ \quad 19 \qquad = \quad \underline{+45}$$

**H A N D S**

$$\underline{+1} \quad = \quad 1$$

$$26 \qquad\qquad\qquad + \qquad\qquad 183 \quad = \quad 209$$

(God)                 (Spear of Destiny)

This phrase carries some important energies: the Word (represented twice) and the energies of God and the Spear of Destiny. The Spear of Destiny has been symbolically bestowed upon many throughout history: Jesus, Arthur, Charlemagne, Lincoln, and Jefferson, to name a few. At this time it is being given to many to manifest the principle of the Group Avatar and lift humanity to its next higher level in the evolution of its consciousness.

# Appendix *VIII*

## *Strength*

*And I saw seven angels which stood before God and*
*to them were given seven trumpets.*

Rev. 8:2

This verse signifies the magical transcendence of the number 7 leading to Christ Consciousness. Number 77 symbolized by seven angels (the first seven) were given seven trumpets (the second seven).

|     |   | 55  |   |    |   |     |     |   |     |    |   |     |    |   |     |     |   |     |
|-----|---|-----|---|----|---|-----|-----|---|-----|----|---|-----|----|---|-----|-----|---|-----|
|     |   | 55  |   |    | + |     |     |   | 116 |    |   |     |    | = | **161** |
| 19  | + | 22  | + | 14 |   |     | 20+ | 18 | + | 13+ | 16 | + | 20+ | 19 |     |
| **S** | | **E** | | **V** | **E** | **N** | **T** | **R** | **U** | **M** | **P** | **E** | **T** | **S** |
|     |   | 5   | + | 5  |   | +   |     | 21 |   |     | +  | 5 |     |    | = | **+36** |
|     |   |     |   |    |   |     |     |    |   |     |    |   |     |    |   | ***197*** |

36 = The Return                                  (Nov. 11, 1949)

The phrase carries as its Expression the energy of the number 197 —the mystical vibration hidden in the November 11, 1949, Mt. Shasta event. Additional symbolism related to this number are: The 197 steps from the entrance to the Great Pyramid to the pit, and the 197 steps from the entrance of the Pyramid of Palenque in the Yucatan to the Holy of Holies.

*And the angel took the censer, and filled it with fire of*
*the altar, and cast it unto the earth: and there were voices*
*and thunderings and lightnings and an earthquake.*

Rev. 8:5

| 20+ | 8 | + | 14+ | 4 | + | 18 | + | 14+ | 7+ | 19 = | **104** (freedom) |
|-----|---|---|-----|---|---|----|---|-----|----|------|-------------------|
| **T** | **H** | **U** | **N** | **D** | **E** | **R** | **I** | **N** | **G** | **S** |
|     | 21 |  |   | + | 5 | + | 9 |   |   | = +**35** (organization) |
|     |   |  |   |   |   |   |   |   |   | **139** (Cosmic Christ) |

```
12  +   7+  8+  20+ 14  +   14+ 7+  19   = 101 (visionary)
L   I   G   H   T   N   I   N   G   S
9       +           9                    = +18
                                         119 (altruistic visionary)
```

Revelation 8:5 is a typical Revelation passage that, interpreted literally, possesses a negative meaning. In the language of the subconscious this passage carries a positive message, which is that our angelic potential begins with a renewed sense of purpose. Metaphorically speaking, we become like a sun in our daily lives. By becoming a sun, we experience the freedom and power in life's organization, leading to the attainment of cosmic Christ Consciousness. We also focus our individual attention on visionary ideals. Our new perspective leads to the sudden awareness that each person is a potential messiah with the exercise of proper motive and self-sacrifice.

> *The first angel sounded, and there followed hail and fire mingled with blood, and they were cast upon the earth: and the third part of trees was burnt up, and all green grass was burnt up.*

> Rev. 8:7

```
    20 (female)            24 (responsibility)          18 (altruistic)
8   +       12        6   +   18           2+  12  +        4
H   A   I   L         F   I   R   E         B   L   O   O   D
1+  9                 9   +   5             15+ 10
+10 (male)            +14 (freedom)         +30
30                    38                    48
(communication)       (visionary)          (master communicator)
```

```
    20+ 8   +   18+ 4   +   16  +   18+ 20  =   104
    T   H   I   R   D       P   A   R   T       (New
            9           +       1           =   +10 beginning)
                                                114
                                            (Practical visionary)
```

```
    2   +   18+ 14+ 20  +       16  =   70 (Illumined intellect)
    B   U   R   N   T       U   P
        21                  +   21  =   +42 (World responsibility)
                                        112
                            (Highest form of creative principle)
```

This verse represents the newly acquired quality of the integrated male/female leading to a confidence in our ability to communicate. The balance of freedom and responsibility in our lives results in a new futuristic outlook. All of these factors create a birth of altruism and increasing communication abilities. The end result is a very powerful initiation into our role as practical visionary. The illumined intellect combined with a sense of worldly responsibility leads to the attainment of the highest level of creativity.

> *And the name of the star is called Wormwood: and the third part of the waters became wormwood; and many men died of the waters, because they were made bitter.*

Rev. 8:11

|  | *54* (Sun) |  |  | *27* (Power to create in service |
|---|---|---|---|---|
| 23 + | 18+ 13 | | 23 + | 4        to others) |
| **W** | **O    R    M** | | **W    O** | **O    D** |
|  | *15* (Responsibility) | | 15 + 15 | = *30* (Communication) |

The word "wormwood" symbolizes the world server exemplifying the power of the Sun combined with the power to create in service to others. This passage is symbolic of an accelerated step forward in world service.

> *And the fourth angel sounded, and the third part of the sun was smitten, and the third part of the moon, and third part of the stars; so as the third part of them was darkened, and the day shone not for a third part of it, and the night likewise.*

Rev. 8:12

| 19+ 13 | + | 20+ 20 | + | 14 | = | *86* (Pyramid/Arthur) |
|---|---|---|---|---|---|---|
| **S    M** | **I** | **T    T** | **E** | **N** | | |
| 9 | | + | 5 | | = | *±14* (Freedom) |
|  | | | | | | *100* (New beginning) |

| 4 | + | 18+ 11 | + | 14 | + | 4 | = | *51* (Michael) |
|---|---|---|---|---|---|---|---|---|
| **D** | **A** | **R    K** | **E** | **N** | **E** | **D** | | |
| 1 | + | | 5 | + | 5 | | = | *+11* (Visionary) |
|  | | | | | | | | *62* |

(Organization for feminine empowerment)

The words "smitten" and "darkened" are both traditionally thought of as being negative, but here the esoteric meaning is revealed as positive in both words. "Smitten" symbolizes a newfound freedom of expressing the principle of the inner pyramid is symbolized. The inner pyramid extends from the heart chakra (#4) to the Crown chakra (#7). Through the practice of a commitment to meditation this process is activated. The Michael energy is represented in the Personality of "darkened," another indication of the higher energies at work in this chapter.

## APPENDIX IX

### The Hermit

Chapter 9 of the Book of Revelation is, according to traditional interpretation, one of the more negatively-charged chapters in the book. A discussion of the esoteric meanings of various key words and passages will show how the original intent of the coded text actually introduces the world server to true altruistic service.

> And the fifth angel sounded, and I saw a star fall from heaven unto the earth: and to him was given the key of the bottomless pit.

Rev. 9:1

```
                                                              (Return)
           55                    +         50         +          36   =   141
  2   +   20+ 20   +    13      12  +   19+ 19        16   +     20
  B    O    T    T    O    M     L    E    S    S      P    I      T
  15        +    15    +    5                    +      9    =    +44
                                                            (Altruism) 185
```

141 = Practical responsibility
44 = Master organizer
185 = Individualized Earth power

The essence of this Chapter is the bottomless pit. Its meaning in the language of the Mystery Schools relates to individual world service. Here we have the energies of the "return" and practical responsibility within the Personality of "bottomless pit," combined with the energies of altruism and the Master organizer, resulting in the ultimate Earth power. In our analysis, this represents the return of the World Server utilizing in a practical manner responsibility in an altruistic sense to organize on the highest levels for attainment of earthly goals.

> *And he opened the bottomless pit; and there arose a*
> *smoke out of the pit, as the smoke of a great furnace; and the*
> *sun and the air were darkened by reason of the smoke of the*
> *pit.*

```
                  20+  23                              =   43
                  T    W    O                                       85
        15  =              15
120               23   +   19                          =   42
                  W    O    E    S
        20  =         15+  5
                  13   +   18                          =   31
51 {              M    O    R    E
        20  =         15   +   5
                  8    +   18      +   6+  20   +   18  =  +70
86 {              H    E    R    E    A   F   T   E   R
       +16  =          5   +   5+  1          +   5
        71                                                  186
      (Thoth)                                    (Higher octave of Arthur)
                  51 = Michael        85 = Earth Power
          86 = Pyramid, Arthur     120 =(Archangel Michael, Sanat Kumara
```

This passage again speaks of empowerment from the inner planes. Christ Consciousness, Messianic power, Arthurian and Pyramid energies are all symbolized by the language in this verse. The big energy referred to by the "two woes" is the achievement of Earth power through the activation of the Group Avatar principle.

> *And the rest of the men which were not killed by these*
> *plagues yet repented not of the works of their hands, that*
> *they should not worship devils, and idols of gold, and silver,*
> *and brass, and stone, and of wood: which neither can see,*
> *nor hear, nor walk.*
>
> Rev. 9:20

> *Neither repented they of their murders, nor of their*
> *sorceries, nor of their fornication, nor of their thefts.*
>
> Rev. 9:21

As you can see, the 9th Chapter is full of language that has traditionally held a negative connotation. When we decipher the occult meanings of these words — and we must keep in mind that the author(s) of Revelation wrote from the occult or higher perspective — we find that the intended message was one of upliftment for humanity. A further example of this is the following analysis of several traditionally negative words.

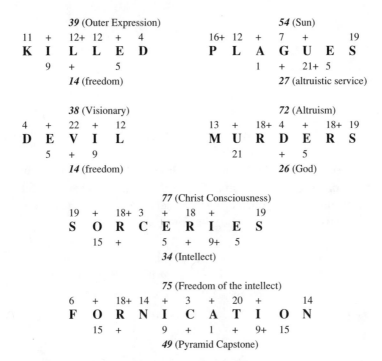

*39* (Outer Expression)

| 11 | + | 12+ | 12 | + | 4 |
|----|---|-----|----|---|---|
| K  | I | L   | L  | E | D |

9 + 5
*14* (freedom)

*54* (Sun)

| 16+ | 12 | + | 7 | + | | 19 |
|-----|----|---|---|---|---|----|
| P   | L  | A | G | U | E | S  |

1 + 21+ 5
*27* (altruistic service)

*38* (Visionary)

| 4 | + | 22 | + | 12 |
|---|---|----|---|----|
| D | E | V  | I | L  |

5 + 9
*14* (freedom)

*72* (Altruism)

| 13 | + | 18+ | 4 | + | 18+ | 19 |
|----|---|-----|---|---|-----|----|
| M  | U | R   | D | E | R   | S  |

21 + 5
*26* (God)

*77* (Christ Consciousness)

| 19 | + | 18+ | 3 | + | 18 | + | 19 |
|----|---|-----|---|---|----|---|----|
| S  | O | R   | C | E | R  | I | E | S |

15 + 5 + 9+ 5
*34* (Intellect)

*75* (Freedom of the intellect)

| 6 | + | 18+ | 14 | + | 3 | + | 20 | + | 14 |
|---|---|-----|----|---|---|---|----|---|----|
| F | O | R   | N  | I | C | A | T  | I | O | N |

15 + 9 + 1 + 9+ 15
*49* (Pyramid Capstone)

If we look at the energies of the Motivation (sum of consonants) and Personality (sum of vowels) expressed by these words, the occult or hidden message can be deduced as follows:

1. "Killed" means the "outer expression of freedom."
2. "Plagues" symbolizes the "great power to serve others through the consciousness of the Sun (Son)."
3. "Devils" represents the authority to experience freedom from an organizational standpoint.
4. "Murders" represents the Motivation of an altruistic use of God Consciousness manifesting through a philanthropic organizational focus.
5. "Sorceries" carries the vibration of an intellectual expression of Christ Consciousness.
6. "Fornication" represents the intellectual freedom to create motivated by the energies represented by the Capstone of the Great Pyramid.

These extremely negatively charged words in reality carry a positive (higher vibrational) meaning when examined in the light of the secret language of the Mystery Schools.

# APPENDIX X

## *Wheel of Fortune*

Chapter 10 of the Book of Revelation relates to the symbolism of the Wheel of Fortune card of the Tarot. The number 10 pertains to the attainment of enlightenment: the principle represented by Jesus and Buddha. The following passage refers to the angelic principle:

> *And I saw another mighty angel come down from heaven, clothed with a cloud: and a rainbow* was *upon his head, and his face* was *as it were the sun, and his feet as pillars of fire:*
>
> Rev. 10:1

Obviously, this is a positive verse, even from a literal standpoint. In this chapter humanity's angelic potential is suggested. The rainbow upon the head and the face beaming as if it were the sun describes a major breakthrough in consciousness.

|  |  | 14 | + |  | 20+ | 8 | + | 18 | = | *60* (The Word) |
|---|---|---|---|---|---|---|---|---|---|---|
| *81* | { | **A** | **N** | **O** | **T** | **H** | **E** | **R** | | |
|  | 21 = | 1 | + | 15 | + | | 5 | | | |
|  |  | 13 | + | 7+ | 8+ | 20+ | 25 | | = | 73 |
| *82* | { | **M** | **I** | **G** | **H** | **T** | **Y** | | | |
|  | 9 = | | 9 | | | | | | | |
|  |  | 14+ | 7 | + | | 12 | | | = | *+33* (Master Mason) |
| *+39* | { | **A** | **N** | **G** | **E** | **L** | | | | |
| *202* | +6 = | 1 | | + | 5 | | | | | |
|  | *36* (Return) | | | | | | | | *166* | |

(Master communicator)

81 = Horus    82 = Feminine organization    202 = Master Builder

The number 10 is the symbol of major new beginnings and with the word "pillars" symbolizes another new level of Christ Consciousness.

| 16 | + | 12 + 12 | + | 18 + 19 | = **77** (Christ Consciousness) |
|---|---|---|---|---|---|
| **P** | **I** | **L    L** | **A** | **R    S** | |
| 9 | | + 1 | | | = **10** (Major new beginning) |

This Revelation chapter is the birth of something big on the many levels of the inner world, and of a new mental and emotional perspective on the earth. The next three verses, 2 through 4, give additional insight into the nature of this birth.

*And he had in his hand a little book open: and he set his*
*right foot upon the sea, and* his *left* foot *on the earth,*
*And cried with a loud voice, as* when *a lion roareth:*
*and when he had cried, seven thunders uttered their voices.*
*And when the seven thunders had uttered their voices,*
*I was about to write: and I heard a voice from heaven saying*
*unto me, Seal up those things which the seven thunders*
*uttered, and write them not.*

Rev. 10:2-4

In verse 10:3 the "seven thunders" is significant as it represents the second level of the Messiah's return—the spiritual unity of religions, nations and peoples.

(Master leader)

| | | | | | | | | | |
|---|---|---|---|---|---|---|---|---|---|
| | *55* | | | | | *83* | | | |
| 19 | + | 22 | + | 14 | 20+ 8 | + | 14+ 4 | + | 18+ 19 |
| **S** | **E** | **V** | **E** | **N** | **T    H** | **U** | **N    D** | **E** | **R    S** |
| | 5 | + 5 | | | | 21 | + 5 | | |
| | *±10* | | | | | *±26* | | | |
| | **65** | | + | | | **109** | = | **174** | |

(Higher octave of Messiah)

"Their voices" is revealing as the number 133 represents ultimate earth power and this is the sum of the numerical value of these two words. Looking at the subconscious message behind the words, the combining of the values of "seven thunders" and "their voices" numerologically translates as the principle of one of the planetary goals, that of great earth power to emerge after the spiritual unity of religions, nations and peoples.

```
                                                              (The Sphinx)
                46              +              44          =      90
        20+  8   +        18        22  +        3    +   19
         T   H   E    I   R         V   O    I   C    E    S
                5+   9                 15+  9   +    5
                14              +              29          =     +43
                                                               133
                                                         (The Ankh)
```

In Verse 10:4, another reference to "seven thunders" (meaning spiritual unity) and the term "seal up" represents the perfect balance of male/female polarities symbolized by "Messiah". This principle assists in the process of unification.

```
            31            +   16        =    47 (Merging of Heart & Mind)
        19  +        12            16
         S   E   A    L        U    P
            5+   1             21
            +6            +   +21       =   +27
            37            +   37        =   74 (Messiah)
```

Verses 9 and 10 of Chapter 10 reveal additional references to the Messiah, however it is couched in apparently ominous terms.

```
(Michael) 51            +            60  (The Word)
        2   +  12+ 12+ 25        2   +  20+ 20  +   18
         B   E   L   L   Y        B   I   T   T   E   R
         5                        9   +       5
                                 14
                                 74  (Messiah)
```

Revelation 10:10 represents the start of a major new beginning in a two-fold manner. The first 10 represents our feminine energy and the second represents the masculine. This represents the introduction of our covenant (destiny and purpose in life) at our second birth, the birth of our light body. This is represented by the Ark of the Covenant, and the phrase "my belly was bitter" is the phrase in this verse that relates to this principle.

```
        13                              =   13
        M  Y
25  =       25
         2 +    12+ 12+ 25              =   51
         B   E   L   L   Y
5  =       5
        21  +   19                      =   42
        W   A   S
1  =       1
         2  +  20+ 20  +  18            =  +60  (The Word)
         B   I   T   T   E   R
+14 =      9 + 5              (Master Communicator)
45                     +               166   =   211


        20+ 8                           =   28
        T  H  E
5  =       5
        18+ 11                          =   29
        A   R   K
1  =   1
        6                               =   6
        O  F
15 =   15
        20+ 8                           =   28
        T  H  E
5  =       5
         3  +  22  +  14  +  14+20       =  +73
         C   O   V   E   N   A   N   T
+21 =  15 + 5   + 1
47                     +                164   =   211
```

(Merging of Heart & Mind)

The encoding of the energy of the Ark of the Covenant in this verse represents a major acceleration in our consciousness and a rededication to our chosen path in life relating to our destiny.

# APPENDIX XI

## *Justice*

Revelation Chapter 11 corresponds to the eleventh card of the Major Arcana of the Tarot, Justice. The principles associated with this card are:

- Benevolence and proper use of powers
- Idealism
- The refinement of ideals and the creation of the future
- Visionary
- Reformation of old and outdated ideals
- Guided by intuition and revelation
- Artistic and inventive genius
- Existence on the highest plane of intellect and spirituality
- Avant-garde approach toward invention and art
- Dual in nature and ability to see both sides
- Balance in feminine/masculine natures
- Capability of achieving great fame as a result of artistic and humanitarian effort
- A well-developed understanding of human condition

*And there was given me a reed like unto a rod: and the angel stood, saying, Rise, and measure the temple of God, and the altar, and them that worship therein.*

*But the court which is without the temple leave out, and measure it not; for it is given unto the Gentiles: and the holy city shall they tread under foot forty* and *two months.*

Rev. 11:1-2

$$
\begin{array}{l}
\textbf{A} \\
1 \;=\; 1 \\
18 \;+\; 4 \qquad = \quad \textbf{\textit{22}} \text{ (Master builder)} \\
\textbf{R} \quad \textbf{E} \quad \textbf{E} \quad \textbf{D} \\
10 \;=\; 5+ \; 5 \\
12 \;+\; 11 \qquad = \quad 23 \\
\textbf{L} \quad \textbf{I} \quad \textbf{K} \quad \textbf{E} \\
14 \;=\; 9 \;+\; 5 \\
14+ \; 20 \qquad = \quad 34 \\
\textbf{U} \quad \textbf{N} \quad \textbf{T} \quad \textbf{O} \\
\text{(Return)} \;\; \textbf{\textit{36}} \;=\; 21 \;+\; 15
\end{array}
$$

$$
\begin{array}{l}
\textbf{A} \\
1 \\
18 \;+\; 4 \qquad = \quad \underline{\textbf{\textit{+22}}} \text{ (Master builder)} \\
\textbf{R} \quad \textbf{O} \quad \textbf{D} \\
\underline{+15} \;=\; 15 \\
76 \qquad\qquad + \qquad \textbf{\textit{101}} \;=\; \textbf{\textit{177}}
\end{array}
$$

(New Messiah) (Higher octave of Christ)

The number 101 represents the Personality of the New Messiah and 177 represents the higher vibration of Christ. This reflects a bestowal of spiritual illumination upon the initiate by his/her inner angelic presence. It is an amulet of energy symbolizing the Motivation of Christ Consciousness and the Personality of the New Messiah.

> *And I will give* power *unto my two witnesses, and they shall prophecy a thousand two hundred* and *threescore days, clothed in sackcloth.*
> *These are the two olive trees, and the two candlesticks standing before the God of the earth.*
> Rev. 11:3-4

There are a number of references to high spiritual energies within these two verses.

```
            A
  1   =     1
            20+  8        +    19  +   14+  4          =    65
            T    H   O    U    S    A    N    D
  37  =               15+  21  +   1
            20+  23                                    =    43
            T    W    O
  15  =               15
            8    +    14+  4+   18  +   4               =    48
            H    U    N    D    R    E    D                      } 74
  26  =          21        +    5                                (Messiah)
                 14+  4                                =    18
            A    N    D
  1   =     1
            20+  8+   18        +    19+  3   +   18    =    86  (Pyramid)
            T    H    R    E    E    S    C    O    R    E
  30  =               5+   5   +         15  +   5
            4    +    25+  19                           =   +48
            D    A    Y    S
  +1  =     1
  111                                                       308  (Noah)
(Individual
Word Power)


            19   +    3+   11+  3+   12  +    20+  8    =   76
            S    A    C    K    C    L    O    T    H
            1         +              15             =   +16
                                                           92
                                                  (Maitreya Buddha)
```

The unfolding process within each spiritual aspirant is that of the achievement of Christ Consciousness. In Rev. 11:3, the time period of 1,260 days is mentioned in this verse. Again, this is a symbolic representation of a very high-powered spiritual energy consisting of the Noah vibration merging with the Christ energy resulting in an illumined perspective.

The wearing apparel (sackcloth) is the same vibration of the Maitreya (the New Age Christ).

```
            13   +         20 + 18  +   25       =   76
            M    A    I    T    R    E    Y    A
                 1+   9    +         5   +    1   =  +16
                                                      92
```

*And if any man will hurt them, fire proceedeth out of*
*their mouth, and devoureth their enemies: and if any man*
*will hurt them, he must in this manner be killed.*

Rev. 11:5

```
                    14+  4              =   18
              A     N    D
    1    =    1
                    6                   =   6
              I     F
    9    =    9
                    14+  25             =   39
              A     N    Y
    1    =    1
                    13 + 14             =   27
              M     A    N
    1    =    1
                    23 + 12+ 12         =   47
              W     I    L    L
    9    =    9
                    8  + 18+ 20         =   46
              H     U    R    T
   21    =         21
                    20+ 8  +  13        =  +41
              T     H    E    M
   +5    =          5                   (2nd octave of Thoth)
   47              +                    224   =   271
(Merging of Heart & Mind)              (Spear of Longinus)
```

The Spear of Longinus refers to the spear used by the Roman soldier, Gaius Cassius, or Longinus, who was given the task of ensuring that Christ had died at the crucifixion. His spear was one which was said to have been perpetually sharp and to have never rusted, and legend has it that the spear drew "blood and water" (St. John 19:34-37) out of the lifeless body of Jesus Christ (recall that a dead body does not bleed) which was considered a miracle. It was at this moment that Gaius Cassius converted to Christianity and his spear, the Spear of Longinus, became the Holy Lance or the Spear of Destiny. An interesting feature of the decoding process is that the verses many times have to be looked at in segments to find the symbolism. This is not unusual to a symbologist as it is understood that symbolism is represented in concepts, not in the words themselves.

> *These have power to shut heaven, that it rain not in the days of their prophecy: and have power over waters to turn them to blood, and to smite the earth with all plagues, as often as they will.*
> *And when they shall have finished their testimony, the beast that ascendeth out of the bottomless pit shall make war against them, and shall overcome them, and kill them.*
>
> Rev. 11:6-7

                              14+4           =    18
                        **A N D**
                1   =   1
                        8  + 22           =    30
                        **H A V E**
                6   =   1 + 5
                        16 + 23  + 18     =    57
     *77*  {              **P O W E R**
  (Christ)     20   =   15   + 5
                        22 + 18           =    *40*  (Buddha)
     *60*  {              **O V E R**
   (Word)     20   =   15 + 5
                        23 + 20 +  18+19   =   +80
     *86*  {              **W A T E R S**
(Pyramid; Arthur)   +6   =        1  + 5
                53                        *225* (Nov. 11, 1949)

The combined energies of Christ, Word and Pyramid/Arthur in one verse suggests the potential of religions and nations working together.  The anonymous author(s) of Revelation represented a catalyst for a new future, one that will be realized in our time.

                20                        =    20
                **T    O**
        15   =        15
                20    +    18+  14        =    52
                **T    U    R    N**
        21   =        2 1
                20+ 8    +    13          =    41
                **T    H    E    M**
        5    =        5
                20                        =    20
                **T    O**
        15   =        15
                2+  12       +    4       =    +18
                **B    L    O    O    D**
        +30  =        15+  15
         *86*                                  *151*
(Pyramid, Arthur)        (Lord of Hosts, Jesus Christ, Holy Spirit, etc.)

This phrase carries the energy of 151, which we have seen many times throughout the Revelation text.  The term Holy Spirit expresses the principle of 151.  Adding the energies of the Pyramid and Arthur to the higher energy of the Holy Spirit increases the power of the vibration of this phrase.

```
            20 + 8                                              =    28
            T    H    E
   5   =              5
            2      +      19 + 20                               =    41
            B    E    A    S    T
   6   =         5 + 1
            20 + 8   +   20                                     =    48
            T    H    A    T
   1   =    1
            19 + 3   +   14 + 4   +   20 + 8    =    68
            A    S    C    E    N    D    E    T    H
  11   =    1     +     5     +     5
                         20                                     =    20
            O    U    T
  36   =    15 + 21
                         6                                      =    +6
            O    F
  +15  =    15                                  (The Ark of the Covenant)
  74  (Messiah)                                          211
```

"The beast that ascendeth out of" is an important phrase as it relates to the Ark of the Covenant. The modern Ark of the Covenant is our covenant with our individual destiny, and is combined with the Messiah vibration, representing the search for the purpose of service on the earth plane.

> *And they of the people and kindreds and tongues and*
> *nations shall see their dead bodies three days and an half,*
> *and shall not suffer their dead bodies to be put in graves.*
>
> Rev. 11:9

```
            19+ 8    +    12+ 12                  =    51  (Michael)
            S    H    A    L    L
   1   =              1
            19                                    =    19
            S    E    E
  10   =         5+   5
            20+ 8    +         18                 =    46
            T    H    E    I    R
  14   =         5+   9
            4    +         4                      =    8
            D    E    A    D
   6   =         5+   1
            2    +    4    +         19           =    +25
            B    O    D    I    E    S
  +29  =         15   +    9+   5                    (Spear of Destiny)
  60                      +                 149      =    209
 (Word)                             (Higher octave of Capstone)
```

The overlighting energy of Michael is an integral part of the Personality (the higher octave of the Capstone) of this phrase. Combined with the energy of "the Word" as its Motivation, this phrase is an Expression of the Spear of Destiny, also called the Spear of Longinus referred to earlier.

According to the records of the Essene Order Jesus did not die on the cross as has long been believed. During the 18-year period between Jesus' twelfth and thirtieth years, he traveled and studied at the feet of the Masters of various traditions. While in Egypt he learned how to withdraw the conscious mind from the physical body at will. This was part of his initiation into the Mysteries at the Great Pyramid, where he took the name of Issa. The technique, known as suspended animation, was used by Jesus during his crucifixion on Mt. Golgotha.

|  |  | 14 + 4 |  |  | = | 18 |
|  |  | **A** **N** **D** |  |  |  |  |
| 1 | = | 1 |  |  |  |  |
|  |  | 7 + 18 + | 20 |  | = | 45 |
|  |  | **G** **R** **E** **A** **T** |  |  |  |  |
| 6 | = | 5+1 |  |  |  |  |
|  |  | 6 + | 18 |  | = | 24 |
|  |  | **F** **E** **A** **R** |  |  |  |  |
| 6 | = | 5+1 |  |  |  |  |
|  |  | 6 + 12+ 12 |  |  | = | 30 |
|  |  | **F** **E** **L** **L** |  |  |  |  |
| 5 | = | 5 |  |  |  |  |
|  |  | 16 + 14 |  |  | = | 30 |
|  |  | **U** **P** **O** **N** |  |  |  |  |
| 36 | = | 21 + 15 |  |  |  |  |
|  |  | 20+ 8 + 13 |  |  | = | +41 |
|  |  | **T** **H** **E** **M** |  |  |  |  |
| +5 | = |  | 5 |  |  | (Master Mystic) |
| 59 |  |  | + |  | **188** = | **247** |

(Year of Jesus' Ascension
in Great Pyramid)

The number 247, the Expression of this phrase, represents the age that Jesus attained in his earthly life. Here is an example of how sacred truth is hidden in the text of religious works, a practice that was undertaken to preserve the true history of our spiritual traditions.

> *And the same hour was there a great earthquake, and*
> *the tenth part of the city fell, and in the earthquake were*
> *slain of men seven thousand: and the remnant were*
> *affrighted, and gave glory to the God of heaven.*

Rev. 11:13

In this verse, in the phrase "And the same hour was there," the symbolism related to Thomas Jefferson is present. Thomas Jefferson, author of the Declaration of Independence, symbolizes the power to be, feel and speak our truth. His writing this document, in effect, freed a nation.

|  |  | 20+ | 8 |  |  |  | = | 28 |
|  |  | **T** | **H** | **E** |  |  |  |  |
|  | 5 = |  |  | 5 |  |  |  |  |
|  |  | 19 | + | 13 |  |  | = | 32 |
|  |  | **S** | **A** | **M** | **E** |  |  |  |
|  | 6 = |  | 1 | + | 5 |  |  |  |
|  |  | 8 | + | 18 |  |  | = | 26 |
|  |  | **H** | **O** | **U** | **R** |  |  |  |
| (Thomas | **36** = |  | 15+ | 21 |  |  |  |  |
| Jefferson) |  | 23 | + | 19 |  |  | = | 42 |
|  |  | **W** | **A** | **S** |  |  |  |  |
|  | 1 = |  | 1 |  |  |  |  |  |
|  |  | 20+ | 8 | + | 18 |  | = | +46 |
|  |  | **T** | **H** | **E** | **R** | **E** |  |  |
|  | +10 = |  |  | 5 | + | 5 |  |  |
|  | 58 |  |  |  |  |  |  | **174** (Individual Messiah) |

Each time "earthquake" appears in Revelation, it represents a symbol the Messiah within each of us. The energy of Archangel Michael is also represented in the 11th verse, an expression of will power. This will power is directed toward abiding by the laws of the earth plane, such as following a discipline of right diet, exercise and selfless service.

|  |  | **A** |  |  |  |  |  |  |  |  |  |  |
|  | 1 = | 1 |  |  |  |  |  |  |  |  |  |  |
|  |  | 7 + | 18 | + |  | 20 |  |  |  |  | = | 45 |
| 51 { | **G** | **R** | **E** | **A** | **T** |  |  |  |  |  |  |  |
|  | 6 = |  | 5+ | 1 |  |  |  |  |  |  |  |  |
|  |  | 18 + | 20 + | 8 + | 17 | + |  | 11 |  | = | +74 (Messiah) |  |
|  | **E** | **A** | **R** | **T** | **H** | **Q** | **U** | **A** | **K** | **E** |  |  |
|  | +33 = | 5 + | 1 |  | + |  | 21 + | 1 | + | 5 |  |  |
|  | **40** |  |  |  |  |  |  |  |  | **119** |  |  |
|  | (Buddha) |  |  |  |  |  |  |  |  | (subconscious) |  |  |

51 = Michael    107 = Messiah

The word "earthquake" appears twice in this verse, emphasizing the importance of the principle which it represents. Not only that, but the Personality, Motivation and Expression of "a great earthquake" and "were slain of men" are identical, indicating that the principle represented by these two phrases are emphasized by Revelation's author(s) for some reason.

| (Michael) | | 23 | + | 18 | | = | 41 |
|---|---|---|---|---|---|---|---|
| *51*  { | | **W** | **E** | **R** | **E** | | |
| | 10  = | | 5 | + | 5 | | |
| (Master Leader) | | 19+ | 12 | + | 14 | = | 45 |
| *55*  { | | **S** | **L** | **A** | **I** | **N** | |
| | 10  = | | | 1+ | 9 | | |
| | | | 6 | | | = | 6 |
| | | **O** | **F** | | | | |
| | 15  = | 15 | | | | | |
| | | 13 | + | 14 | | = | +27 |
| | | **M** | **E** | **N** | | | |
| | +5  = | | 5 | | | | |
| | *40* | | | | | | *119* |
| | (Buddha) | | | | | | (subconscious) |

*And the nations were angry, and thy wrath is come, and
the time of the dead, that they should be judged, and that
thou shouldest give reward unto thy servants the prophets,
and to the saints, and them that fear thy name, small and
great; and shouldest destroy them which destroy the earth.*

Rev. 11:18

| | | 14 | + | 20 | | + | 14+ | 19 | | = | 67 |
|---|---|---|---|---|---|---|---|---|---|---|---|
| *92*  { | | **N** | **A** | **T** | **I** | **O** | **N** | **S** | | | |
| | 25  = | | 1 | + | 9+ | 15 | | | | | |
| | | 23 | + | 18 | | | | | | = | 41 |
| *51*  { | | **W** | **E** | **R** | **E** | | | | | | |
| | 10  = | | 5 | + | 5 | | | | | | |
| | | 14+ | 7+ | 18+ | 25 | | | | | = | +64 |
| | | **A** | **N** | **G** | **R** | **Y** | | | | | |
| | +1  = | 1 | | | | (Higher octave of the Star) | | | | | |
| | *36* | | + | | | | | | *172* | = | *208* |
| | (Return) | | | | | | | | | | (Lunar Cycle) |

92 = Maitreya Buddha      51 = Michael

Powerful and positive are two words that describe this verse.  The
energies of Michael and Maitreya Buddha are encoded along with the Return
of the Lunar Cycle and the higher octave of the Star within its text.

|  |  | 14+ 4 |  |  |  | = | 18 |
|---|---|---|---|---|---|---|---|
|  |  | **A N D** |  |  |  |  |  |
| 1 | = | 1 |  |  |  |  |  |
|  |  | 20+ 8 |  |  |  | = | 28 |
|  |  | **T H Y** |  |  |  |  |  |
| 25 | = | 25 |  |  |  |  |  |
|  |  | 23+ 18 | + | 20+ 8 |  | = | 69 |
|  |  | **W R A** | | **T H** |  |  |  |
| 1 | = | 1 |  |  |  |  |  |
|  |  | 19 |  |  |  | = | 19 |
|  |  | **I S** |  |  |  |  |  |
| 9 | = | 9 |  |  |  |  |  |
|  |  | 3 + 13 |  |  |  | = | +16 |
|  |  | **C O M E** |  |  |  |  |  |
| +20 | = | 15 + 5 |  |  |  |  | (God) |
| 56 |  | + |  |  | 150 | = | 206 |
| ("Light") |  |  |  | (The Devil —10th power) |  |  |  |

This phrase represents the merging of the "Devil" and the "Light" within us. In other words, this is the combining of the energies of past lifetime experience and the principle of the Light, which is information. Overcoming past-life karma and integrating the energy of the Light leads to the attainment of God consciousness.

> *And the temple of God was opened in heaven, and there was seen in his temple the ark of his testament; and there were lightnings, and voices, and thunderings, and an earthquake, and great hail.*
>
> Rev. 11:19

|  |  | 20+ 8 |  |  |  |  |  | = | 28 |
|---|---|---|---|---|---|---|---|---|---|
|  |  | **T H E** |  |  |  |  |  |  |  |
| 5 | = | 5 |  |  |  |  |  |  |  |
|  |  | 18+ 11 |  |  |  |  |  | = | 29 |
|  |  | **A R K** |  |  |  |  |  |  |  |
| 1 | = | 1 |  |  |  |  |  |  |  |
|  |  | 6 |  |  |  |  |  | = | 6 |
|  |  | **O F** |  |  |  |  |  |  |  |
| 15 | = | 15 |  |  |  |  |  |  |  |
|  |  | 8 + 19 |  |  |  |  |  | = | 27 |
|  |  | **H I S** |  |  |  |  |  |  |  |
| 9 | = | 9 |  |  |  |  |  |  |  |
|  |  | 20 + | 19+ 20 | + | 13 | + | 14+ 20 | = | +106 |
|  |  | **T E** | **S T** | | **A** | | **M E N T** |  |  |
| +11 | = | 5 + |  |  | 1 | + | 5 |  | (Julius Caesar) |
| **41 (Freedom)** |  |  |  |  |  |  | **196** |  |  |

Julius Caesar was the personification of the achievement of ultimate power on earth, in mundane terms. He failed the tests of this power and served as an example of the misuse of power to the rest of us. These tests are as follows:

1. Sex Test—This was his extra-marital relationship with Cleopatra. (He had a Roman wife at that time.)
2. Money Test—He used Roman money in commercial trade with Egypt without the approval of the Roman Senate.
3. Power Test—He adopted the title "Dictator of Rome" leading to his assassination on the Ides of March (March 15).

Brutus, who betrayed Caesar, was Caesar's "Judas." This is a representation of the Gnostic Christian crucifixion experience which occurs in the life of each initiate, usually manifesting on the mental and emotional level. This test is passed when we bless those who crucify us.

$$
\begin{array}{llllllllll}
 & & & 14+ & 4 & & & & & = & 18 \\
 & & & \textbf{A} & \textbf{N} & \textbf{D} & & & & & \\
1 & = & 1 & & & & & & & & \\
 & & & 20+ & 8 & + & 18 & & & & = & 46 \\
 & & & \textbf{T} & \textbf{H} & \textbf{E} & \textbf{R} & \textbf{E} & & & \\
10 & = & & & & 5 & + & 5 & & & \\
\text{(Michael)} & & & 23 & + & 18 & & & & = & 41 \\
51 \{ & & & \textbf{W} & \textbf{E} & \textbf{R} & \textbf{E} & & & & \\
10 & = & & & 5 & + & 5 & & & & \\
 & & & 12 & + & 7+ & 8+ & 20+ & 14 & + & 14+ & 7+ & 19 & = & \underline{+101} \\
 & & & \textbf{L} & \textbf{I} & \textbf{G} & \textbf{H} & \textbf{T} & \textbf{N} & \textbf{I} & \textbf{N} & \textbf{G} & \textbf{S} \\
\underline{+18} & = & 9 & + & 9 & & & & & & \\
39 & & & & & & & & & & \textbf{\textit{206}} \\
 & & & & & & & & & & \text{(God)}
\end{array}
$$

Here again appears the Michael energy and in relationship to the principle of God. This is another expression of these same energies we have seen throughout this chapter.

                                                      (Freedom of the Master Builder)

$$
\begin{array}{lllllllllll}
18 & + & & & & 104 & & & & & = & \textbf{122} \\
14+ & 4 & & 20+ & 8 & + & 14+ & 4 & + & 18 & + & 14+ & 7+ & 19 \\
\textbf{A} & \textbf{N} & \textbf{D} & \textbf{T} & \textbf{H} & \textbf{U} & \textbf{N} & \textbf{D} & \textbf{E} & \textbf{R} & \textbf{I} & \textbf{N} & \textbf{G} & \textbf{S} \\
1 & & & & 21 & & + & 5 & + & 9 & & & = & \underline{+36} \\
 & & & & & & & & & & & & & \textbf{\textit{139}} \\
 & & & & & & & & & & & & \text{(Cosmic Christ)}
\end{array}
$$

| 7+ | 18 | + | | 20 | | 8 | + | | 12 | = | 65 |
|----|----|---|---|----|---|---|---|---|----|---|----|
| **G** | **R** | **E** | **A** | **T** | | **H** | **A** | **I** | **L** | | |
| | | 5+ | 1 | | | | 1+ | 9 | | = | +16 |

**81** (Horus)

This phrase represents the return of the Cosmic Christ combined with the energy of Horus (the Egyptian Christ prototype). It is an expression of the achievement of higher awareness which gifts us with the vision to perform our work with humility, selflessness and love however grand or lowly it may seem.

# Appendix *XII*

## *The Hanged Man*

The vibration of the number 12 is that of transformation and the alignment and balance of light and shadow, which will take us to the next level of our evolution. The key verse in Revelation Chapter 12 is the first:

> *And there appeared a great wonder in heaven; a woman clothed with the sun, and the moon under her feet, and upon her head a crown of twelve stars:*

Rev. 12:1

```
         A
  1  =    1
         23   +   13   +   14              =    50
         W    O    M    A    N
 16  =        15   +    1
         3+   12   +   20+  8    +    4     =    47
         C    L    O    T    H    E    D
 20  =        15   +        5
         23   +   20+  8                    =    51 (Michael)
         W    I    T    H
  9  =        9
         20+  8                             =    28
         T    H    E
  5  =        5
         19   +   14                        =    +33 (Highest degree
         S    U    N                                 of Masonry)
+21  =        21
  72                                             209
(Resurrection of the Feminine)                  (Spear of Destiny)
```

This verse has already been discussed at length in Chapter 7 of this book, but its significant numerological features bear repeating. Most significantly, this phrase indicates that mastery will not be achieved unless we operate from our heart center. And its key component, the personality of the phrase vibrates to the energy of the Spear of Destiny. The Spear of Destiny symbolizes our awakening to service in a spiritual sense. The image of a female figure radiating the light of the sun is an expression of the feminine principle serving through nurturing. And within that image is the motivation of the resurrection of the feminine. Also inherent within this phrase is the highest degree attainable in Masonry, the 33rd degree, symbolizing mastery.

The phrase, "And the moon under her feet" bears the motivation of Christ Consciousness, an expression for the opening of the seven male and seven female chakras. The moon represents the subconscious mind and it is placed "under her feet" to symbolize her mastery of her subconscious.

```
                        14+  4                        =    18
                 A      N    D
        1   =    1
                        20+  8                         =   28
                 T      H    E
        5   =            5
                        13        +  14                =    27
                 M      O    O    N
        30  =           15+  15
                        14+  4    +   18               =   36 (Return)
                 U      N    D    E    R
(God)   26  =    21          +   5
                 8      +   18                          =   26 (God)
                 H      E    R
        5   =            5
                 6           +   20                     =   +26 (God)
                 F      E    E    T
       +10  =           5+   5
        77                                                 161
```
(Christ Consciousness)

Further examination of the Revelation 12:1 verse reveals even more remarkable energies operating in this coded text, energies which bear a promise for Earth's people. Encoded within this phrase are the energies of the Sphinx (90) and the symbolism of the number of critical mass (144,000). In this case this number (144) does not refer to the number of people, but symbolizes Abraham who was the father of many nations. It was upon him that the mantle of the covenant was bestowed to assure humanity that it would not have to endure another cataclysm like the biblical flood. The Sphinx is a symbol of power and represents the evolution of humanity.

Also part of this combination of energies are the vibrations of the Return (36), Christ Consciousness (77), God (26) and Buddha (40). This collection of powerful symbols merely underscores the importance of this verse.

```
                      14+  4                    =   18
                   A   N   D
        1   =   1
                      16   +   14               =   40
                   U   P   O   N
       36   =  21   +   15
                   8   +   18                    =   26
                   H   E   R
        5   =       5
                   8   +        4                =   12
                   H   E   A   D
        6   =       5+  1

                   A
        1   =   1
                   3+  18   +   23+ 14           =   58
                   C   R   O   W   N
       15   =               15
                       6                         =   6
                   O   F
       15   =  15
                   20+ 23   +   12+ 22           =   77
                   T   W   E   L   V   E
       10   =           5   +       5
                   19+ 20   +   18+ 19           =  +76
                   S   T   A   R   S
       +1   =           1
       90                                           313
```

*144*
(Abraham)

(The Sphinx)

The highly significant energies continue throughout this chapter, for example in the next verse, we find evidence of universal archetypes.

*And she being with child cried, travailing in birth, and pained to be delivered.*

Rev. 12:2

```
          20+ 18  +   22   +        12  +  14+ 7   =    93
           T   R   A    V    A    I    L    I    N   G
 20  =             1   +   1+  9   +   9
                  14                                 =    14
           I   N
  9  =      9
                   2   +  18+ 20+ 8                   =   +48
           B   I   R    T    H
 +9  =      9
 38                                                       155
(Noah)                                         (Lincoln Power #)
```

Two powerful historical prototypes are present in this verse: Lincoln, who preserved freedom in the United States and Noah, who preserved the remnants of civilization at the time of the flood. This verse represents the "travail" of preserving by birthing freedom for humanity.

```
(Lord)        16         +  14  +  4                =    34
 49 {                P    A    I    N    E    D
  15  =              1+   9   +   5
                    20                               =    20
                     T    O
  15  =             15
                     2                               =    2
                     B    E
   5  =              5
                     4   +  12  +  22  +  18  +  4   =   +60
                     D    E    L    I    V    E   R   E   D
 +24  =              5   +   9   +   5   +   5
 59                              +                        116  =   175
                                               (Office of the Christ)
```

The word "pained" represents the same energy as "Lord." The Lord (our Christed Light Body) is delivered by immaculate conception. We then share as co-holders the office of the Christ (Group Avatar) with other Christ-conscious souls on the planet.

# Appendix *XIII*

## *Death*

The number 13 represents the principle of love projected wherever personal energy is directed. This is represented by the twelve forces encircling a singular powerful entity. *Mem* is the 13th letter of the Hebrew alphabet, representing the feminine/Mother mystery. The processes symbolized by this mystery include birth, death, sublimation and transfiguration. The Book of Revelation is keyed to the completion of this feminine four-fold process as symbolized by the vision of the "woman clothed with the sun."

The 13th chapter is a turning point in consciousness as the initiate is symbolized as having committed to achieving his/her destiny. Key planetary figures in history have symbolized the number 13: Hercules, Arthur and Jesus. As they spearheaded the spiritual adventure, the door to higher consciousness is open to us.

The terminology of the first two verses (13:1 and 13:2) symbolizes the ultimate potential lying within each individual. The encoding of terms like "Spear of Destiny," "Maitreya Buddha," "the New Messiah," "Michael" and "the World Teacher" are prototypal goals for which the initiate must strive in search of self-mastery. These are just some of the energies we find hidden within these verses. The following examples and analyses illustrate this point:

> *And I stood upon the sand of the sea, and saw a beast rise up out of the sea, having seven heads and ten horns, and upon his horns ten crowns, and upon his heads the name of blasphemy.*
>
> Rev. 13:1

```
                14+ 4                    =   18
                A   N   D
1   =   1

                I
9   =   9
                19 + 20   +    4         =   43
                S   T   O   O   D
30  =                15 + 15
                     16  +  14           =   30
                U   P   O   N
36  =   21  +   15
                20+ 8                    =   28
                T   H   E
5   =                5
                19  +  14+ 4            =   37
                S   A   N   D
1   =            1
                     6                   =   6
                O   F
15  =   15
                20+ 8                    =   28
                T   H   E
5   =                5
                19                       =   +19
                S   E   A
+6  =            5 + 1
108                                      209
(altruism)                          (Spear of Destiny)
```

```
                8   +   22  +  14+ 7     =   51 (Michael)
                H   A   V   I   N   G
10  =               1   +   9
                19  +   22  +   14       =   55
                S   E   V   E   N
10  =               5   +   5
                8   +       4+ 19        =   +31
                H   E   A   D   S
+6  =               5+  1
26                                           137
(God)
```

|  | (Christ Consciousness) | | (Master Communicator) | |
|---|---|---|---|---|
| 34 | + | 77 | = | *111* |

| 20 | + | 14 | 3+ | 18 | + | 23+ | 14+ | 19 |
|----|---|----|----|----|---|-----|-----|----|
| **T** | | **E** | **N** | **C** | **R** | **O** | **W** | **N** | **S** |

| 5 | + | 15 | = | +20 |
|---|---|----|---|-----|

*131* (Freedom)

The Spear of Destiny and the principle of altruism are key energies in verse 13;1, especially as the energy of Michael and God, Christ Consciousness and the Master Communicator combined with Freedom are encoded in the same context. This is the esoteric definition of the Group Avatar and the calling for which it is being birthed.

> *And the beast which I saw was like unto a leopard, and*
> *his feet were as the feet of a bear; and his mouth was as the*
> *mouth of a lion, and the dragon gave him his power.*

Rev. 13:2

| 23 | + | 19 | | = | 42 |
|----|---|----|---|---|----|
| **W** | | **A** | **S** | | |

| 1 | = | | 1 | | |
|---|---|---|---|---|---|

| 12 | + | 11 | | = | 23 |
|----|---|----|---|---|----|
| **L** | | **I** | **K** | **E** | |

| 9 | = | | 9 | | |
|---|---|---|---|---|---|

| 14+ | 20 | | = | 34 |
|-----|----|---|---|----|
| **U** | **N** | **T** | **O** | |

| 36 | = | 21 | + | 15 |
|----|---|----|---|----|

**A**

| 1 | = | 1 | |
|---|---|---|---|

| 12 | + | 16 | + | 18+ | 4 | = | +50 |
|----|---|----|---|-----|---|---|-----|
| **L** | **E** | **O** | **P** | **A** | **R** | **D** |

| +21 | = | 5+ | 15 | + | 1 |
|-----|---|----|----|---|---|
| *68* | | | | | *149* |

(Embodied Christ Consciousness)                          (The New Messiah)

|  |  |  | (Pyramid, Arthur) | |
|---|---|---|---|---|
| 18 | + | 27 | + | 41 | = | *86* |

| 14+ | 4 | 8 | + | 19 | 13 | + | 20+ | 8 |
|-----|---|---|---|----|----|---|-----|---|
| **A** | **N** | **D** | **H** | **I** | **S** | **M** | **O** | **U** | **T** | **H** |

| 1 | + | 9 | + | 15+ | 21 | = | +46 |
|---|---|---|---|-----|----|---|-----|

*132*

(The World Teacher)

```
                          19              =    19
                    A     S
       1   =   1
                    20+   8              =    28
                    T     H     E
       5   =   5
                    13          +   20+  8    =    41
                    M     O     U     T     H
      36   =        15+   21
                          6              =    6
                    O     F
      15   =   15

                    A
       1   =   1
                    12          +   14       =   +26
                    L     I     O     N
     +24   =        9+    15
      82                                   120
                          (Archangel Michael, Sanat Kumara)
                                            (Davidic Covenant)
     18     +         28      +          43           =     89
     14+  4         20+   8         4+   18   +   7   +   14
   A  N   D      T    H    E     D    R    A    G    O    N
   1       +              5   +          1    +   15      =   +22
                                                            111
      22 = Master Builder                  (Master Communicator)
```

In addition to the numerological symbolism encoded within Rev. 13:2 outlined above (the energies in bold type), the lion, bear and dragon which appear in this verse are symbolic of the higher spiritual principles of courage, resurrection, and wisdom, respectively.

> *Here is wisdom. Let him that hath understanding count*
> *the number of the beast; for it is the number of a man, and*
> *his number is six hundred three score and six.*
>
> Rev. 13:18

This single verse has been misinterpreted so often that the number 666 has taken on a perverse connotation. The author(s) of Revelation encoded this particular verse with higher meaning known only to the initiated. The number 666 actually represents the crowning accomplishment of complete acceptance of responsibility on the physical, mental, emotional and spiritual levels. (See Chapter 6)

|        |   | 14 | + | 13+ | 2 | + | 18 | = | 47 |
|--------|---|----|---|-----|---|---|----|---|----|
|        |   | **N** | **U** | **M** | **B** | **E** | **R** | | |
| 26 | = | | 21 | | + | 5 | | | |
|        |   | 6 | | | | | | = | 6 |
|        |   | **O** | **F** | | | | | | |
| 15 | = | 15 | | | | | | | |
|        |   | 20+ | 8 | | | | | = | 28 |
|        |   | **T** | **H** | **E** | | | | | |
| 5 | = | | | 5 | | | | | |
|        |   | 2 | | + | 19+ | 20 | | = | +41 |
|        |   | **B** | **E** | **A** | **S** | **T** | | | |

+6  =        5+  1                                    (Thomas Jefferson)

52                          +              *122*  =  *174*

(Freedom of the feminine                  (Individualized Master Builder)
leading to illumination)


|        |   | 6 | + | 18 | | = | 24 |
|--------|---|---|---|----|---|---|----|
|        |   | **F** | **O** | **R** | | | |
| 15 | = | | 15 | | | | |
|        |   | | 20 | | | = | 20 |
|        |   | **I** | **T** | | | | |
| 9 | = | 9 | | | | | |
|        |   | | 19 | | | = | 19 |
|        |   | **I** | **S** | | | | |
| 9 | = | 9 | | | | | |
|        |   | 20+ | 8 | | | = | 28 |
|        |   | **T** | **H** | **E** | | | |
| 5 | = | | | 5 | | | |
|        |   | 14 | + | 13+ | 2 | + | 18 | = | 47 |
|        |   | **N** | **U** | **M** | **B** | **E** | **R** |
| 26 | = | | 21 | + | | 5 | | |
|        |   | 6 | | | | | | = | 6 |
|        |   | **O** | **F** | | | | |
| 15 | = | 15 | | | | | |
|        |   | **A** | | | | | |
| 1 | = | 1 | | | | | |
|        |   | 13 | + | 14 | | = | +27 |
|        |   | **M** | **A** | **N** | | | |

+1  =        1

81                                          171

(Personality of Sphinx, Horus)            (Thoth, Moses)


Several famous personages are hidden within this oft-quoted verse. Thoth, representing "thought," the Personality of Sphinx, or the Egyptian expression of the Beast, and Horus, the Egyptian Christ figure. The energy of Thomas Jefferson also appears representing the principle of freedom.

# APPENDIX *XIV*

## *Temperance*

*And I looked and lo, a lamb stood on the Mount Sion
and with him an hundred forty and four thousand, having
his father's name written in their foreheads.*

Rev. 14:1

This verse evokes the energy of Buddha which potentially resides within each individual. The creative principle symbolized by the 1:12 ratio is also part of the energy of this verse.

|       |   | **A** |   |      |    |   |      |
|-------|---|-------|---|------|----|---|------|
| 1     | = | 1     |   |      |    |   |      |
|       |   | 12    | + | 13+  | 2  | = | 27   |
|       |   | **L** | **A** | **M** | **B** | | |
| 1     | = | 1     |   |      |    |   |      |
|       |   | 19+   | 20 | +   | 4  | = | 43   |
|       |   | **S** | **T** | **O** | **O** | **D** | |
| 30    | = |       |   | 15 + 15 | | | |
|       |   | 14    |   |      |    | = | 14   |
|       |   | **O** | **N** | | | | |
| 15    | = | 15    |   |      |    |   |      |
|       |   | 20+   | 8 |      |    | = | 28   |
|       |   | **T** | **H** | **E** | | | |
| 5     | = |       |   | 5    |    |   |      |
|       |   | 13    | + | 14+  | 20 | = | 47   |
|       |   | **M** | **O** | **U** | **N** | **T** | |
| 36    | = |       | 15+ | 21 | | | |
|       |   | 19    | + | 14   |    | = | +33  |
|       |   | **S** | **I** | **O** | **N** | | |
| +24   | = | 9+    | 15 |      |    |   |      |
| *112* |   |       |   |      |    |   | *192* |
| (World Creative Principle) | | | | | | | (Buddha) |

The phrase "and with him" is a seemingly insignificant one until we examine its numerological meaning. It contains within it the dynamic motivation of the Sun, the personality and the expressive nature of the Sphinx which reside within each person as a potentiality.

```
                                                              (The Sphinx)
         18        +        51              +        21      =    90
         14+ 4            23  +  20+ 8            8   +   13
     A   N   D         W   I    T   H          H   I    M    (The Sun)
     1             +        9               +        9       =   +19
                                                                 109
                                                     (Higher octave of the Sun)
```

The expression,""having his father's name" reveals the powerful relationship of the Sun and the Moon, the balance between our male and female natures.

```
              8   +   22   +   14+ 7        =    51
              H    A    V    I    N   G
     10  =         1   +   9
              8   +   19                    =    27
              H    I    S
      9  =         9
              6   +   20+ 8   +   18+ 19    =    72
              F    A    T   H    E   R'  S
      6  =         1        +   5
              14  +   13                    =   +27      (The moon
              N    A    M   E                            reflecting the
     +6  =         1   +   5                             Sun's light)
     31                         +               177  =  208
                                     (Individual Christ Consciousness)
```

In addition, the author(s) encoded the energy of Horus (the Egyptian Christ prototype) and the Word into this verse:

```
         46              +                   55              =   101
     20+ 8   +       18       6   +   18  +   8   +       4+  19
     T   H   E   I   R        F    O   R   E   H   E   A   D   S
         5+  9           +        15  +   5   +   5+  1       =    40
         +14                          +26                    (Buddha)
         60   (Word)                  81   (Horus)
```

*And there followed another angel saying, "Babylon is fallen, is fallen, that great city, because she made all nations drink of the wine of the wrath of her fornication."*

Rev. 14:8

The number 148 is an occult representation of the Pyramid which appears on the back of the U.S. one dollar bill; it consists of 48 stones and one that is missing, the capstone. This symbol is an esoteric representation of the link between the destiny of the United States and the Pyramid (of Egyptian origin) as well as the Eagle (a symbol of Israel) and the role these nations have played in the quest for peace. The two sons of Abraham, Ishmael (the Arab nation) and Isaac (the Jewish patriarch) are the source of the enmity that has persisted for thousands of years between these two nations which has yet to be resolved.

|  |  | 19 | + | 25 | + | 14+ | 7 |  |  | = | 65 |
|---|---|---|---|---|---|---|---|---|---|---|---|
|  |  | **S** | **A** | **Y** | **I** | **N** | **G,** |  |  |  |  |
| 10 | = |  | 1 | + | 9 |  |  |  |  |  |  |
|  |  | 2 | + | 2+ | 25+ | 12 | + | 14 |  | = | 55 |
|  |  | **B** | **A** | **B** | **Y** | **L** | **O** | **N** |  |  |  |
| 16 | = |  | 1 |  | + |  | 15 |  |  |  |  |
|  |  |  | 19 |  |  |  |  |  |  | = | 19 |
|  |  | **I** | **S** |  |  |  |  |  |  |  |  |
| 9 | = | 9 |  |  |  |  |  |  |  |  |  |
|  |  | 6 | + | 12+ | 12 | + | 14 |  |  | = | +44 |
|  |  | **F** | **A** | **L** | **L** | **E** | **N** |  |  |  |  |
| +6 | = |  | 1 |  | + | 5 |  |  |  |  | (Spear of Destiny) |
| 41 |  |  |  | + |  |  |  |  |  | 183 | = | *209* |

Here, again, we find the energy of the Spear of Longinus encoded in this chapter, as we have found in so many others. This energy represents the divine spiritual power given to the Group Avatar. Its symbolism includes peace, prosperity and world healing which are accomplished through the conscious (speech), subconscious (habitual) and superconscious (prayer). The avatar uses the energy of the Spear of Longinus to achieve healing on the planetary level through use of these three aspects of human nature.

The phrase "of her fornication" interpreted literally would appear to represent at the least an immoral act. When we examine it under the light of numerological analysis it represents an entirely different principle. The Personality of this phrase carries the same energy as "The Messiah," and the Motivation of the word "fornication" (its vowels) is equivalent to the Expression of "Lord."

|  |  | 6 |  |  |  |  |  |  |  |  | = | 6 |
|---|---|---|---|---|---|---|---|---|---|---|---|---|
|  |  | **O** | **F** |  |  |  |  |  |  |  |  |  |
| 15 | = | 15 |  |  |  |  |  |  |  |  |  |  |
|  |  | 8 | + | 18 |  |  |  |  |  |  | = | 26 |
|  |  | **H** | **E** | **R** |  |  |  |  |  |  |  |  |
| 5 | = | 5 |  |  |  |  |  |  |  |  |  |  |
|  |  | 6 | + | 18+ | 14 | + | 3 | + | 20 | + | 14 | = +75 |
| (Lord) |  | **F** | **O** | **R** | **N** | **I** | **C** | **A** | **T** | **I** | **O** | **N** |
| + *49* | = | 15 |  | + | 9 | + | 1 | + | 9+ | 15 |  | (The Messiah) |
| 69 |  |  |  |  |  |  |  |  |  |  |  | *107* |

# APPENDIX XV

## The Devil

*And I saw another sign in heaven, great and marvelous,*
*seven angels having the seven last plagues, for in them is*
*filled up the wrath of God.*

Rev. 15:1

Throughout my analysis of Revelation I was aware of the frequency in which the word "and" appears in the text. "And" is a coordinating conjunction used often in biblical text to introduce a sentence to emphasize the statement being made. (See *Appendix VI* for a discussion of the significance of "and.") For our purposes, at times, dropping the introductory conjunction offers a more concise interpretation of the material, and in no way detracts from the meaning of the phrase being analyzed. My analyses throughout the Book of Revelation reflect this alternate approach to interpretation.

|  |  | **I** |  |  |  |  |  |  |
|---|---|---|---|---|---|---|---|---|
| 9 | = | 9 |  |  |  |  |  |  |
|  |  | 19 | + | 23 |  |  | = | 42 |
|  |  | **S** | **A** | **W** |  |  |  |  |
| 1 | = | 1 |  |  |  |  |  |  |
|  |  | 14 | + | 20 + 8 | + | 18 | = | 60 |
|  |  | **A** | **N** | **O** | **T** | **H** | **E** | **R** |
| 21 | = | 1 | + | 15 | + | 5 |  |  |
|  |  | 19 | + | 7 + 14 |  |  | = | 40 |
|  |  | **S** | **I** | **G** | **N** |  |  |  |
| 9 | = | 9 |  |  |  |  |  |  |
|  |  | 14 |  |  |  |  | = | 14 |
|  |  | **I** | **N** |  |  |  |  |  |
| 9 | = | 9 |  |  |  |  |  |  |
|  |  | 8 | + | 22 | + | 14 | = | +44 |
|  |  | **H** | **E** | **A** | **V** | **E** | **N** |  |
| +11 | = | 5 + 1 | + | 5 |  |  |  |  |
| **60** |  |  | + |  |  | 160 | = | **220** |
| (Word) |  |  |  |  |  |  |  | (Master builder) |

The phrase "I saw another sign in Heaven" represents the emergence of the power of the feminine through the Word—speech, thought, prayer, and action—as the feminine is integrated as a new dynamic within humanity.

Julius Caesar represents karma related to the power and sex tests which he failed in terms of his relationship with Cleopatra. This energy keeps cropping up throughout the Revelation text, perhaps as a reminder of the importance of wise decision-making as our deeds performed in this life will have repercussions throughout all earthly lifetimes. The following phrase is a representation of this energy:

```
            7+   18   +        20                    =    45
            G    R    E    A   T
    6    =            5+   1
            14+  4                              =    18
            A    N    D
    1    =  1
            13   +   18+  22   +   12   +        19   =   +84
            M    A    R    V    E    L    O    U   S            (Julius
    +42  =       1    +        5    +   15+  21                 Caesar)
    49                             +              147  =   196
    (Capstone)                         (Merging of Heart and Mind)
```

The two words "last plagues" represent the energies of the Sun in a philanthropic sense used to achieve the consciousness of the Egyptian Horus principle, and within the personality of the phrase is the energy of Michael.

```
    (Michael)
        51            +                54              =   105
    12  +  19+  20        16+  12   +   7    +        19
    L   A   S   T        P    L    A    G    U    E   S
        1             +                1    +   21+  5      =   +28
                                                            133
            (Higher octave of 33rd degree of Masonry)
```

The number 36 is an important one in numerology. Wherever it shows up in an analysis it represents the return of something. In the phrase "the wrath of God," 36 is the vibration of its Motivation.

```
    28        +            69        +        6    +        11   =   114
    20+  8            23+  18   +   20+  8             6        7    +   4
    T    H    E       W    R    A    T    H        O    F       G    O    D
         5    +                1             +   15        +    15   =   +36
                                                                      150
            70  (Illumined intellect; 10th power)
            36 = Return      114 = Saint Michael
```

The number 150 represents the 10th power of independence and freedom leading to responsibility. This symbolizes the individual taking responsibility on all levels, and the word "wrath" is the energy of the 10th power of illumined intellect.

> *And the temple was filled with smoke from the glory of God, and from his power, and no man was able to enter into the temple till the seven plagues of the seven angels were fulfilled.*

> Rev. 15.:8

```
             14+  4                              =   18
          A    N    D
  1   =   1
             20+  8                              =   28
          T    H    E
  5   =             5
             20  +  13+  16+  12                 =   61
          T    E    M    P    L    E
  10  =             5         +         5
             23  +  19                           =   42
          W    A    S
  1   =             1
             6   +  12+  12  +   4               =   34
          F    I    L    L    E    D
  14  =             9         +   5
             23  +  20+  8                        =   51
          W    I    T    H
  9   =             9
             19+  13  +   11                      =   +43
          S    M    O    K    E
  +20  =            15  +   5
  60                                                277
 (Word)                              (2nd stage of Christ return)
```

This is a powerful phrase symbolizing that the Motivation of the Word combined with the second stage of the Christ return (the unity of religions, nations and peoples) will take humanity one step closer to manifesting heaven on earth.

```
                    6+   18   +   13      =    37
                    F    R        O   M
        15   =                        15
                    20+  8                   =    28
                    T    H    E
         5   =                         5
                    7+   12   +   18+ 25   =    62
                    G    L        O   R   Y
        15   =                        15
                              6              =    6
                    O    F
        15   =      15
                    7    +    4           =    +11
                    G    O    D
       +15   =      15                          (Spear of Destiny)
        65                    +          144   =   209
 (Balance of Freedom &Responsibility)   (Master Builder of Philanthropy)
```

Here again appears the Spear of Destiny.  In this case, the energy of the Master Builder of philanthropy and the balance between Freedom and Responsibility will lead to the achievement of the energy represented by the Spear of Destiny.

```
                    20                       =    20
                    T    O
        15   =      15
                    14+  20   +   18         =    52
                    E    N    T    E    R
        10   =      5    +    5
                    14+  20                  =    34
                    I    N    T    O
        24   =      9    +         15
                    20+  8                    =    28
                    T    H    E
         5   =                     5
                    20   +    13+ 16+ 12      =    +61
                    T    E    M    P    L    E
       +10   =      5    +              5
        64 *                                       195
```

* The number 64 is the energy of "Southeastern France," where La ValDieu and Rennes le Chateau are located.  These places are the historical home of the Cathars and the Knights Templar.  The author(s) of the Book of Revelation were sensitive to the universal nature of spirituality and reflected this sensitivity in encoding themes from many locations and traditions within its text.

|  |  | 6 |  |  |  |  |  |  |  | = | 6 |
|---|---|---|---|---|---|---|---|---|---|---|---|
|  |  | **O** | **F** |  |  |  |  |  |  |  |  |
| 15 | = | 15 |  |  |  |  |  |  |  |  |  |
|  |  | 20+ | 8 |  |  |  |  |  |  | = | 28 |
|  |  | **T** | **H** | **E** |  |  |  |  |  |  |  |
| 5 | = |  |  | 5 |  |  |  |  |  |  |  |
|  |  | 19 | + | 22 | + | 14 |  |  |  | = | 55 |
|  |  | **S** | **E** | **V** | **E** | **N** |  |  |  |  |  |
| 10 | = |  |  | 5 | + | 5 |  |  |  |  |  |
|  |  | 14+ | 7 | + | 12+ | 19 |  |  |  | = | 52 |
|  |  | **A** | **N** | **G** | **E** | **L** | **S** |  |  |  |  |
| 6 | = | 1 |  | + | 5 |  |  |  |  |  |  |
|  |  | 23 | + | 18 |  |  |  |  |  | = | 41 |
|  |  | **W** | **E** | **R** | **E** |  |  |  |  |  |  |
| 10 | = |  | 5 | + | 5 |  |  |  |  |  |  |
|  |  | 6 | + | 12+ | 6 | + | 12+ | 12 | + | 4 | = | +52 |
|  |  | **F** | **U** | **L** | **F** | **I** | **L** | **L** | **E** | **D** |  |  |
| +35 | = | 21 |  | + | 9 | + |  | 5 |  |  |  |  |
| *81* |  |  |  | + |  |  |  |  |  | 234 | = | *315* |
| (Horus) |  |  |  |  |  |  |  |  |  | (Ides of March) |  |

Here again, Horus appears representing the navel chakra, John the Baptist, the River Jordan as the initiator of emotional integrity. The Expression of this phrase is the energy of the Ides of March — the transference of power resulting in a change of destiny during Caesar's time. This represents great change with far-reaching ramifications.

# APPENDIX XVI

## The Tower

It is in Chapter 16 of the Book of Revelation that the word "Armageddon" makes its one and only appearance. The apocalyptic vision that has been associated with this word has been so often reinforced that it has come to be synonymous with death, destruction and chaos. If Armageddon can be understood to mean an ending of current conditions and the rebirth of humanity in a spiritual sense it is easy to understand how it can have an inherently positive meaning. This is the interpretation that I have chosen to focus upon.

The number 16 corresponds to the 16th card of the Tarot, the Tower. This card symbolizes a life crisis which must be confronted and overcome; a challenge which the individual faces in his/her growth. There are many phrases within the 16th Chapter that carry important energy, but I will focus on just a few to give a sample of the energies operating within it. A more in-depth discussion of the meaning of Armageddon is given in Chapter 7.

> *And I heard a great voice out of the temple saying to the seven angels,*
> *"Go your ways and pour out the vials of the wrath of God upon the earth."*
>
> Rev. 16:1

```
                    6                       =    6
                O   F
    15   =      15
                20+ 8                       =    28
                T   H   E
    5    =              5
                23+ 18  +   20+ 8           =    69
                W   R   A   T   H
    1    =              1
                    6                       =    6
                O   F
    15   =      15
                7   +   4                    =   +11
                G   O   D
   +15   =      15
    51                                          120
 (Michael)                          (Sanat Kumara, Archangel Michael)
```

The number 120 comes up repeatedly in the text of Revelation. This is the energy of Archangel Michael and Sanat Kumara. Michael is the Archangel of the Aquarian Age and Sanat Kumara is a highly evolved Venusian being who supervised the early development of planet Earth. As inner-world energies they represent part of the unfolding of the end-of-the-age process in which humanity discards obsolete patterns and adopts a higher awareness and greater spiritual perspective.

*And there were voices and thunders and lightnings such as was not since men were upon the earth; so mighty an earthquake and so great.*

Rev. 16:18

```
                14+ 4                       =    18
            A   N   D
    1   =   1
                20+ 8   +   18              =    46
            T   H   E   R   E
   10   =           5   +   5
                23  +   18                   =   41
            W   E   R   E
   10   =       5   +   5
                22  +   3   +   19          =   +44
            V   O   I   C   E   S
  +29   =       15+ 9   +   5
    50                                          149
(10ᵗʰ Power of Freedom)                    (The New Messiah)
```

The energy of the New Messiah (Group Avatar) is combined with Freedom magnified to the 10th power. The author(s) of Revelation encoded the energy of the New Messiah throughout the Book with the understanding of its importance and the intention of bringing it into manifestation.

|     |   |     |   |    |    |     |    |   |     |                  |
|-----|---|-----|---|----|----|-----|----|---|-----|------------------|
| 19  | + |     |   | 73 |    |     |    | = | 92  | (Maitreya)       |
| 19  |   | 13  | + | 7+ | 8+ | 20+ | 25 |   |     |                  |
| **S** | **O** | **M** | **I** | **G** | **H** | **T** | **Y** |   |     |              |
| 15  | + |  9  |   |    |    |     |    | = | +24 |                  |
|     |   |     |   |    |    |     |    |   | 116 | (Responsibility) |

|     |   |    |   |                   |   |     |     | (Master mystic) |
|-----|---|----|---|-------------------|---|-----|-----|-----------------|
|     |   |    |   | (Messiah)         |   |     |     |                 |
|     | 14 | + |   | *74*              |   |     | =   | *88*            |
| 14  |   |    |   | 18 + 20 + 8 + 17  |   | + 11|     |                 |
| **A** | **N** | **E** | **A** | **R**  **T**  **H**  **Q** | **U** | **A** **K** | **E** |  |
| 1   | + | 5+ | 1 | +                 | 21+ 1 | + 5 | = | +34           |
|     |   |    |   | *33*              |   |     | *122* |              |
|     |   |    |   | (Master Mason)    |   |     | (Feminine master |
|     |   |    |   |                   |   |     | mind for Freedom) |

Whenever the word "earthquake" appears it reinforces the principle of the Messiah. My personal view is that this principle is intended to refer to a group prototype rather than one individual.

# APPENDIX *XVII*

## *The Star*

*And there came one of the seven angels which had the
seven vials, and talked with me, saying unto me, Come
hither; I will shew unto thee the judgment of the great whore
that sitteth upon many waters.*

Rev. 17:1

|  |  | 14 |  |  |  |  | = | 14 |
|---|---|---|---|---|---|---|---|---|
|  |  | **O** | **N** | **E** |  |  |  |  |
| 20 | = | 15 | + | 5 |  |  |  |  |
|  |  | 6 |  |  |  |  | = | 6 |
|  |  | **O** | **F** |  |  |  |  |  |
| 15 | = | 15 |  |  |  |  |  |  |
|  |  | 20+ 8 |  |  |  |  | = | 28 |
|  |  | **T** | **H** | **E** |  |  |  |  |
| 5 | = |  |  | 5 |  |  |  |  |
|  |  | 19 | + | 22 | + | 14 | = | 55 |
|  |  | **S** | **E** | **V** | **E** | **N** |  |  |
| 10 | = |  | 5 | + | 5 |  |  |  |
|  |  | 14+ 7 | + | 12+ 19 |  |  | = | +52 |
|  |  | **A** | **N** | **G** | **E** | **L** **S** |  |  |
| +6 | = | 1 | + | 5 |  |  |  | (Ark of the Covenant) |
| **56** |  |  |  | + |  |  | ***155*** = ***211*** |  |

(Lincoln's Power #)

This phrase contains two outstanding energies. The number 211
represents the energy of the Ark of the Covenant, the ancient Jewish symbol of
patriarchal power to fulfill the highest humanitarian service. Individually it is
our commitment (covenant) to fulfill our chosen destiny. The number 155
represents the energy exemplified by Abraham Lincoln as it is his power
number. On a personal level, it represents our liberation from addictions we
have carried with us since birth and our ability to assist others in becoming

liberated from addictions as well.

Motivation                                                                Personality

```
           20+  8                                              =    28
           T    H    E
   5   =             5
           10   +    4+   7+   13   +    14+  20    =    68
           J    U    D    G    M    E    N    T
  26   =        21        +         5
                6                                    =    +6
           O    F
 +15   =   15
  46                                                      102
```

```
           20+  8                                    =    28
           T    H    E
   5   =             5
           7+   18   +              20               =    45
           G    R    E    A    T
   6   =             5+   1
           23+  8    +    18                         =    +49
           W    H    O    R    E
 +20   =            15   +    5               (Magical Power)
  31                 +                        *122*   =   *153*
                                             (Individual Feminine
                                              Master Builder)
```

***Sum of Motivations***            ***Sum of Personalities***
*46 + 31 = 77*                       *102 + 122 = 224*
(Christ)                             (Spear of Longinus)

Here is an apparently negative phrase which carries a very different energy than would be perceived by a casual glance. The Personality of this phrase carries the same energy as the Spear of Longinus (See Epilogue). The Motivation of the phrase equals that of the energy of "Christ" and the Expression of the sub-phrase "the great whore" represents Magical Power. The combination of these energies relates to the magical powers of the Spear and its part in the crucifixion event and the elevation of the spirit.

> *And upon her forehead was a name written, MYSTERY, BABYLON THE GREAT, THE MOTHER OF HARLOTS AND ABOMINATIONS OF THE EARTH.*
>
> Rev. 17:5

*Revelation For Our Time*

```
                14+   4                              =   18
          A     N     D
  1   =   1
                16  +  14                            =   30
          U     P     O     N
  36  =   21  +  15
                 8  +  18                            =   26
          H     E     R
  5   =   5
                 6  +  18  +   8  +         4   =   +36
          F     O     R     E     H     E     A     D
  +26 =   15  +   5  +   5+  1
  68                                        110 (The Christ)
```

(Body of Christ)

The energies present in this phrase are the Motivation of the "Body of Christ" and the Personality, or outer expression, is "The Christ." The number 17 (Chapter number) represents the 17th level related to the connection of the first chakra (#1) to the crown chakra (#7). This is achieved through meditation and selfless service.

```
                                        (Sanat Kumara, Archangel Michael)
                13+ 25+ 19+ 20   +    18+ 25   =    120
                M   Y   S   T    E    R   Y,
        5   =                    5
(Moses, Thoth)  2  +  2+  25+ 12  +   14    =    55
  71  {         B   A   B   Y   L   O   N
        16  =       1       +       15
                20+ 8                        =    28
                T   H   E
        5   =               5
(Michael)       7+  18  +        20           =    45
  51  {         G   R   E   A   T
        6   =           5+  1
```

The phrase (the "name"), "Mystery, Babylon the great, the mother of harlots and abominations of the earth" is capitalized in the King James Bible for emphasis. The word 'Mystery" has the Personality of Sanat Kumara and Archangel Michael, as well as the authority to communicate at the 10th level. Babylon carries the Expression of Moses and Thoth (possibly the same soul in different embodiments). On a personal level, these energies represent the principle of the integration of the seventh and first chakras and performance of service unconditionally.

```
        20+ 8                        =    28
         T   H   E
  5  =           5
        13  +  20+ 8  +  18         =    59
         M   O   T   H   E   R
 20  =         15  +     5
         6                           =    6
         O   F
 15  =        15
         8  +  18+ 12  +  20+ 19    =   +77  (Christ)
         H   A   R   L   O   T   S
+16  =         1  +        15            (The Star)
 56                    +                170   =   226
(Light)                                    (2nd level of
                                         God Consciousness)
```

This phrase is another that apparently has a negative connotation, but a numerological analysis reveals its true energies. This represents another opportunity to free the woman from the bondage of outworn negative symbols. The energy of "Christ" within the Personality of "The Star" is significant for the symbolism of illumination which it bears. Additionally, the Motivation of "Light" reinforces this principle, and the Expression of this phrase carrying the energy of God Consciousness symbolizes the principle of ultimate power.

> *And the angel said unto me, Wherefore didst thou marvel? I will tell thee the mystery of the woman, and of the beast that carrieth her, which hath the seven heads and ten horns.*
>
> Rev. 17:7

```
         14+ 4               =   18
         A   N   D
  1  =   1
         20+ 8               =   28
         T   H   E
  5  =           5
         14+ 7  +  12        =   33
         A   N   G   E   L
  6  =   1  +     5
         19 +     4          =   23
         S   A   I   D
 10  =   1+  9
         14+ 20             =   34
         U   N   T   O
 36  =   21 +    15
         13                 =   +13
         M   E
 +5  =        5                (The New Messiah)
 63                 +          149   =   212 (Lincoln)
```

The energy of the New Messiah symbolizes the Personality of this phrase. Its Expression is that of Lincoln. This phrase is an example of the energies that are repeatedly brought into form throughout history in order to seed the divine principles which are part of the hierarchical plan.

```
                                            (Archangel Michael, Sanat Kumara)
              13+  25+  19+  20    +     18+  25   =    120
              M    Y    S    T           R    Y
       5  =
              6                                    =     6
              O    F
      15  =   15
              20+  8                                =     28
36 (Return)   T    H    E
       5  =        5
              23  +  13  +  14                =    +50
              W    O    M    A    N
     +16  =        15  +  1
      84                                          120
                                            (Archangel Michael, Sanat Kumara)
```

This phrase has the energies of Archangel Michael and Sanat Kumara in two places, emphasizing their significance, and the vibration of "Return," indicating the return of these two vibrational principles. The inclusion of the word "woman" is particularly significant for its association with the return of these energies.

```
              20+  8                      =    28
              T    H    E
       5  =        5
              19  +  22  +  14           =    55  ⟍
              S    E    V    E    N
      10  =        5  +  5                          (Pyramid, Arthur)
              8  +      4+  19            =    31  ⟋      86
              H    E    A    D    S
       6  =        5+  1
              14+  4                      =    18  ┐
              A    N    D                              (Communication
       1  =   1                                        on highest level)
              20  +  14                   =    34       111
              T    E    N
21 (World)     5  =   5                                     │
              8  +  18+ 14+ 19            =    +59  ┘
              H    O    R    N    S
     +15  =        15
      42                                          225
```

                                    (11/11/49—the advent of the New Messiah)
      Expression of 'and ten horns': 111 + 21 = **132** (The World Teacher)

Arthurian legend and the ancient pyramid are represented by "seven heads." The "World" is the Motivation of the phrase "the ten horns"; its Personality is communication on the highest level. These energies combined give us the World Teacher. These two phrases, "seven heads" and "ten horns" show up in other verses of Revelation, emphasizing the importance of their energies.

> *The beast that thou sawest was, and is not; and shall ascend out of the bottomless pit, and go into perdition: and they that dwell on the earth shall wonder, whose names were not written in the book of life from the foundation of the world, when they behold the beast that was, and is not, and yet is.*

> Rev. 17:8

"The bottomless pit" appears in Chapter 9. See *Appendix IX* for an analysis of this phrase. It is significant that this verse alludes to "the beast" that "was, and is not" ascending. If we follow our premise that "the beast" (Satan, AntiChrist, Devil) does not exist ("is not"), yet in the minds of humanity he is given life through the power of belief, then he "was" (past tense), and "is not" (present tense—no longer exists) and "shall ascend" (transmute) out of the bottomless pit. This verse holds an optimistic vision for the transmutation of the planetary thoughtform of evil into a positive form.

```
                    14+ 4                        =    18
                 A   N   D
         1  =    1
                 7                               =    7
                 G   O
        15  =    15
                 14+ 20                          =    34
                 I   N   T   O
        24  =    9  +      15
(The Christ)     16 +  18+ 4  +   20  +      14   =   +72
110 {            P   E   R   D   I   T   I   O   N
       +38 =     5  +      9  +   9+  15
        78                +                  131  =   209
                                        (Spear of Destiny)
```

Here, again, we find the Spear of Destiny encoded in another verse. The word "perdition" carries the energy of "the Christ," and its inclusion in this phrase represents the relationship between achieving Christ Consciousness and the Spear of Destiny.

*And the ten horns which thou sawest upon the beast,*
*these shall hate the whore, and shall make her desolate and*
*naked, and shall eat her flesh, and burn her with fire.*

Rev. 17:16

|  |  | 20+ | 8 | + | 19 |  | = | 47 |
|  |  | **T** | **H** | **E** | **S** | **E** |  |  |
|  | 10 = |  | 5 | + | 5 |  | (Michael) |  |
|  |  | 19+ | 8 | + | 12+ 12 | = | **51** |  |
|  |  | **S** | **H** | **A** | **L** | **L** |  |  |
|  | 1 = |  | 1 |  |  |  | } 79 (Sword) |  |
|  |  | 8 | + | 20 |  | = | 28 |  |
| 7 (Thought) { |  | **H** | **A** | **T** | **E** |  |  |  |
|  | 6 = | 1 | + | 5 |  |  |  |  |
|  |  | 20+ | 8 |  |  | = | 28 |  |
|  |  | **T** | **H** | **E** |  |  |  |  |
| (Freedom of | 5 = |  | 5 |  |  |  | } 77 (Christ) |  |
| the Feminine) |  | 23+ | 8 | + | 18 | = | **49** |  |
| 25 { |  | **W** | **H** | **O** | **R** | **E** |  |  |
|  | 20 = |  | 15 + 5 |  |  |  |  |  |

Expression of "shall hate":  79 + 7 = **86**  (Arthur, Pyramid)

There are many powerful symbols in this phrase. The words "shall
hate" invoke the energies of the Sword and the power of thought to yield the
energy of Arthur and the Pyramid. "The whore" carries the energy of Christ
and merges it with the freedom of the feminine, two principles which will be
fully realized when humanity completes its present evolutionary step.

# APPENDIX XVIII

## The Moon

*And he cried mightily with a strong voice, saying, Babylon the great is fallen, is fallen, and is become the habitation of devils, and the hold of every foul spirit, and a cage of every unclean and hateful bird.*

Rev. 18:2

```
                              14+  4                      =   18
                          A   N   D
            1  =          1
                              20+ 8                       =   28
                          T   H   E
            5  =                  5
(Return)                  8  +   12+ 4                    =   24
   36                     H   O   L   D
           15  =              15
                              6                           =    6
                          O   F
           15  =             15
                              22 +   18+ 25              =   65
                          E   V   E   R   Y
           10  =          5  +   5
                              6                           =    6
                          F   O   U   L
           36  =             15+ 21
                              19+ 16 +   18 +   20   =  +73
                          S   P   I   R   I   T
          +18  =                  9  +   9
           100                                              232
```

(Major new Beginning)                    (Feminine Illumined Intellect)

This phrase symbolizes a major new beginning for the feminine intellect. This vision perceives a future where the woman will take personal, group and planetary leadership positions.

*For all nations have drunk of the wine of the wrath of
her fornication, and the kings of the earth have committed
fornication with her, and the merchants of the earth are
waxed rich through the abundance of her delicacies.*

Rev. 18:3

```
                 6                                             =    6
           O   F
  15   =   15
           8   +   18                                         =   26
           H   E   R
   5   =        5
           6   +   18+ 14  +   3  +   20  +          14   =   +75
 (Lord)    F   O   R   N   I   C   A   T   I   O   N
  +49  =   15  +        9  +   1  +   9+  15
   69                                                            107
(Responsibility)                                            (The Messiah)
```

The Personality here is the energy of the Messiah, coupled with the
Motivation of responsibility, which also carries within it the energy of the
Lord. It is interesting that "Lord" is the Motivation of the word "fornication."
Our literal use of this word is certainly derogatory at best, yet when we
examine its subconscious meaning we find a very different translation.

*And the kings of the earth, who have committed
fornication and lived deliciously with her, shall bewail her,
and lament for her, when they shall see the smoke of her
burning.*

Rev. 18:9

```
           23+ 8                                              =   31
           W   H   O
  15   =           15
           8   +   22                                         =   30
           H   A   V   E
   6   =       1   +   5
           3   +   13+ 13  +   20+ 20  +   4                  =   73
           C   O   M   M   I   T   T   E   D
  29   =       15  +        9  +        5
           6   +   18+ 14  +   3  +   20  +          14   =   +75
           F   O   R   N   I   C   A   T   I   O   N
  +49  =       15  +        9  +   1  +   9+  15
   99                                   +                        209
(altruism)                                              (Spear of Destiny)
```

99+ 209 =  **308** (Noah)

The Spear of Destiny appears again and this time with the energy of altruism. Their combination yields an Expression of the energy of Noah.

|  (Michael) |  |  |  |  |  |  |  | (Saint Michael) |  |
|---|---|---|---|---|---|---|---|---|---|
|  *51* |  | + |  | 37 |  | + |  | 26 | = *114* |
| 19+ 8 | + | 12+ 12 | 2 | + | 23 + | 12 | 8 | + 18 |  |
| **S  H** | **A** | **L  L** | **B** | **E** | **W  A** | **I  L** | **H** | **E  R** |  |
|  1 |  | + |  | 5 | + 1+ 9 | + |  | 5 | = *21* |
|  |  |  |  |  |  |  |  |  | (World) |

Saint Michael and its shortened form, Michael, are emphasized in this phrase which has a Motivation represented by the energy of the World, the 21st card of the Tarot.

> *And a mighty angel took up a stone like a great millstone and cast* it *into the sea, saying, Thus with violence that great city Babylon be thrown down, and shall be found no more at all.*
>
> Rev. 18:21

|  |  | 20+ 8 | + | 19 |  |  | = | 47 |
|---|---|---|---|---|---|---|---|---|
|  |  | **T  H** | **U** | **S** |  |  |  |  |
|  | 21 = |  | 21 |  |  |  |  |  |
|  |  | 23 | + | 20+ 8 |  |  | = | *51* (Michael) |
|  |  | **W** | **I** | **T  H** |  |  |  |  |
|  | 9 = |  | 9 |  |  |  |  |  |
|  |  | 22 |  | + 12 + | 14 + 3 |  | = | +*51* |
|  |  | **V** | **I** | **O  L  E** | **N  C** | **E** |  |  |
| +34 = |  | 9+ 15 | + | 5 + | 5 |  |  |  |
| *64* |  |  |  |  |  |  |  | *149* |
| (Rennes-Le-Chateau) |  |  |  |  |  | (The New Messiah) |  |  |

Michael appears twice again in this verse, indicating that the author(s) of Revelation felt this was an important energy. This double Michael energy is a part of the Personality which resonates to the vibration of the New Messiah. The energy of Rennes-Le-Chateau, a region in France which has deep connections to the Grail, is encoded in the Motivation.

> *And in her was found the blood of prophets, and of saints, and of all that were slain upon the earth.*
>
> Rev. 18:24

|  |  | 14+ 4 |  |  |  | = | 18 |
| | | **A** **N** **D** | | | | | |
| 1 | = | 1 | | | | | |
| | | 14 | | | | = | 14 |
| | | **I** **N** | | | | | |
| 9 | = | 9 | | | | | |
| | | 8 + 18 | | | | = | 26 |
| | | **H** **E** **R** | | | | | |
| 5 | = | 5 | | | | | |
| | | 23 + 19 | | | | = | 42 |
| | | **W** **A** **S** | | | | | |
| 1 | = | 1 | | | | | |
| | | 6 + 14+ 4 | | | = | +24 | |
| | | **F** **O** **U** **N** **D** | | | | | |
| +36 | = | 15+ 21 | | | | | |
| *52* | | | | | | *124* | |

(Freedom of the Feminine)    (The New Messiah Personality)

|  |  | 20+ 8 |  |  |  | = | 28 |
| | | **T** **H** **E** | | | | | |
| 5 | = | 5 | | | | | |
| | | 2+ 12 +   4 | | | | = | 18 |
| | | **B** **L** **O** **O** **D** | | | | | |
| 30 | = | 15+ 15 | | | | | |
| | | 6 | | | | = | 6 |
| | | **O** **F** | | | | | |
| 15 | = | 15 | | | | | |
| | | 16+ 18 + 16+ 8 + 20+ 19 | | | = | +97 | |
| | | **P** **R** **O** **P** **H** **E** **T** **S** | | | | | |
| +20 | = | 15 + 5 | | | | | |
| *70* | | | | | | *149* | |

(10th power of Illumined Intellect)    (The New Messiah)

  The energy of the New Messiah is found twice in this verse. Combined with the freedom of the feminine leading to the 10th power (higher octave) of the illumined intellect, this represents a unique combination of prototypical energies, one which will become manifest as the feminine is empowered on earth.

# APPENDIX XIX

## The Sun

*For true and righteous* are *his judgments: for he hath judged the great whore, which did corrupt the earth with her fornication, and hath avenged the blood of his servants at her hand.*

Rev. 19:2

```
     28           +              45              +              49        = 122
20+  8          7+  18  +         20        23+  8   +   18
 T   H   E       G   R   E   A   T       W   H   O   R   E
     5   +          5+  1          +              15   +   5  = +31
                                                                153
```

122 = Freedom/Feminine Empowerment
31 = Practical Grounding        153 = Magical power #

This phrase symbolizes the practical grounding of the freedom of feminine empowerment. Its significance is emphasized by the encoding of the energy of the magical power number, 153. This is another example of where the author(s) integrated higher-plane principles within apparently negative terms.

```
                                                    (The Cosmic Christ)
     27        +              112              =     139
 8  +  19       19  +  18+ 22  +  14+ 20+ 19
 H   I   S       S   E   R   V   A   N   T   S   (Responsibility)
 9        +       5  +     1              =     +15
                                                154
                                        (The Christ Office)
```

Here we have the symbolism of the Cosmic Christ combined with responsibility culminating in the Christ Office (Group Avatar). This is the goal of the initiate, to achieve Christ Consciousness through the adoption of the

Personality of Christ and responsible action.

```
                                    (Christ)        (The Star)
        41        +           52      +        77      =    170
23  +   18           13  +  14+ 25        3+  18  +   23+ 14+ 19
W  E    R   E        M   A   N   Y        C   R   O   W   N   S   (God)
    5   +   5   +        1            +           15           =   +26
                                                                    196
                                                           (Julius Caesar)
                                                    92  (Maitreya Buddha)
```

The energy of Julius Caesar is again encoded into Revelation in this phrase. The author(s) must have felt that this energy (Caesar's karma) was an important principle to repeat it in the text. The combination of Caesar's and Maitreya's energies is apparently an attempt to resolve the negative aspect of the Caesar energy. Note, too, that a component energy of the word "crowns," for which the energy of Maitreya Buddha is the Expression, is that of Christ.

> *And I saw the beast, and the kings of the earth, and their*
> *armies, gathered together to make war against him that sat*
> *on the horse, and against his army.*

Rev. 19:19

```
                        14+  4            =    18
                        A    N    D
        1    =    1

                        I
        9    =    9
                        19  +  23         =    42
                        S    A    W
        1    =    1
                        20+  8            =    28
                        T    H    E
        5    =         5
                        2   +     19+ 20  =    +41
                        B    E    A    S    T
        +6   =         5+   1
        22                         +           129  =   151
    (Master Builder)                                (See below)
```

In this verse the author sees himself as the mirror of the beast in a positive sense. In the early chapters of Revelation he sees himself struggling with this image, but in the later chapters he is able to embrace it as a function of the reflection of the Sun energy. The beast, represented by the vibration of 151 (the expression of the radiance of the Sun), is elevated to the vibration of Christ the King, Michael embodiment, the pipecarrier, the Davidic Covenant. (See Chapter 10 for a complete discussion.) These are all expressions of the same energy.

$$
\begin{array}{llllll}
 & & 20+8 & + & 20 & = & 48 \\
 & & \mathbf{T} & \mathbf{H} \quad \mathbf{A} & \mathbf{T} & & \\
1 & = & & 1 & & & \\
 & & 19 & + \quad 20 & & = & 39 \\
 & & \mathbf{S} & \mathbf{A} \quad \mathbf{T} & & & \\
1 & = & 1 & & & & \\
 & & 14 & & & = & 14 \\
 & & \mathbf{O} & \mathbf{N} & & & \\
15 & = & 15 & & & & \\
 & & 20+8 & & & = & 28 \\
 & & \mathbf{T} & \mathbf{H} \quad \mathbf{E} & & & \\
5 & = & & 5 & & & \\
 & & 8 & + \quad 18+19 & & = & \underline{+45} \\
 & & \mathbf{H} & \mathbf{O} \quad \mathbf{R} \quad \mathbf{S} & \mathbf{E} & & \\
\underline{+20} & = & 15 & + \quad 5 & & & \\
42 & & & & & & \mathbf{174} \text{ (Thomas Jefferson)}
\end{array}
$$

It is quite remarkable that the energy of Thomas Jefferson is encoded into a document that was written over 2,000 years ago. This indicates to me that the energy represented by Thomas Jefferson (the democratic ideal) was and is an important aspect of the rise in consciousness and an appropriate metaphor for the dawning Aquarian Age.

> *And the beast was taken, and with him the false prophet that wrought miracles before him, with which he deceived them that had received the mark of the beast, and them that worshipped his image. These both were cast alive into a lake of fire burning with brimstone.*
>
> Rev. 19:20

"The mark of the beast" is such an oft-quoted phrase that it is important to address it in this discussion. This mark of the beast has long been interpreted as a mark of evil, but in our analysis, in the language of the subconscious, it carries a very different meaning.

```
              20+  8                    =    28
               T   H   E
       5  =             5
              13  +  18+ 11             =    42
               M   A   R   K
       1  =             1
                       6                =    6
               O   F
      15  =   15
              20+  8                    =    28
               T   H   E
       5  =             5
               2  +       19+ 20       =   +41
               B   E   A   S   T
      +6  =            5+  1
       32                   +                145  =   177
   (Destiny of U.S.A.)                (Individualized Christ Consciousness)
```

The Expression of this phrase carries the energy of the individualized Christ Consciousness.  This is the key to the process of unfoldment.

```
              14+  4                                  =   18
               A   N   D
       1  =    1
              20+  8  +  13                           =   41
               T   H   E   M
       5  =            5
              20+  8  +  20                           =   48
               T   H   A   T
       1  =            1
              23  +  18+ 19+  8  +  16+ 16  +   4   = +104
               W   O   R   S   H   I   P   P   E   D
      +29  =       15   +       9   +       5  (Ark of the Covenant)
       36                   +              211  =  247
   (Return)          (Jesus' age at ascension in Pyramid initiation)
```

This phrase represents the energy of the return of the Ark of the Covenant and its esoteric relationship to the age at which Jesus made his ascension during his initiation in the Great Pyramid.

| | | | | | | | |
|---|---|---|---|---|---|---|---|
| | | 20+ | 8 | + | 19 | = | 47 |
| | | **T** | **H** | **E** | **S** | **E** | |
| | 10 = | | | 5 | + | 5 | |
| | | 2 | + | 20+ | 8 | = | 30 |
| | | **B** | **O** | **T** | **H** | | |
| | 15 = | | 15 | | | | |
| (Michael) | | 23 | + | 18 | | = | 41 |
| *51* { | | **W** | **E** | **R** | **E** | | |
| | 10 = | | 5 | + | 5 | | |
| | | 3 | + | 19+ | 20 | = | 42 |
| | | **C** | **A** | **S** | **T** | | |
| | 1 = | | 1 | | | | |
| (Lord) | | 12 | + | 22 | | = | +34 |
| *49* { | | **A** | **L** | **I** | **V** | **E** | |
| | +15 = | 1 | + | 9 | + | 5 | |
| | *51* | | | | | | *194* |
| | (Michael) | | | | | | (Covenant) |

Here we have the covenant of Michael, which is "alive," a synonym for "Lord." All this is immersed within language that bears an outward description of Hell, but when broken down to its esoteric symbolism, it represents a most positive principle.

# APPENDIX XX

## Judgment

*And shall go out to deceive the nations which are in the four quarters of the earth, Gog and Magog, to gather them together to battle: the number of whom is as the sand of the sea.*

Rev. 20:8

| 18 | + |  | 51 |  | + | 7 | + |  | 20 | = | 96 |
| 14+ | 4 | 19+ | 8 | + | 12+ 12 | 7 |  |  |  | 20 |  |
| **A** | **N  D** | **S** | **H** | **A** | **L   L** | **G   O** |  | **O** | **U   T** |  |  |
| 1 |  | + |  | 1 |  | + | 15 | + | 15+ 21 | = | +53 |

**149**

(The New Messiah)

The symbology of the New Messiah must have been a concept that the author(s) understood for it to have been encoded so often in Revelation. This energy is that of the Group Avatar which will usher in the Aquarian Age. This is yet another example of the occult use of language to express a higher principle.

*And the devil that deceived them was cast into the lake of fire and brimstone, where the beast and the false prophet are, and shall be tormented day and night for ever and ever.*

Rev. 20:10

```
              14+ 4                        =    18
          A   N   D
  1    =   1
              20+ 8                        =    28
          T   H   E
  5    =           5
              4  +  22  +  12              =    38
          D   E   V   I   L
 14    =       5  +  9
              20+ 8  +  20                 =    48
          T   H   A   T
  1    =           1
              4  +  3  +      22  +  4     =    33
          D   E   C   E   I   V   E   D
 24    =       5  +  5+ 9  +  5
              20+ 8  +  13                 =   +51 (Michael)
          T   H   E   M
 +5               5                        (God) (2nd level of Light)
(Freedom) 50                 +             206  =   256
```

This phrase carries the Personality of the triple-digit energy of the freedom of God leading to the 2nd octave of Light. This is another example of an apparently negative verse carrying a positive message.

*And the sea gave up the dead which were in it; and death and hell delivered up the dead which were in them: and they were judged every man according to their works.*

Rev. 20:13

```
                  20+ 8              =    28
                  T   H   E
              5 =         5
                  19                 =    19
                  S   E   A
              6 =      5+ 1
                  7  + 22            =    29
                  G   A   V   E
              6 =  1  + 5
                  16                 =    16
                  U   P
             21 = 21
                  20+ 8              =    28
                  T   H   E
              5 =         5
(Freedom)         4  +      4     =   +8 (Independence)
  14/5  {         D   E   A   D
  (Practicality) +6 =      5+ 1          (Christ Consciousness)
(Capstone of the Pyramid) 49      +      128  =   177
```

This phrase has the Motivation of the Capstone of the Pyramid leading to the Expression of Christ Consciousness (the opening of the seven male and seven female chakras). The word "dead" carries a symbolic (subconscious) meaning of independence and practicality resulting in the attainment of freedom. The death of the cocoon is the birth of the butterfly.

```
                    4   +  12  +  22  +  18  +   4   =    60
                    D      E      L      I      V      E      R      E      D
        24   =      5   +   9  +   5   +   5
                   16                                      =    16
                    U      P
        21   =     21
                   20+  8                                  =    28
                    T      H      E
         5   =                     5
                    4   +          4                       =    +8
                    D      E      A      D
        +6   =      5+  1
         56                                                      112
        (Light)                                    (Roundtable, creative principle)
```

The Personality of the "Roundtable" as well as the creative principle are important components of this phrase. The Roundtable is a symbol of equality in organizational structure, dating back to the reign of Arthur. This energy coupled with the Motivation of "Light" is a significant combination of energies reflecting the power that is available for those with the proper intent.

> *And whosoever was not found written in the book of life*
> *was cast into the lake of fire.*
>
> Rev. 20:15

This phrase contains within it some very ancient prototypical energies. It has as its Motivation the God principle and the Personality of the Sun God, Ra. Together they lead to the attainment of the number of critical mass, 144(000). The Egyptian god, Horus symbolizes the energy behind the trial of the three perennial tests—money, sex and power—in the second phrase. The successful completion of these tests results in the symbolism of the lady clothed with the Sun: The inner woman expressing the Sun principle on earth, the ideal to which we all aspire.

```
              23    +    19         =    42
              W    A    S
     1    =         1
              3     +   19+  20     =    42
              C    A    S    T
     1    =         1
                        14+  20     =    +34
              I    N    T    O
   +24   =    9    +         15
    26  (God)                           118  (Ra)
```

```
                        20+  8           =    28
                        T    H    E
     5                            5
                        12   +   11      =    33
                        L    A    K    E
     6    =              1    +    5
                        6                =    6
                        O    F
    15    =             15
                        6    +   18      =    +24
                        F    I    R    E
   +14    =             9    +    5
    40  (Money, Sex, Power Tests)        81  (Horus)
```

**26 + 40 = 144**  (symbolic 144,000 - critical mass)

**118 + 81 = 121**  (Lady clothed with the Sun)

# APPENDIX XXI

## The World

> *But the fearful, and unbelieving, and the abominable,*
> *and murders, and whoremongers, and sorcerers, and*
> *idolaters, and all liars, shall have their part in the lake*
> *which burneth with fire and brimstone: which is the second*
> *death.*

Rev. 21:8

This verse is one of the most negative, fear-inducing verses in the Revelation text if we look at it only from a literal standpoint. But, again, when we examine it in the language of the subconscious, numerology, it possesses a clearly positive message.

```
                        14+  4                                    =   18
                    A    N   D
            1   =   1
                        20+  8                                    =   28
                    T    H   E
            5   =            5
(Messiah)               2  +  13  +  14  +  2+  12               =  +43
      74 {           A    B    O    M    I    N    A    B    L    E
          +31  =    1  +  15  +   9  +   1  +       5
           37                     +                           89  =  126
                                                       (Davidic Covenant)
                    126 = Individualized God Consciousness
```

The word "abominable" has the energy of the Messiah as its Expression. The Personality of this phrase carries the energy of the Davidic Covenant; its Expression is a higher octave of God, representing the promise for the fulfillment of the Davidic Covenant leading to God Consciousness.

(Archangel Michael, Sunat Kumara)

| 23+ | 8 | + | 18 | + | 13 | + | 14+ | 7 | + | 18+ | 19 | = | *120* |
|---|---|---|---|---|---|---|---|---|---|---|---|---|---|
| **W** | **H** | | **O** | | **R** | | **E** | **M** | **O** | **N** | **G** | **E** | **R** | **S** |

| | 15 | + | 5 | + | 15 | + | | 5 | | | = | *40* |

(Buddha)

| | 14+ | 4 | | | = | 18 |
|---|---|---|---|---|---|---|
| | **A** | **N** | **D** | | | |

| 1 | = | 1 |

| | 19 | + | 18+ | 3 | + | 18 | + | 18+ | 19 | = | +95 |
|---|---|---|---|---|---|---|---|---|---|---|---|
| | **S** | | **O** | **R** | | **C** | | **E** | **R** | **E** | **R** | **S** |

| +25 | = | 15 | + | 5 | + | 5 | (Visionary Freedom) |
| **26** | | | + | | | *113* = *139* |

(God)          (Cosmic Christ)

(Altruistic leadership)

| 18 | + | | 73 | | = | *91* |
|---|---|---|---|---|---|---|
| 14+ | 4 | | 4 | + | 12 | + | 20 | + | 18+ | 19 |
| **A** | **N** | **D** | **I** | **D** | **O** | **L** | **A** | **T** | **E** | **R** | **S** | (Practical) |
| 1 | | | + | 9 | + | 15 | + | 1 | + | 5 | | = | +31 |

122

(Feminine leadership)

The Personality of "Whoremongers" represents the energies of Archangel Michael and Sanat Kumara. "And sorcerers" combines the Motivation of God and the Personality of Visionary Freedom to yield the Cosmic Christ. There are clearly highly positive energies hidden within otherwise apparently negative terms. "Idolaters" represents the practicality of altruistic leadership resulting in a new level of planetary leadership for the woman—a considerably different translation than the traditional definition of the word "idolaters."

| | | 23+ | 8 | + | 3+ | 8 | = | 42 |
|---|---|---|---|---|---|---|---|---|
| | | **W** | **H** | | **I** | **C** | **H** | |

| 9 | = | | 9 |

| | | 19 | | | = | 19 |
| | | **I** | **S** |

| 9 | = | 9 |

| | | 20+ | 8 | | = | 28 |
| | | **T** | **H** | **E** |

| 5 | = | | 5 |

(Word)

| | 19 | + | 3 | + | 14+ | 4 | = | *40* |
|---|---|---|---|---|---|---|---|---|
| 60 { | **S** | **E** | **C** | **O** | **N** | **D** |

| 20 | = | 5 | + | 15 | (Destiny of U.S.A.) |

| | 4 | + | 20+ | 8 | = | +32 |
| | **D** | **E** | **A** | **T** | **H** |

| +6 | = | 5+ | 1 | (Organization) |
| **49** | | | + | *161* | = | *210* |

(Capstone)          (10th power of The World)

"The second death" is in reality the use of the Word to achieve a new world. This is a verse of good news: a new world is coming, a better world represented by the energies of organization and the capstone of the Great Pyramid, and the destiny of the United States of America.

> *And there came unto me one of the seven angels which had the seven vials full of the seven last plagues, and talked with me, saying, Come hither, I will shew thee the bride, the Lamb's wife.*

Rev. 21:9

```
                6    +   12+  12                        =   30
                F    U    L    L
21   =          21
                6                                        =   6
                O    F
15   =          15
                20+  8                                   =   28
                T    H    E
5    =               5
                19   +   22   +   14                     =   55
                S    E    V    E    N
10   =          5  +  5
                12   +   19+  20                         =   51
                L    A    S    T
1    =          1
                16+  12   +   7   +        19            =   +54
                P    L    A    G    U    E    S
+27  =          1    +   21+  5           (Spear of Longinus)
79              +                           224   =   303
(Sword)              303 = 33rd degree of Masonry
```

Here again we have the energy of the Spear of Longinus as the Personality of "full of the seven last plagues." This is a powerful subconscious message which also carries the energy of the Sword in its Motivation. The resulting Expression bears the higher octave of the 33rd degree of Masonry. See Epilogue for detailed information about the relationship between the Sword and the Spear of Longinus.

> *And he carried me away in the spirit to a great and high mountain, and shewed me that great city, the holy Jerusalem, descending out of heaven from God.*

Rev. 21:10

```
         20+ 8                                    =   28
          T   H   E
 5   =            5
          8   +  12+ 25                           =   45
          H   O   L   Y
15   =           15
                              (Master organizer)
         28                          44
         10  +  18  +        19  +  12  +  13  =  +72
          J   E   R      U   S   A   L   E   M
+32  =           5   +      21 +  1  +   5
52               |          +                       145 =   197
                 |                                       (11/11/49)
                              +27
         33                    71
         +27              (Thoth, Moses)
         60  (Word)
```

The holy Jerusalem is a vision of the sought-after unity among nations, wherein there will be created a Roundtable of Nations. This is the principle of unity through diversity.

```
         18  +        14+ 4+ 20  +   2+ 12         =   70
          R   O   U   N   D   T   A   B   L   E
42   =           15+ 21      +       1  +      5
                 6                                 =   6
          O   F
15   =           15
         14  +  20  +        14+ 19               =  +67
          N   A   T   I   O   N   S
+25  =           1   +   9+ 15
82                           +                       143 =   225
                                                        (Nov. 11, 1949)
```

*Single-digit derivation of conception date of the Group Avatar:*

**11** - **11** - **1949**
*2*       *2*        *5*  [1 + 9 + 4 + 9 = 23/5]

## APPENDIX XXII

## *The Fool*

*I am Alpha and Omega, the beginning and the end,*
*the first and the last.*

Rev. 22:13

```
              I  .
     9  =     9 .
             13          .          =   13
             A   M
     1  =    1
             12+ 16+ 8               =   36
             A   L   P   H   A
     2  =    1       +       1
             14+ 4                   =   28
             A   N   D
     1  =    1
             13  +   7               =   +20
(The World)  O   M   E   G   A
    +21 =    15  +   5   +   1
     34              +           87  =   121
```
(Woman clothed with the Sun)

This oft-quoted verse is interpreted as a statement spoken by God to "John" (the supposed author of Revelation) as a sort of self-description. Esoterically, when we break down the three phrases which compose the verse there are energies involved which are indicative of higher spiritual principles. The vibration of the "woman clothed with the Sun" (Rev. 12:1) is important as it reveals the significance of feminine power.

In addition to the "woman clothed with the sun," the energies of the Davidic covenant, the World (21st card of the Tarot) and the Spear of Destiny are present and emphasized again in this last chapter of Revelation. The principles represented by each of these are an integral part of the achievement of higher consciousness.

```
        20+ 8                              =   28
         T   H   E
5   =            5
         2  +  7  +  14+ 14  +  14+ 7  =   58
         B   E   G   I   N   N   I   N   G
23  =           5  +  9  +       9
         14+ 4                          =   18
         A   N   D
1   =    1
         20+ 8                              =   28
         T   H   E
5   =            5
         14+ 4                          =   +18
         E   N   D
+5  =    5                          (10th power of Responsibility)
39                         +                    150   =   189
                                            (Davidic covenant)


             20+ 8                         =   28
              T   H   E
    5   =             5
              6   +  18+ 19+ 20       =   63
              F   I   R   S   T
    9   =     9
              14+ 4                        =   18
              A   N   D
    1   =     1
              20+ 8                         =   28
              T   H   E
    5   =             5
              12  +  19+ 20          =   +51
              L   A   S   T
    +1  =             1             (Master Mystic)
    21                    +              188   =   209
(The World)                             (Spear of Destiny)
```

*For I testify unto every man that heareth the words of the prophecy of this book, If any man shall add unto these things, God shall add unto him the plagues that are written in this book.*

Rev. 22:18

| | | | 6 | + | 18 | | | | | = | 24 |
|---|---|---|---|---|---|---|---|---|---|---|---|
| | | | **F** | **O** | **R** | | | | | | |
| 15 | = | | | 15 | | | | | | | |

| | | | **I** | | | | | | | | |
|---|---|---|---|---|---|---|---|---|---|---|---|
| 9 | = | | 9 | | | | | | | | |
| | | | 20 | + | 19+ | 20 | + | 6+ | 25 | = | 90 |
| | | | **T** | **E** | **S** | **T** | **I** | **F** | **Y** | | |
| 14 | = | | | 5 | + | | 9 | | | | |
| | | | 14+ | 20 | | | | | | | |
| | | | **U** | **N** | **T** | **O** | | | | = | 34 |
| 36 | = | | 21 | + | | 15 | | | | | |
| | | | 22 | + | 18+ | 25 | | | | = | 65 |
| | | | **E** | **V** | **E** | **R** | **Y** | | | | |
| 10 | = | | 5 | + | 5 | | | | | | |
| | | | 13 | + | 14 | | | | | = | +27 |
| | | | **M** | **A** | **N** | | | | | | |
| +1 | = | | 1 | | | | | | | | |
| **74** (Messiah) | | | | | | | | | | **92** (Buddha) | |

This verse represents the attainment of the universal perspective of Buddha Consciousness, and the recognition of the Messianic principle. It is a symbolic representation of creating on the earth plane in a spirit of service to others.

The word "plagues" carries the vibration of the "Sun" as its Personality. This combines with the Motivation of the altruistic use of power to serve humanity resulting in the higher consciousness of the Egyptian Christ figure, Horus.

| 16+ | 12 | + | 7 | + | | 19 | = | **54** (Sun) |
|---|---|---|---|---|---|---|---|---|
| **P** | **L** | **A** | **G** | **U** | **E** | **S** | | |
| | 1 | + | 21+ | 5 | | | = | +27 (altruism) |
| | | | | | | | | **81** (Horus) |

> *The grace of our Lord Jesus Christ be with you all.*
> *Amen.*

                                                          Rev. 22:21

It is interesting that the first verse of Revelation (1:1) includes a reference to Jesus, and the last verse, this one, does as well. This is an obvious tribute to the attainment of Christ Consciousness, which all can achieve. Revelation is the journey that every soul can take, complete with tests, to reach self-mastery.

The Book ends with the word "Amen," a commonly used finale to any prayer. This little word contains within its vibration the power of the master number 33.

|     | 13 | + | 14 | = | *27* (Power to create for others) |
|-----|----|---|----|---|-----------------------------------|
| **A** | **M** | **E** | **N** | | |
| 1 | + | 5 | | = | *+6* (Responsibility) |
| | | | | | *33* (World Service) |

# NOTES

## Chapter 1

1. Hall, Manley P., *The Secret Teachings of All Ages*, (Los Angeles, CA; Philosophical Research Society, 1988) p. III.

2. Anderson, Martin R., *Tales of the Returning Messiah and the Universal Christ* (self-published, n.d.) p. 27.

3. Hall, p. CLXXXV.

4. Anderson, p. 51.

5. ———, p. 51.

6. ———, p. 16.

7. Gaskell, G.A., *The Dictionary of All Scriptures and Myths* (New York, NY: Julian Press, 1960) pp. 129-30.

8. Gaskell, p.132.

## Chapter 2

1. Zajak, John, *The Delicate Balance* (Cornerstone Books). Interviewed by Art Bell on his "Dreamland" radio program. Interview published in The Dreamland Report," *After Dark* newsletter, Vol. I, No. 2, Feb 1995.

2. Zajak.

3.  Bauval, Robert and Adrian Gilbert, *The Orion Mystery* (New York, NY: Crown Publishers, 1994)

4.  Alford, Alan F., *Gods of the New Millennium* (Walsall, England: Eridu Books, 1996)

5.  Jochmans, Joseph Robert, "Is It True What They Are Saying About the Year 2000?" *The Mountain Astrologer*, Dec./Jan 1995.

6.  Jochmans.

7.  Hickey, Isabel, M., *Astrology, A Cosmic Science* (Sebastopol, CA: CRCS Publications, 1992)

8.  Lemesurier, Peter, *The Great Pyramid Decoded* (Rockport, MA: Element Books, 1996)

9.  Van Auken, John, *The End Times: Prophecies of Coming Changes* (Virginia Beach,VA: Inner Vision, 1994) p. 74.

10. Bey, Hamid, *A Coptic Home Study Course,* "Lesson I, The Pyramid Mysteries" (Coptic International, n.d.)

## *Chapter 3*

1.  Hall, Manley P., *The Secret Teachings of All Ages*, (Los Angeles, CA: Philosophical Research Society, 1988) p. CXXIX.

2.  Arrien, Angeles, *The Tarot Handbook* (Sonoma, CA: Arcus Publishing, 1987)

3.  Hall, Ibid.

4.  Greer, Mary K., "Tarot and Astrology," *The Mountain Astrologer*, April/May 1997.

# Chapter 4

1. Hall, Manley P., *The Secret Teachings of All Ages*, (Los Angeles, CA: Philosophical Research Society, 1988) p. XLIII.

2. ——, p. XLII.

3. Robert Schoch, Ph.D.,"How Old is The Sphinx? New Findings in Egypt," *Future History*, Winter 1992, Vol. 1, pp. 2-4.

4. ——, Ibid.

# Chapter 5

1. Eisler, Riane, *The Chalice and the Blade,* (San Francisco, CA: HarperCollins,1988) p. xvi.

2. ——, p. xiv.

3. ——, p. xvii.

4. Andrews, Ted, *The Occult Christ* (St. Paul, MN: Llewellyn, 1993) p 71.

5. ——, p. 72.

6. ——, p. 73.

7. Eisler, p. 169.

8. ——, p. 170.

9. ——, p. 176.

10. ——, p. 186.

11. ——, p. 190.

12. ——, pp. 188-189.

13. ——, p. 197.

14. ——, p. 199.

15. ——, p. 200.

16. ——, p. 203.

17. ——, p. xx.

18. Hall, Manley P., *The Secret Destiny of America*, (Los Angeles, CA: Philosophical Research Society, 1944) p. 23.

19. ——, pp. 128-130.

20. ——, p.130.

21. Hieronimous, Robert, Ph.D., *America's Secret Destiny* (Rochester, VT: Destiny Books, 1989) pp. 24, 30.

22. ——, p. 34.

23. ——, p. 28.

24. ——, p. 42.

25. Hall, pp. 149-153.

26. ——, pp. 166-167.

27. ——, p.167.

28. Hieronimous, p. 42.

# *Chapter 6*

1. Carus, Paul, *The History of the Devil and the Idea of Evil* (LaSalle, IL: Open Court Publishing, 1974) p.14.

2. ——, p.28.

3. ——, p. 193.

4. ——, pp. 201-2.

5. ——, p. 203.

6. ——, p. 219.

7. ——, p. 137.

8. ——, p. 141.

9. ——, p. 278.

10. ——, p. 282.

11. ——, p. 395.

12. ——, p. 401.

13. Walsch, Neale Donald.*Conversations with God* (New York, NY: G.P. Putnam's Sons, 1995) p. 155.

14. ——, p. 53.

15. Carus, p. 450.

# *Chapter 7*

1. Campbell, Joseph, *The Power of Myth* (New York: Doubleday, 1988) p. 17.

2. Krishna, Gopi, *Kundalini: The Evolutionary Energy in Man* (Berkeley, CA: Shambhala, 1967). ©1967. Reprinted by arrangement with Shambhala Publications, Inc., Boston.

3. Krishna, pp. 247-8.

4.  Thayse, Harris, *American Dream* (unpublished manuscript)

# Chapter 8

1.  Joel D. Wallach, M.D.,"Dead Doctors Don't Lie" Audiotape

# Chapter 9

1.  Mascetti, Manuela Dunn and Lorie, Peter, *Nostradamus: Prophecies for Women* (New York, NY: Simon & Schuster, 1995) p. 189.

2.  Drosnin, Michael, *The Bible Code* (New York, NY: Simon & Schuster, 1997)

3.  Van Auken, John, *The End Times: Prophecies of Coming Changes* (Virginia Beach, VA: Inner Vision, 1994) p. 77.

4.  Cannon, Dolores, *Conversations with Nostradamus: Vol. II* (Tehachapi, CA: America West Publishers, 1990) p. 317.

5.  ——, p. 135.

6.  ——, p. 200.

7.  ——, p. 308.

8.  Mascetti, and Lorie, pp. 32-3.

9.  ——, p. 47.

10. ——, p. 53.

11. ——, p. 187.

12. Van Auken, p. 39.

13. ——, p. 40.

14. ——, p. 42.

15. ——, p. 62-4.

16. ——, p. 65.

# Chapter 10

1. Gaskell, G.A., *Dictionary of All Scriptures and Myths* (New York, NY: Julian Press, 1960) pp. 755-6.

2. Bailey, Alice, *Initiation, Human and Solar* (New York, NY: Lucis Publishing, 1922) pp. 150-9. Copyright Lucis Trust.

3. Saraydarian, H., *Hierarchy and the Plan* (Agoura, CA: Aquarian Educational Group, 1975) pp. 16-21.

4. Bailey, p. 129.

5. ——, p. 131.

6. United Research Center, Black Mountain, NC, 1996, Phone (704) 669-6845.

# Conclusion

1. His Holiness the Dalai Lama, *A Policy of Kindness: An Anthology of Writings by and about the Dalai Lama* (Ithaca, NY: Snow Lion, 1990) p. 113-114.

2. Bailey, Alice, *Initiation, Human and Solar* (New York, NY: Lucis Publishing, 1922) pp. 20-4. Copyright Lucis Trust.

3. ——, p. 7.

4. Okawa, Ryuho, *The Laws of the Sun* (Rockport, MA: Element Books, 1996) p.39. Copyright © Ryuho Okawa 1994. Used by permission of Element Books, Inc.

5. World Goodwill, *The New Group of World Servers* (pamphlet)

6. Lanza, Fred, "Spiritual Unity of Nations," *Sun Up Newsletter*, Volume 1, No. 1, September 1992.

7. Sherman, Harold, *The Green Man and His Return* (Amherst, WI: Amherst Press, 1979) p. 63.

# *Epilogue*

1. Buechner, Col. Howard A., and Capt. Wilhelm Bernhart, *Adolf Hitler and the Secrets of the Holy Lance* (Metairie, LA: Thunderbird Press, 1988)

2. Ravenscroft, Trevor, *The Spear of Destiny* (York Beach, ME: Samuel Weiser, 1973)

3. Buechner and Bernhart.

# BIBLIOGRAPHY

Alford, Alan F. *Gods of the New Millennium* (Walsall, England: Eridu Books, 1996).

Anderson, Martin R. *Tales of the Returning Messiah and the Universal Christ* (self-published, n.d.)

Andrews, T. *The Occult Christ* (St. Paul, MN: Llewellyn, 1993).

Arrien, Angeles. *The Tarot Handbook* (Sonoma, CA: Arcus Publishing, 1987).

Bailey, Alice. *Initiation, Human and Solar* (New York, NY: Lucis Publishing, 1922).

Bauval, Robert and Adrian Gilbert. *The Orion Mystery* (New York, NY: Crown Publishers, 1994).

Bey, Hamid. *A Coptic Home Study Course,* "Lesson I, The Pyramid Mysteries" (Coptic International, n.d.).

Buechner, Col. Howard A., and Capt. Wilhelm Bernhart. *Adolf Hitler and the Secrets of the Holy Lance* (Metairie, LA: Thunderbird Press, 1988).

Campbell, Joseph. *The Power of Myth* (New York: Doubleday, 1988).

Cannon, Dolores. *Conversations with Nostradamus: Vol. II* (Tehachapi, CA: America West Publishers, 1990).

Carus, Paul. *The History of the Devil and the Idea of Evil* (LaSalle, IL: Open Court Publishing, 1974).

Drosnin, Michael. *The Bible Code* (New York, NY: Simon & Schuster, 1997).

Eisler, Riane. *The Chalice and the Blade,* (San Francisco, CA: HarperCollins, 1988).

Gaskell, G.A.,*The Dictionary of All Scriptures and Myths* (New York, NY: Julian Press, 1960).

Greer, Mary K."Tarot and Astrology," *The Mountain Astrologer*, April/May 1997.

Hall, Manley P. *The Secret Destiny of America*, (Los Angeles, CA: Philosophical Research Society, 1944).

——. *The Secret Teachings of All Ages*, (Los Angeles, CA: Philosophical Research Society, 1988).

Hickey, Isabel, M. *Astrology, A Cosmic Science* (Sebastopol, CA: CRCS Publications, 1992).

Hieronimous, Robert, Ph.D. *America's Secret Destiny* (Rochester, VT: Destiny Books, 1989).

His Holiness the Dalai Lama. *A Policy of Kindness: An Anthology of Writings by and about the Dalai Lama* (Ithaca, NY: Snow Lion, 1990).

Jochmans, Joseph Robert."Is It True What They Are Saying About the Year 2000?" *The Mountain Astrologer*, Dec./Jan 1995.

Krishna, Gopi. *Kundalini: The Evolutionary Energy in Man* (Berkeley, CA: Shambhala, 1967).

Lanza, Fred. "Spiritual Unity of Nations," *Sun Up Newsletter*, Volume 1, No. 1, September 1992.

Lemesurier, Peter. *The Great Pyramid Decoded* (Rockport, MA: Element Books, 1996).

Mascetti, Manuela Dunn and Peter Lorie. *Nostradamus: Prophecies for Women* (New York, NY: Simon & Schuster, 1995).

Okawa, Ryuho. *The Laws of the Sun* (Rockport, MA: Element Books, 1996).

Ravenscroft, Trevor. *The Spear of Destiny* (York Beach, ME: Samuel Weiser, 1973).

Saraydarian, H. *Hierarchy and the Plan* (Agoura, CA: Aquarian Educational Group, 1975).

Schoch, Robert, Ph.D. "How Old is The Sphinx? New Findings in Egypt," *Future History*, Winter 1992, Vol. 1.

Sherman, Harold. *The Green Man and His Return* (Amherst, WI: Amherst Press, 1979).

Thayse, Harris. *American Dream* (unpublished manuscript).

United Research Center, Black Mountain, NC, 1996, Phone (704) 669-6845.

Van Auken, John. *The End Times: Prophecies of Coming Changes* (Virginia Beach, VA: Inner Vision, 1994).

Walsch, Neale Donald. *Conversations with God* (New York, NY: G.P. Putnam's Sons, 1995).

World Goodwill. *The New Group of World Servers* (pamphlet).

Zajak, John. *The Delicate Balance* (Cornerstone Books). Interviewed by Art Bell on his *Dreamland* radio program. Interview published in "The Dreamland Report," *After Dark* newsletter, Vol. I, No. 2, Feb. 1995.

# ABOUT THE AUTHOR

JOHN DAVIS is Director of Coptic International, a modern philosophy based on the Mystery Schools of ancient Egypt. The Coptic organization has conducted personal power workshops and Great Pyramid initiation seminars nationwide for many years under John's leadership. He is also President of World Light Travels, a metaphysical travel company devoted to exploring Earth's Power Places, and has led 17 tours to Egypt alone. He has twenty years experience in the investigation of the ancient Kabala and related sciences such as the Science of Numbers (Numerology) over the course of which he has interpreted more than 8,000 personality profiles. John has also written *Messiah and the Second Coming* (1982) and has devoted the last 16 years to the development of the Spiritual Unity of Nations (S.U.N.), for which he serves as Director, an organization dedicated to "The World as One Family," and to which this book is dedicated.

John lives in Grand Rapids, Michigan, with his wife Nancy and a delightfully spirited little canine called Sunny, and has been known to make a great cup of coffee.

## The World As One Family

PEOPLE ARE LIKE *flowers. They have different colors and shapes. But within all is the same light of love. This divine essence binds us all as one family. The mother/fatherhood of God and the sister/brotherhood of humanity has been taught by all great philosophies and religions. When this oneness is more fully understood and practiced, then the barriers of division will disappear and there will be peace and prosperity for all.*

# ADDITIONAL INFORMATION

INFORMATION ABOUT Coptic International, World Light Travels, the Spiritual Unity of Nations, and John's personal numerology readings can be obtained by calling 800/704-2324 or by writing to:

John Davis
PO Box 9061
Wyoming, MI 49509


or you can E-mail John at:

copticsun@AOL.com